Fourth Down
And
Life To Go

More Testimonials
for *Fourth Down And Life To Go*
and Tony Franklin

"Powerful book, gripping stories, and meaningful lessons. My coach, my friend, my mentor. You can take it to the bank, if Coach Franklin says it happened, it happened."
Pookie Jones—1993 Peach Bowl MVP,
University of Kentucky Captain, 1992-1994

"Biting! Great reading! Reminds me of the "old days" in the SEC. Every coach and business leader should be required to read this book."
Ron Greene—1978 SEC Coach of the Year

"Classic Franklin. Brutally honest and straight to the point. I couldn't put it down!"
Rush Propst—1998 Alabama High School Coach of the Year,
2000 Alabama 6A State Champions Coach

Fourth Down
And
Life To Go

**Lessons Learned From
The Good, The Bad, and The Ugly Experiences
of Kentucky Football (1996-2001).**

By Tony Franklin

Published by
BadCoaches, Inc.
2220 Nicholasville Road
Suite 110, PMB 160
Lexington, Kentucky 40503

Printed in the United States of America by United Graphics, Inc.
Matton, Illinois

Franklin, Tony L.
Fourth Down And Life To Go: Lessons Learned from the Good, the Bad, and the
Ugly Experiences of Kentucky Football

Design by PageCrafters, Inc.

Although the author and publisher have extensively researched all sources to
insure the accuracy and completeness of the information contained in this book,
and we believe all dates, conversations, and grammatical placements to be accurate, the author and publisher acknowledge that errors can be made irregardless of
the number of proofreadings taking place. The author and publisher assume no risk
or liability for those unintentional errors if they have occurred. All events recalled
are believed to be accurate and the author and publisher assume no liability or risk
for any possible inaccuracies in the recalling of stories and events.

Library of Congress Cataloging-in-Publication Data

Franklin, Tony L., 1957-
    Fourth down and life to go: lessons learned from the good, the bad,
and the ugly experiences of Kentucky football / Tony L. Franklin.
        p. cm.
ISBN 0-9714280-0-X
1. University of Kentucky—Football—History. 2. Mumme, Hal. 3.
Franklin, Tony L., 1957- 4. Football coaches—Kentucky. I. Title.
    GV958.U5274 F73 2001
    796.332'092—dc21

2001006035

DEDICATION

To my three daughters—don't ever be afraid to stand alone and fight for what you believe to be right, no matter what the cost.

To my wife, who supported me in my desire to do the right thing even though she knew it would probably cost us our prior livelihood.

ACKNOWLEDGMENTS

The following people played a role in helping to make this book possible through their support at sometime in my life.

To my mother and father who have always loved and supported me through the good times and the bad and who taught me to fight for what you believe in.

To my brother Bobby who has been my best friend for 44 years of my life and who has always supported me whether I was right or wrong.

To the high school football coaches in the state of Kentucky who supported me before, during, and after my coaching tenure at UK.

To Rush Propst of Hoover High School in Alabama, who I would take in a fox hole to fight for me on any day.

To Dusty Bonner whose courage and leadership taught me valuable lessons in life.

To my many friends in Mayfield, Kentucky who taught me a long time ago the meaning of true friendship, a lesson I will never forget.

To Steve Aull, a great friend and mentor whose advice I have used for over 20 years.

To Sandy Wiese for having the courage to tell the truth when saying nothing would have been a much easier route to take.

To Kwyn Jenkins for being a role model for my three girls while playing the role of my fourth daughter.

To the current and former players at UK whose talent, hard work, and courage enabled myself and my family to enjoy a livelihood produced by your efforts.

To Don and Carol Pinska who have supported me in all of my ventures as I moved their daughter and grandchildren all over this state.

To Jerry and Ann English who have remained loyal friends for 18 years.

To Bobbie Jo Franklin and her late husband Jimmy for providing me love and shelter at difficult times.

To my Aunt Barbara and Uncle Billy Mitchell for constantly being solid family.

To Robert and Anna Barclay for critically proofing my book and being loyal friends.

To Jill and David Morris for always being "dead-on" honest and true friends.

To Joe Morris for helping a friend when he was in need.

To Joe and Nedra Boitnott for providing shelter and help to my family when needed.

To Al Giordano for teaching me what a "real coach" is supposed to be.

To Chrysti Carol-Crick Propes for being a wonderful role model for my children.

To Eddie Hodges for always providing a perfect round of golf at just the right time.

To my dear friends in the state of Alabama who always listen without judgement and provide sound, caring advice.

To Roger Fields who was a great mentor and friend in times of need.

To Bob Counts who taught me the art of resiliency through his own life of comebacks.

To Jake Hallum who desperately tried to help me in coaching when others turned their backs.

To the late Randy Jones whose positive outlook on every day of life continues to inspire me.

To Beth Franklin who has consistently given me unconditional love, advice, and help.

To Mike and Jamie Franklin for being sincere critics, neighbors, and family.

To Jane Pedley who always calls me and comforts me when she knows I need a friend.

To Charlie Phelps who gives the best $8.00 haircut in America, to go along with sound counseling sessions while in his chair.

To Tracy Rivette who introduced our daughter to the Lexington Children's Theater and kicked off her acting career.

To Mark and Holly West who provided sound friendship, advice, and listening skills during a time of turmoil.

To Debbie Burgess Bell for being a steady friend to my wife and I for 18 years.

To Joan, Ted, Jennifer, and Meghan King for being steady and stable friends to my wife and children.

To Joe and Phyllis Warren for being the best neighbors anyone could ever hope for.

To the community of Princeton, Kentucky for consistently embracing my parents and family and for making me proud to call you my hometown.

To the late Ernie Rickard and Curt Jones whose friendship and fond memories are sources of inspiration to me 26 years after their untimely passing.

To William and Alex Hardin at Mailboxes Etc. for giving incredible quality and professional work in helping make this book happen.

To Meghan Haney and Jessica Vaught who provided friendship and genuine caring during my four years with Kentucky Football.

To David Klein who dedicated his life to helping people with ulcerative colitis and saved my daughter with his advice.

To Paul Leahy who hired me at Mayfield High and provided me with an opportunity of a lifetime to meet and become friends with the unique people of Mayfield, Kentucky.

To Jim Lowry who helped me with my daughter when most of the Kentucky associated people turned me away after my early departure from the university.

To Paul Orberson who provided sound advice and friendship during turbulent times.

To Janetta Owens who taught me survivor skills second to none.

To Quaintance Clark who showed a consistently loving heart.

To Father Ed Bradley who showed up 20 years after our friendship began to remind me of his faith and belief in me.

To Tom Culpepper who gave a great vote of confidence by naming me one of the Top 10 Recruiters in the South.

To Greg Carter of St. Martin Deporres High in Detroit who exemplifies every great characteristic of coaching.

To Richard McFee who taught me how to never give up on a person or a player.

To Cutty Cutsinger who told me about some guy named Hal Mumme many years ago and renews our friendship with yearly phone calls.

To Glen Cohen who listened to my story about my experiences at Kentucky and passionately expressed his desire to fight for me.

To Marvin O'Koon and Les Keene of Pre-Paid Legal Services who gave me good sound legal advice and sent me to Glen Cohen.

To Jon Fleishaker who refreshed and reacquainted me with the First Amendment to the Constitution while protecting me in writing this book.

To Alex Panaretos who had the courage to tell the truth.

To Scott and Tina Schlosser for providing true friendship and sound advice.

To Mark Brady for being a valuable first mentor.

Table of Contents

INTRODUCTION

My good friend Chris Hatcher, former University of Kentucky assistant football coach, called me on May 9, 2001 to send me a message from my former boss, Hal Mumme. "Tell Franklin he had better back off and take a chill pill," Hatcher informed me verbatim of Mumme's message to me.

I laughed at Hatcher and said, "You're kidding!"

"No, I'm not, that's the message. I'm just delivering it for Mumme," Hatcher responded.

I told Hatcher, "Tell Mumme my phone number is listed and I still live in the same house. He doesn't have to call you with his threats towards me, he can call me directly or better yet, he can come by." I told Hatcher. "Also tell him if writing a book that will reveal his true character and preparing a lawsuit against him is backing off and taking a chill pill then I am definitely following his orders."

I had no idea what had brought about the recent interest by Mumme until the next day, May 10, 2001 when UK Assistant Athletic Director for Compliance Sandy Bell called and told me a NCAA investigator was coming to town and had requested the opportunity to meet with me. Mumme's call now made sense. My guess is that Hal's good friend, former UK Athletic Director C.M. Newton, informed him of the NCAA coming to Lexington. I would venture to predict he was told by Newton he better make sure Franklin doesn't tell his story or Mumme could end up with a NCAA record which would hurt his chances of being a Division I head coach again.

The threat by Mumme is one of many reasons I am writing this book. From February, 1997 until October 2000, I enjoyed some of the greatest times in my life while coaching football at the University of Kentucky. I also witnessed a disgusting abuse of power by Hal Mumme and other Kentucky officials. It reminded me of being a child again and having to go to recess with a group of bullies. My father taught me at a young age that bullies eventually must be confronted and that most of them are cowards. He also taught me to protect people weaker than I when they can't protect themselves. The people who misused their power need to be exposed for what they did, and I will do my best in this book to do just that.

In order to tell a story that is believable, a person must tell all of the truth, not just part of it. I must tell the good things some bad people did even if I have a strong dislike for them personally. This book is fair to all concerned. If there are positive stories I remember which should be told, then I will tell them.

My four years of coaching football at Kentucky were also full of colorful memories about great football games and the wonderful young men whom I had the privilege of coaching. The pageantry and excitement of SEC football is something every Kentucky fan should experience, and in this book I try to give the reader an up-close view of some of those occurrences. I let the reader get to know the players, staff, and coaches in ways that may surprise them.

Everyone's life is full of good, bad, and ugly incidences. My four years at Kentucky were no different, thus, in this book I reveal some wonderful, some bad, and some really ugly experiences recalled from my notes I kept for the four years while coaching at Kentucky. I've tried to protect any young person who could be hurt by a story by not revealing a name, unless it has already appeared in the UK compliance report to the NCAA or in other media outlets. If I have chosen not to use an adult's name in a referenced story, it is because I feel that person does not deserve recognition for one of two reasons: either they deserve name protection because of their good qualities or their name doesn't warrant ever entering a book because of their bad qualities.

On more than one occasion in this book I will tell of my own poor decisions. In no way do I wish to leave anyone with the impression I was without fault. That is simply not true. Some readers will blast some of my actions I am most proud of and view me as disloyal, self-promoting, and unethical. Potential future employers will read things that will make them never consider hiring me. That's okay because this is a true story and true stories have people with faults and I definitely have mine.

Five primary goals have consumed me in writing this book:

1. Inform bullies and abusers in the work place they better be more careful when deciding to consistently berate and degrade their employees. They need to understand one day they will do it to the wrong person and a huge price to pay may be in their future. They can eventually be publicly exposed and expelled.

2. Inform the public at all state universities they should closely watch those selected to lead. What the public sees is not necessarily the reality of what is happening. Taxpayers are the largest donators collectively, not some over-zealous boosters. Use your collective power to make those officials accountable for their actions.

3. Many good people were hurt by certain representatives of the University of Kentucky and their selfish actions. Some of those people are continually subjected to rumors about why they are no longer employed at UK. The story of their good deeds and strong character needs to be told.

4. The players, games, and pageantry of UK football provide interesting stories fans, family, and all can and should enjoy and from which they can learn. What happens to us in life should not dictate our quality of life, but rather how we respond to what happens to us should be the primary indicator of the quality our lives. Therefore, everything that happens to us in life should teach us a lesson, which brings me to the fifth goal in writing this book.

5. A valuable life-changing lesson can and should be learned from each chapter of this book. I've attached the lesson I have learned and each reader can learn at the end of every chapter, as well as a summary of all twenty-one lessons near the end of this book.

Read *Fourth Down and Life To Go* with an open mind and a critical heart. I hope you enjoy it, but I mainly hope you learn a lesson which will help improve the quality of your life. If you are a bully and abuser of others in life, I hope you finish this book and realize you had better change your ways because one day you should be and will be exposed.

Enjoy and learn,
Tony Franklin

For more information go to www.badcoaches.com

Part I
The Good . . .

CHAPTER 1

THE HIRING,
DREAM IT—PLAN IT—ACT IT

Lesson 1—No matter how outlandish or impossible your dream seems you can accomplish it with a solid plan and by taking immediate and consistent action! However, be careful what you dream. It may come true.

The Crazy Idea

It was September 28, 1996, and I was sitting in my lounge chair in Harrodsburg, Kentucky, watching Kentucky lose to Florida 0-65. I asked my wife Laura to come into the living room where I informed her it was over. She asked me what I meant and I told her Kentucky would fire Head Football Coach Bill Curry sometime in the next few weeks. As she started to leave the room I told her, "I'm going to call Hal Mumme and get him the Kentucky coaching job." She looked back at me and burst out laughing. For the next few months I got that response several times.

The next few weeks would open the doors to an incredible journey that would last four years. It was full of tremendous excitement, passion, emotion, love, adrenaline rushes, and learning. At the same time those four years would show me some of the worst times in life, full of lying, cheating, deception, and backstabbing.

Finding Hal Mumme

Hal Mumme was the Head Football Coach at Valdosta State University in Georgia, an NCAA Division II team. His offenses were fast paced and exciting and they were breaking records on a weekly basis. Sports Illustrated had recently featured Mumme and his Blazers in a big game against North Alabama and he was the hottest Division II coach in America looking to climb the ladder to the big time.

3

My relationship with Mumme began in 1990 when I called a friend of mine, Cutty Cutsinger in Duncanville, Texas, and asked him to help me find a place for a couple of receivers to play college football. Calloway County High was my present employer, and, as the Head Football Coach and also former owner of a college scouting service, my contacts led me to Hal in Mount Pleasant, Iowa. Cutty said, "Call Hal Mumme at Iowa Wesleyan, he'll take anybody."

That phone call to Mt. Pleasant, Iowa would begin a relationship that lasted 11 years but would end with deep bitterness by both parties. I made two trips to Mt. Pleasant over the next two seasons and my 1990 quarterback, Rob Dennis, signed a scholarship to attend Iowa Wesleyan University.

Hal eventually mysteriously lost his job at Iowa Wesleyan after a 10-2 season. Following a brief stint in a fledging professional football spring league, Mumme landed on his feet at Valdosta State University. From 1992 to 1996, Mumme won enough football games and broke enough offensive records to gain a reputation for being exciting, creative, and a winner.

I kept up with Mumme each year and occasionally we would talk. Mumme had previously made a trip to Murray, Kentucky, with his assistant Mike Leach (the current head coach at Texas Tech University), to recruit Rob Dennis. We had gone to the world famous "Big Apple" to have a few beers and talk football and Mumme had talked to me about maybe coaching with him at Iowa Wesleyan. He would again bring up that possibility while coaching at Valdosta State.

Mumme was good about returning phone calls and he seemed to have a folksy appeal which made high school coaches comfortable in his presence. I believed he was going to be a big time college coach one day. It seemed he had just enough cockiness, confidence, and brashness to pull it off. All he needed was to get the opportunity and I was sure he would make it work.

The End Of Curry

In 1995, Curry was making a change in his offense and planned to hire a new offensive coordinator. This was the perfect opportunity for me to make a move to help Kentucky break out of an offensive crisis by introducing Mumme to UK. What a perfect marriage this would be! Mumme could come in with Curry and the combination of Curry's integrity and values with Mumme's offensive firepower could put Kentucky at the top of SEC football.

I went to see Jack Fligg, the Director of Football Operations, and asked him to see if he could get Mumme in front of Coach Curry. Mumme had given me permission to pursue the deal because he believed Curry was one of the few head coaches who, if he gave his word, would allow Mumme to actually have control of the offense. Fligg later told me that Coach Curry had already made up his mind to hire Elliott Uzelac to become his Offensive Coordinator by the time Fligg mentioned Mumme to him. It's amazing how things work out sometimes. What an interesting turn of events it would have been had Curry hired Mumme.

Mumme continued on at Valdosta State with a couple of banner seasons and continued to put up big numbers on offense. Kentucky in the meantime struggled offensively and in 1996 after the LSU game, Kentucky Athletics Director C.M. Newton announced that Curry was fired effective at the end of the season.

The Plan

My plan to get Mumme hired began at the conclusion of the Kentucky vs. Florida game in 1996. I called Mumme on the Monday following the game and asked him if he would be interested in becoming the next head coach at the University of Kentucky. Mumme said "Sure" but responded that Kentucky still had a coach. My response to him was I believed Curry would be fired before the end of the season. I asked Mumme to send me his resume, publicity sheets, and football promoting materials so I could formulate a plan to give Mumme a chance if Curry was fired.

My background was basically a high school teacher and football coach, but I always had an entrepreneurial spirit. Several times in my life I had ventured out in an attempt to make a million dollars. One of the those ventures brought me in contact with Anthony Robbins, the world's greatest inspirational coach and achievement teacher. Robbins had a cassette program with marketing guru Jay Abraham. Abraham taught me a marketing principle which enabled me to formulate a plan to get Mumme hired at Kentucky. Robbins' program helped push me to take action.

After consulting with Mumme and receiving his permission to take the initiative, I simply waited to see if my premonition that Curry would be fired was correct. A couple of weeks later, after a 14-41 loss to LSU, Newton fired Curry. It was now time to put my plan into action.

What Newton Left Out

For those of you who read the book, *Newton's Laws* by Newton and Billy Reed, this letter (see Insert A, page 6) may come as a surprise. Newton's book makes no mention of a group of high school coaches who requested a meeting. Newton's book simply details how he got a phone call from Carl Parker, a

Tony Franklin
Mercer County High School
937 Moberly Road
Harrodsburg, KY 40330
(606) 734 - 6360

Coach C.M. Newton,
     A group of concerned high school coaches across the state of Kentucky would like to request 10 minutes of your time. We have a recommendation for the head coaching position and feel that our reasons could be made clear in a brief 10 minute presentation.
     Our choice for that job is a current head college coach with enormous success, having previously turned 2 college programs around, we feel that he can win and win big, **now** !
     We realize that you will get 100's of calls and recommendations and that you are very busy, however our intentions are positive and we only need 10 minutes.
     We strongly wish to support UK football and hope that you grant us this request.

                    Sincerely,

                    Tony Franklin
                    Concerned High School Coaches

Sam Harp - Danville High
John Vandermeer - Covington Holmes High
Craig Clayton - Hopkinsville High
David Barnes - Daviess County High
Tony Franklin - Mercer County High
Joe Beder - Leslie County High

P.S. Coach Harp and Coach Franklin will be the coaches making the presentation. Their nights and weekends would be best. (UK - Georgia date) If possible - both coaches will be at the game.

Insert A. Letter to C.M. Newton

former Vanderbilt University football player who knew Newton and had coached with Mumme. At the time, Parker was the Valdosta State radio game day announcer. That phone call spurred Newton to research Mumme and after reviewing his resume, according to Newton, he decided to go see Mumme.

    That's a great story, but several things seem to be missing. When Newton received my Fed Ex letter requesting a meeting, he called the Mercer County High School football office and left a message. I was, at that time, the Head Football Coach at Mercer County High. When I entered the locker room that afternoon, Todd Davis, our trainer said, "You've got a message from C.M. Newton on the phone."

I couldn't help but smile and I replied, "I wonder what he wants."

David Barnes, Craig Clayton, and Joe Beder didn't have a clue who Mumme was, but like me, they wanted a coach at Kentucky whom they felt would build excitement. They trusted me when I asked permission to use their names in my letter. Barnes and Clayton were from my home school of Caldwell County and were both successful head coaches and lifetime friends. Beder was Kentucky Quarterback Tim Couch's high school coach during Couch's senior season, and, although I didn't personally know Joe, I sent him a video of Mumme's Valdosta State teams and Joe liked what he saw. I asked Joe to get a video to Couch's dad also, which Joe was able to do.

Covington Holmes Coach, John Vandermeer had known Mumme when John was an assistant and eventually the Head Coach at Olivet Nazarene University. They had competed against each other and John thought Hal was a great coach and would be a good fit at UK. He enthusiastically supported the push for Mumme.

Harp is one of the most successful head coaches in the history of Kentucky high school football. His Danville teams have won five state championships and he had a couple of teams that were better than anybody in the state, regardless of class. Sam had also been President of the Kentucky High School Football Coaches Association and was highly respected as a leader among the state's football coaches. Sam had met Mumme at a clinic and was excited about the possibility of a small college coach with high school roots leading the Wildcats. I persuaded Sam to join me in this venture and he played a prominent role in an approximate 45-minute meeting with Newton on the Saturday before the Kentucky vs. Georgia game in 1996.

I returned Newton's call and he agreed to a meeting with Sam and me. I then called Mumme to tell him we had accomplished our goal of getting a sit-down meeting with Newton.

Plan B

Meanwhile, Plan B was also going into effect. Larry Vaught, Sports Editor of *The Advocate-Messenger* in Danville, had agreed to meet with me and hear my suggestions for a new Head Football Coach at Kentucky. I had grown to deeply respect Larry's abilities as a journalist during my years as a high school coach. Every Thanksgiving my family would travel to Danville for a holiday celebration with my wife's sister Nedra and her husband, Joe Boitnott. Every year I would read Larry's articles and be impressed with his coverage of high school sports. My job with Mercer County High provided me numerous opportunities to work with Larry, and I was impressed with his quality of work and insight into college and high school sports.

Mumme had suggested I talk to a local media person rather than a statewide publication. This would help start a grass-roots movement if it caught on. Vaught listened with an open mind as I described Mumme's credentials and provided his background information. Larry decided it would be a bold move if Newton would simply hire the best coach available, not caring what level he was coaching. The article ran in not only *The Advocate-Messenger*, but also *The Cats' Pause*. Larry did such a good job presenting the case to hire someone like Mumme that some Kentucky fans actually began to wonder if maybe it was a sound possibility.

The Meeting

Harp and I drove to Lexington to meet with Newton Saturday morning, October 26, 1996. Newton did not know who the candidate was until I revealed his name during our presentation. I had planned a three-part presentation and it worked without flaw.

The presentation consisted of my opening with seven points:

1. Unique System—I compared Mumme with Lavell Edwards, Head Football Coach at Brigham Young University, and described what Kentucky could do passing just as BYU had done in the WAC. Mumme's Division II passing records were similar to BYU's.

2. Recruiting—Mumme believed in 'position recruiting' rather than recruiting by geographic area. Each position coach would recruit his own players.

3. Coaching History—Mumme had taken over Iowa Wesleyan and Valdosta State and dramatically improved their records.

4. Practice Philosophy—All practices would be less than two hours and no tackling or blocking below the waist.

5. Injuries—Jim Madaleno, Mumme's eventual trainer at Kentucky and Valdosta State, had been a trainer for the New York Giants when they won the Super Bowl. The combination of Mumme's limited contact philosophy and Madaleno's experience had kept injury rates low. Mumme also had never lost a quarterback to injury during his college head-coaching career.

6. Staff—Mumme's Defensive Coordinator Mike Major was a Larry Lacewell (Dallas Cowboys) disciple and Offensive Line Coach Guy

Morriss from Mississippi State promised to leave and join Mumme. Claude Bassett formerly of BYU and currently a Texas high school coach would be the Recruiting Coordinator. Mumme also said he would hire one or two high school coaches from the state of Kentucky.

7. Offensive Coordinator—Mumme would be his own offensive coordinator which meant consistency. Nothing would change when coaches left to take other jobs.

During my presentation I told Newton it was Hal Mumme from Valdosta State University whom I was describing. Newton stopped me and said, "I know that name." He stood up and flipped through a list of resumes and said, "That's right, Carl Parker called me about Mumme yesterday." I couldn't believe it! The plan had worked perfect. Earlier in the week, when I got the appointment with Newton, I had called Mumme and asked him if he had anyone that knew Newton which Mumme could get to call prior to our meeting. Mumme told me his radio announcer, Carl Parker, used to coach with him and he had played football at Vanderbilt when Newton was there. I told Mumme to have Parker call and it worked perfectly! To my knowledge, Newton never knew of the connection between Parker's call and our presentation.

Sam talked to Newton about four points:

1. Staff Openness—Sam relayed about how open Mumme had been when he met him at a clinic in Chicago.

2. Consistent System—The emphasis on having an offensive system that did not change from year to year would help high school coaches in Kentucky.

3. Camp—Chase Harp (Sam's son and Danville HS QB), was planning to travel to Valdosta State for QB camp because of the exemplary quality of instruction.

4. Junior Varsity Program—Mumme would implement a JV program. Sam believed this would help promote football in Kentucky. No kid would be rejected from wearing a blue and white uniform and he would get the chance to play in Commonwealth Stadium.

After Sam finished, I closed our meeting with these points:

1. Mumme would continue the academic success of Curry.

2. Football would be fun and exciting.

3. No philosophy changes would take place in mid-stream because of coaching changes.

4. Closeness and camaraderie would take place because players would have fun.

5. A visionary was needed, someone who had experience rising bad programs up from the dead.

The final point needed to be a slam-dunk. Because of my Anthony Robbins and Jay Abraham training programs, I thought I had found the perfect close. I reminded Newton that BYU had run this system for 20 years with great success. I proposed that the athletic director at Virginia Tech had enough courage to hire Frank Beamer from I-AA Murray State University and a long time ago a courageous Athletic Director in the SEC had enough courage to hire an unknown coach from a small, unknown college. I paused and Newton asked, "Who?"

I replied, "The University of Alabama when it chose C.M. Newton of Transylvania University to become its Head Basketball Coach."

Newton responded with a smile and said, "Tell Coach Mumme that Larry Ivy (at that time Assistant Athletic Director and currently Athletic Director) and I are going to jump on a plane to come see him this coming week."

Harp and I stood up and shook hands with Newton and left Memorial Coliseum. We walked outside and down the hallway a good distance before we finally looked at each other with big grins and said, "Can you believe it?" We were in shock! The plan had gone perfectly and Newton had made it clear he was going to hire the best coach regardless of who he was.

Don't Screw It Up

Later that day I called Mumme and told him, "Don't screw it up, it's up to you now." I then relayed the whole story. He couldn't believe it had worked so well. Mumme would not screw it up, at least not the opportunity to get hired.

Newton went to see Mumme because he believed Kentucky needed a dramatic change to invigorate the football program. Newton loved the idea of the JV program and also compared Mumme's no tackling philosophy to a season when legendary Alabama Head Football Coach Bear Bryant had Alabama working non-contact. Newton mentioned other coaches he was considering at that time which included Ron McBride of Utah, Larry

Blakeney at Troy State, and Bobby Wallace at North Alabama. He also said there were several assistants in the NFL and colleges whom he was considering but didn't mention names.

Selling football in the state of Kentucky was a major point Newton was concerned with. He hoped to find a young coach who could spread the field and throw the ball. Newton made one thing clear. He said, "This will not be a Tim Couch hire. We are going to hire the best coach, and I'm in a position where it doesn't matter to me what anybody thinks." Newton reiterated, "This must be a good hire."

The Process

In the weeks that followed, I talked to Mumme numerous times and updated him with information. Kentucky President Charles Wethington would make a presentation to the media and described the qualities they were looking for in the next head coach. I would then call Mumme and relayed that information to him.

Mumme met with Newton on more than one occasion and did a great job selling himself and his ideas. Newton would occasionally call me to ask questions concerning Mumme. Mumme's wife June, and I also began to converse. She made it clear that although she was battling breast cancer she very much wanted this job for the Mumme family.

Mike Gottfried of ESPN; Sherman Lewis, the Offensive Coordinator for the Green Bay Packers; and David Cutcliffe, Offensive Coordinator at the University of Tennessee, were all being mentioned in the final weeks before Newton made his decision. There is no doubt all were capable candidates and could have been good hires, but Mumme had done an admirable job selling his vision and Newton was in a position where he truly could hire whom he wanted and not worry about repercussions.

Mumme's Valdosta State Blazers were advancing to the second round of the play-offs to face Carson Newman. I got calls from both Mumme and Newton to tell me of the decision to offer Mumme the job. When Newton called me prior to the official announcement of Mumme's hiring he asked me how many faxes from high school coaches across the state I could have sent to Kentucky to show the support for Mumme. I told him I could easily get 100 faxes. Newton expressed surprise at the high number I had quoted. He told me he wasn't worried about himself, but he wanted to make sure Mumme knew he was supported. Newton told me to wait for his instructions on when to send the faxes, but he never gave me the go ahead.

There was no way to describe the emotions of seeing an unbelievable chain of events come to a conclusion. As the process had progressed, I had even gotten cold feet about Kentucky hiring Mumme. My gut told me perhaps something was going to happen which would show Mumme had done something wrong at Iowa Wesleyan, thus preventing him from getting the Kentucky job. I called Mumme and asked him point blank, "Are there any skeletons in Iowa that are going to pop out and embarrass Kentucky?" Mumme assured me the only reason he resigned after his 10-2 season at Iowa Wesleyan was because he had signed too many players after the president had told him not to over sign.

I've Got A Job—No, I Don't—Yes, I Do!

My ecstasy over Mumme getting the job soon turned to shock. Early during the process of the Hal Mumme/Kentucky courtship, Mumme had written me a note asking me if I would be interested in coaching running backs at Kentucky if he got the job. Although Mumme had talked to me at both IWC and VSU about coaching vacancies, I was not pursuing him to personally get an opportunity to coach at Kentucky. I had decided years before I would not ever get that opportunity. Mumme's note changed that and from that day forward, I was considered to be a coach on his staff if he got the job.

After Mumme told me he had been offered the job, he then informed me Newton had changed his mind about hiring high school coaches. According to Mumme, Newton had previously okayed my hiring and also suggested he hire a second high school coach from Kentucky. Mumme told me to tell Harp he wanted him to join us at Kentucky. All that had changed now that he had the job. He might be able to hire one of us but he wasn't sure.

I went home that night and told my wife Mumme and Newton had decided I wouldn't have a job at Kentucky after all. Laura is normally a very calm and easygoing person, but she was furious when I told her the news. She had watched this process unfold since day one and she reminded me of my role in the entire process.

That night I wrote Mumme a letter and reminded him about the two separate occasions at other universities when he had approached me about coaching jobs. I also reminded him if I could sell an unknown Division II coach from Valdosta State to Newton, I most certainly could recruit kids to come to Kentucky to play football. I also reminded him about the word called "loyalty" and what its definition is.

The Fed Ex package with my letter enclosed reached Mumme the following day. Later Mumme called to tell me he had spoken to Newton and it was okay to hire me now and that he was "loyal." Sam Harp was not to be so fortunate.

Harp Is Still Waiting

Harp and I drove to Carson-Newman to watch Mumme in his final game at VSU. We went to see Mumme before the game. It was the first time I had seen him in person since a trip to Delta State in 1994 or 1995 to watch Mumme's team play. Mumme walked up and said, "I can't believe you guys did it, you did it!" There was never a thank you and there never would be one to come.

I was later told to tell Harp he wasn't going to get a job at the University of Kentucky. Sam was devastated. I don't know of anyone who had ever prepared harder or who had wanted it more than Sam. Mumme eventually talked to Sam and assured him the first opening on his staff would go to him. Over the next four years, Sam would hear this statement three more times. Harp was never hired at Kentucky.

Why It Happened

I was definitely not the best high school coach in the state of Kentucky, nor was I the most qualified to coach at Kentucky. My primary job criteria was I was not afraid to dream a dream and follow through. Knowing Mumme and putting a plan into action vaulted me into college football, because I helped to make Mumme's dreams come true.

Mumme did not get the job at Kentucky because of what I did for him. He was hired because he was the right coach at the right time at the right place. He was hired because he had paid his dues and had done a quality job coaching football. However, for every Mumme who makes it to his dream job, there are 100 more just as capable and just as qualified who don't ever get that final push over the edge. That final push was my job. Mumme didn't get the UK job because of what I did, but he definitely wouldn't have gotten it without me! Mumme is the only Division II coach in modern history to directly become a head football coach in the SEC.

LESSON #1—Numerous people laughed at me when I would tell them Hal Mumme would be the next Head Coach at Kentucky. Only two people firmly believed there was a chance from day one: Hal Mumme and Tony Franklin. The lesson is no matter how outlandish or impossible the dream is you can accomplish it with a solid plan and by taking immediate and consistent action. However, be careful what you wish for because it may come true!

CHAPTER 2

THE HEAD COACH

Lesson 2—Phenomenal success takes place only when you are willing to step outside of your comfort zone and expand your circle of influence. Nothing spectacular ever takes place without a willingness to risk everything.

I'm So Glad To Be Here

Larry Ivy once commented to me that when Mumme was in the process of agreeing to take the Kentucky job, he didn't even ask about the details of a contract. Ivy commented that he and Newton both had to push Mumme to make sure he understood the details of the contract. Mumme was so thankful to be given the opportunity by Newton and Kentucky he was walking on clouds for the first few months of his contract. There was not a speaking engagement he wouldn't attend if he had the opportunity to sell his vision for Kentucky football.

Call Me, I'll Be There

In 1997 if I told Mumme there was an important function which would help promote Kentucky football with high school coaches or fans, he would attend. The first year was truly a blast of excitement as Mumme would go almost anywhere to promote UK football. Each year after he would decrease in his openness to attend Kentucky high school coaching functions.

In February of 1997 there was a high school coaching clinic in Bowling Green, Kentucky for coaches mainly from the western part of Kentucky. Mumme, Chris Hatcher, and I attended, and Mumme was a huge hit. He sat at a table surrounded by coaches, drinking beer, eating chicken wings, and drawing plays on napkins.

The following day, several coaches went out of their way to tell me how much they appreciated Mumme's presence. Most coaches mentioned how warm and approachable Mumme was. It would only take consistent reinforcement over the years for Mumme to keep this honeymoon with high school coaches going. I had always believed one of Mumme's strongest qualities as a head Division I coach was his camaraderie with high school coaches. He eventually would lose some of their support, but he certainly had it in the beginning.

My hometown of Princeton, Kentucky sponsored a golf tournament every summer in which high school coaches from Western Kentucky played. Some of the local Kentucky boosters decided this would be a good opportunity to spread the new Kentucky coach's philosophy. They asked me to see if Mumme would agree to speak to a group of loyal Kentucky fans.

I told Mumme it would be a perfect opportunity to meet and greet UK fans in far western Kentucky and he agreed to attend. Bassett arranged for most of the entire coaching staff to attend the event and play golf with the high school coaches the following day. The entire event was a success. Mumme won over an entire community with his folksy appeal and candid answers of his plan to build a winning program at Kentucky.

Mumme told the Princeton crowd he would mark his calendar and each summer he would attend this function. He was genuinely overwhelmed with the community's hospitality and openness. Many residents of my hometown would remind me on numerous occasions of Mumme's promise over the next three years. He never attended the event again and some would never forget his failure to honor his commitment to return.

The event in western Kentucky would continue and Bassett would arrange for several Kentucky coaches to attend each summer. Bassett always had an explanation as to why Mumme would not attend, but eventually few people really cared.

The Quarterback Friendly Coach

If you were the starting quarterback in a Mumme offense you were definitely going to be "the man." You better have an arm that was flexible and healed quickly because you would use it more in practice than any QB in America. Mumme believed in the one quarterback system and that QB would take 99% of the practice reps and 100% of the game snaps in most games.

I never believed Mumme was a strong technician in QB skills. He seemed to struggle when coaching fundamentals of QB play, but he didn't have to be good at that phase. QB Coach Chris Hatcher was doing a great job there. Mumme's strength was in teaching a QB confidence and strategy.

From the one-yard line going in or the one-yard line going out, Mumme gave the QB the freedom to call his own play. It didn't matter if it was fourth and one with one minute to go in the game or if it was first and ten in the first quarter. Mumme basically put the game in the hands of his quarterbacks. Most of his QB's were able to excel at this freedom and most thrived under his tutelage.

While coaching the running backs for three years and wide receivers for one season, I wrote the following advice on my meeting room board: "Remember, quarterbacks are never wrong and they never make a bad throw. Expect unmerciful butt chewings from the head coach even when you are right because quarterbacks are never wrong."

Mumme believed a QB in his offense should have unshakable confidence and he coached them to form that confidence. Most of the QB's could handle this, but it definitely upset some of the other players. A ball might hit them in the back and Mumme would blame the receiver. Tim Couch would always step up and take the blame and shield the receivers from Mumme's criticism. It was one of Couch's greatest qualities.

I strongly believe Mumme's method of coaching quarterbacks by installing supreme confidence in them was effective for most of his QB's. The numbers in wins and losses over his career proves it worked most of the time. Overall, Mumme was a productive QB coach.

Cockiness & Confidence

There is a fine line between extreme confidence and pure arrogance. Mumme played on both sides of that line. There were times when his preparation and study of an opponent gave him a cockiness and confidence that exploded on game day with a huge offensive outburst. There were other times when he seemed arrogant and didn't study or game plan nearly enough and we would be much less effective on offense.

There were days when Mumme would watch 15 to 30 minutes of video of an upcoming opponent and write a game plan. Other times he would study for hours before making decisions. He was normally at his best when he had been humiliated the previous game. This would lead to a real breakdown of an opponent and on game day he would be as good as any offensive coach in America. When Mumme got on a roll on a Saturday, he would be unstoppable. If he found your weakness, he would score points quickly and often.

The first year at Kentucky the team needed someone with extreme confidence and Mumme was the perfect fit. There was no sign of intimidation by Mumme for any of the opponents. Kentucky players fed off his confidence and the results proved it.

Offensive Practice Habits (No Contact)

Recruiting offensive players during the four years under Mumme was easy. I strongly believed I could recruit against any college in the nation and have a good chance to get them to Kentucky. Couch provided visibility for our program early on. Couch was much better known than Mumme and his high visibility gave us instant recognition by high school players and coaches. Yet the main reason I was confident in recruiting offensive players was not Couch's presence; it was Mumme's practice philosophy.

I was never a great football player in high school or college, but I was fortunate enough to play and be productive as a running back. The most important factor in my being productive and playing well on Saturdays was my physical well being. If I was beat up and sore there was no way I would be productive. I would have loved to play in Mumme's system because of his practice philosophy.

The criticism Mumme received for his overall practice philosophy was unfounded. The belief there was no contact was simply not true. Mumme's philosophy was to limit full speed hits, but his main emphasis was not to hit below the waist in practice and to stay out of pileups. Most injuries in football came from pileups and below the waist hits.

I could honestly go into a player's home and tell him if he came to Kentucky he would have much less risk of getting injured in his college career than if he chose another school. In four years under Mumme, we probably had fewer injuries at practice than any other Division I team.

Offensive Practice Habits (Repetition)

Any college or high school coach who visited our offensive practices left impressed with the number of practice repetitions we were able to produce in two hours. Mumme's system worked like a clock. Each phase would fit perfectly with the next, and by the end of each practice, each phase of offensive football had been implemented.

The field was broken into six pieces under Mumme's design: Coming Out (goal line to -5-yard line); Yellow Zone (-5-yard line to -20-yard line); Open Field (-20 to +30 yard line); Orange Zone (+30 to +12-yard line); Red Zone (+12 to +5- yard line); Goal Line (+5 to goal line). Every practice week was organized with specific formations and plays for each part of the field. As the season and years went by each player would learn what to expect in each area of the field.

Mumme believed his teams could do the same things over and over again each week and eventually perfect the system. Since defenses only have one week to prepare for his system, there was no way they could stop it if his players perfected it. Kentucky could simply outrep its opponents by its system of practice.

The philosophy of non-tackling below the waist and maximum practice repetitions is what made Mumme's offensive system so effective for many years. It was when he began to change the system and philosophy that the offense began to sputter.

Non-QB Personnel Decisions On Offense

There was no doubt Mumme had the ability to convince his brain to believe anything he wished. It was one of his strengths at times and would eventually be one of his fatal weaknesses.

Each year would start with Mumme talking about some player who was going to be special. Many times that player was not even close to being a contributor. One thing was certain, whatever his motives were for believing in that player, he was going to get a maximum number of opportunities to win a starting position. Some would reward Mumme with stellar performances and careers like James Whalen, while others simply could not play.

Some of the most frustrating moments while coaching at Kentucky were listening to Mumme and Bassett berate a Bill Curry recruited player while promoting one of their own recruits above his ability. For three years I had to fight for Anthony White to continue in his role in the backfield, as Bassett and Mumme were certain each year they could get him on the bench. To Mumme's credit, he would eventually see that White was simply too good of a player to be anywhere but on the field.

Wide receiver Quentin McCord was another classic example of a player whom Mumme never seemed to want on the field. Every receiver would be given multiple opportunities to beat McCord out, but he was simply too good to not be on the field. If his knee had not been hurt before his senior season and he had been healthy enough to practice daily, we would have been a much better team and McCord would have been an All American.

To Mumme's credit although he very badly wanted his recruits to play in front of Curry's recruits, 90% of his decisions on offense would eventually be correct.

Buzz

Buzz Sipes was a WWII veteran who had spent time in the Pacific front. He was a constant figure at practices. If he was missing for a couple of days in a row, players would ask about his absence.

Mumme would occasionally recite history lessons to our players when trying to motivate them and he had a soft spot in his heart for Buzz. He included Buzz in some of our pre-game activities and even had sideline passes for Buzz at some of our home games.

Bassett and Mumme both had some gentle moments of humanity and Buzz was one of Mumme's. For four years he made Buzz feel like he was an important part of the UK family. I would hope that all our grandfathers would be treated with the kindness and respect that Mumme treated Buzz.

Fantasy Camp 2000 (Like A Teenager In Love)

Eddie Gran, the Running Back Coach at Auburn University, had told me about the Fantasy Camp that they had run at Ole Miss and Auburn. He said it was a great way to build camaraderie with alumni and he said all the assistant coaches loved it as well as Tommy Tuberville, their head coach. I had approached Mumme in the spring about hosting one at Kentucky and he agreed to do it.

The 2000 Fantasy Camp at the University of Kentucky was Mumme at his best. I had never seen him so fun loving, full of energy, and friendly. He acted like a teenager in love, full of life and smiling from ear to ear.

Approximately 40 Fantasy Camp participants, aged from 21 to 70+, had paid around $1000 to have two days with Mumme and the Kentucky staff. When they left, each one was satisfied with the attention Mumme had given them. He had been "one of the boys" for two days and, with the exception of a profanity-laced reprimand to one of the campers, Mumme was perfect.

Hiring Coaches

One of Mumme's strongest philosophical characteristics was perceived by some to be one of his truly weakest characteristics. That characteristic was his decisions made in hiring assistant coaches. I strongly believe Mumme's philosophy of hiring high school coaches and coaches from small colleges was a good idea, not a bad idea.

I don't believe Mumme ever believed Division I coaches were a notch above the rest. I believe he truly felt some of the best coaches were high school and small college coaches. With that being said, I also believe Mumme made some incredibly bad choices about coaches whom he chose to hire or to keep and not fire. They were not bad choices because they were high school or small college coaches; they were bad choices because there were much better coaches available.

People tend to not want to leave their comfort zone. When head college football coaches hire assistants, most follow the pattern of hiring someone they know or a friend of someone they know. It is coaches like Bob Stoops of Oklahoma who boldly stepped outside his comfort zone and hired Mike Leach in his first year at Oklahoma that will make championships. Stoops and Leach had briefly met once, according to Leach, but Stoops knew the one offense he hated to face was Mumme's. After talking to Mumme and spending several hours with Leach on the phone, Stoops hired someone he did not really know. The reward was a national championship. Even though Leach left after one year, the offensive system he installed remained.

Mumme could have hired 50 head coaches from Kentucky high schools who, in my opinion, would have been a stronger choices than his choice of Scott Highsmith, a former college roommate and career assistant coach from Texas high schools. By staying within his comfort zone and hiring someone he perceived would be loyal at any cost, he missed an opportunity to honor a promise and hire a much better football coach. By hiring Sam Harp instead of Highsmith, Mumme could have made us a better staff and he would have helped mend some fast-breaking fences with Kentucky high school coaches. Harp was not what Mumme was looking for. He preferred a coach who would seldom, if ever, question him. Mumme told me the main reason he hired Highsmith was his belief that Scott would always be loyal and he would never leave for a better job.

The belief that age and level of coaching was not important in determining the quality of coaching was one admirable quality of Mumme's. His decision-making ability was not as admirable.

Conclusion

Hal Mumme possessed some qualities that helped to make him a great offensive football coach for most of his career. He also possessed the confidence and charisma to sometimes show signs of being an effective leader. His greatest asset, however, was his simple system of teaching offensive football. Top coaches like Sam Harp, Rush Propst, Chris Hatcher, and Bob Stoops have taken his system and combined it with better leadership skills to make championship football teams.

LESSON #2—Phenomenal success takes place only when you are willing to step outside of your comfort zone and expand your circle of influence. Nothing great ever takes place without a willingness to risk everything. Bob Stoops hired Mike Leach as his offensive coordinator without personally knowing Mike. He simply saw something he liked and thought it would work and had enough guts to take a chance. His reward was a National Championship two years later.

CHAPTER 3

Good Guys/Good Coaches

Lesson 3—Leadership does not care who possesses it. There is not an age requirement or experience requirement to be a good leader.

The "Hatch-Man," The Sky Is The Limit

The greatest quarterback coach in all of college football may well be a 28-year old by the name of Chris Hatcher. Tim Couch, Duante Culpepper, Lance Funderburke, and Dusty Bonner all have their names sprinkled in the NCAA record books. Couch and Culpepper have gone on to become multimillionaires in the NFL. Bonner won the Harlon Hill Trophy in 2000 as the best player in all of Division II as well as having led the SEC in several categories and having led Kentucky to the Music City Bowl in 1999. All of them have one thing in common: Hatcher coached them all.

Hatch, as most everyone calls him, grew up in a circle of football coaches. He was lucky the greatest coach he ever knew was with him every day, his father Edgar Hatcher. The state of Georgia is known for its unrelenting passion for football and Edgar Hatcher is well known as one of the best and most passionate football coaches in the state. Chris had been at Edgar's side since birth soaking up every bit of knowledge consumable.

Great coaches almost always have one thing in common, the ability to communicate with their players. Hatch had been one of the best quarterbacks in the history of college football, owning several NCAA records and winning the Harlon Hill Trophy. Many top players struggle as coaches, but Hatch has definitely taken his on field success and transferred it to the quarterbacks he coaches. He communicates his expertise.

Couch was a phenomenal talent who had been extremely well coached in high school by Leslie County coaches Mike Whitaker and Joe Beder. Nineteen ninety-six was not a good year for Couch as he struggled in his freshman season at Kentucky. The implementation of Mumme's system was important in giving Couch the opportunity to succeed, but Hatcher's guidance and advice was crucial. A fine line exists between coaching too much and letting a great player play without hindering him. Hatcher played that balance perfectly and Couch thrived because of it.

Bonner wasn't a heavily recruited player coming out of Valdosta High in Georgia. He was, however, a winner! When given the opportunity to be Couch's successor he followed Hatcher's game plan exactly. Every tidbit of knowledge was consumed for two seasons while waiting in the wings. Behind a struggling and inexperienced group of offensive linemen and receivers, Bonner used every mental and physical advantage Hatcher had taught him to lead Kentucky to the Music City Bowl.

The three years Hatcher coached at Kentucky he was basically a co-offensive coordinator, making practice schedules and helping with game plans and scripts. He was never shy about taking charge and he was pure proof that age has nothing to do with leadership. He was also the Head Junior Varsity Coach and blistered the opposing JV teams with offensive explosions.

Hatcher brought an air of confidence and competitiveness our team needed. He is the most competitive person I've ever known. Our daily jogs always ended in a 200-yard sprint where he would have tripped me at the end in order to win. Racquetball matches regularly had balls drilled into the back of his opponent, and he would dive for a ball he couldn't get. All of his quarterbacks were required to have this same passion and competitiveness and they thrived because of his insistence they compete at everything.

Intimidation is a tactic that never worked against Hatcher. Defensive Coordinator Mike Major tried to intimidate Hatcher during one of our winter workout sessions. Mumme had left Hatcher in charge of our "Wildcat Games" while Mumme was in Hawaii. Major decided he didn't like how Hatcher was running the games and screamed at Hatcher in front of the players. Hatcher went nose-to-nose with Major. When Major saw Hatcher wasn't going to do what was asked of him, he threatened to call Mumme in Hawaii and pull rank over Hatcher. Hatch replied he would go with Major and call Mumme immediately. That call was never made and Hatcher never budged an inch.

Chris is now the Head Coach at Valdosta State and during his first season turned a losing program into a 10-2 record and a spot in the NCAA Division II playoffs. He has the perfect blend of arrogance and humility to be a prominent head coach. His father's influence, and the influence of many of Georgia's top high school coaches, combined with Mumme's offensive system has given Hatcher a unique coaching style. The toughness and defensive mentality of good old-fashioned football was born into his upbringing while Mumme's attacking offensive philosophy gives him a possibility of immense success in coaching.

Follow the career of Hatcher. If he maintains the integrity, values, and humility that his family installed in him, and he now possesses, Hatcher will reach the heights of stardom in college coaching.

Guy Morriss, "Mr. Cool"

Cool, calm, and pensive are all words that describe Guy Morriss. If Guy had an outburst of emotion you can bet he had planned it and it was well thought out in advance. Guy was the Offensive Line Coach and Assistant Head Coach for four years in the Mumme Era and is the new University of Kentucky Head Football Coach.

After playing 15 years in the NFL and coaching at all levels from high school to NCAA Division II, NCAA Division I, and the NFL, Guy was prepared for a quality coaching career. Morriss knew exactly what he had responded to as a player and he felt 18-23 year old men should be treated as men. In four years I didn't hear him raise his voice four times. An air of respect hung over his head and players listened to him with intense focus. There was seldom a need for Guy to raise his voice and when he did, you could hear a pin drop.

Morriss was the consummate teacher who would take every small detail and analyze it to make his offensive line better. Each group of linemen improved dramatically under his tutelage. Two people taught me most of my football knowledge and learning at Kentucky: Chris Hatcher and Guy Morriss. Hatcher taught me the intricate details of the passing game with route combinations and philosophy while Morriss taught me pass protection and defensive front recognition.

The best coaches never stop learning and will take bits of information and implement it regardless of its source. After I had some early success in recruiting, Morriss began to inquire about my techniques and philosophy in recruiting. I showed him letters I had handwritten to top recruits on a weekly basis. Guy took that technique and successfully used it to recruit some of the top offensive linemen in the country. His ego was intact and it was unimportant to him that an old high school coach with no recruiting experience was advising him on how his recruiting techniques were working.

Morriss was frustrated throughout his four years in the Mumme Era, just as several of us were, but he remained focused and did a solid job with his group of linemen. If given a fair opportunity and time to develop his own team he could bring tremendous success to Kentucky football.

Tim Keane, "Bubba," A Coach With Passion

"Hubba Bubba," as Tim Keane was called by his friends, was the electricity needed to start excitement. Defense is played with excitement and emotion and there must be a coach on defense who fuels that emotion. Bubba was that coach for four years with the Kentucky defense.

Bubba came to Kentucky with impressive credentials. He had coached with famed coach, Larry Lacewell, for many years at Arkansas State and eventually at Tennessee. Keane had been a successful defensive coordinator and secondary coach and was well respected throughout college football.

If you walked onto our practice field the first coach you would hear was Bubba. He was loud and consistent. All day long you could hear him emphasizing technique, hustle, and discipline. Bubba's players loved him and respected him. He was a great coach on the field and a good friend and mentor to his players off the field.

The defensive philosophy from year one to year four dramatically changed and Keane's cornerbacks were forced to play man-to-man press coverage on most every snap for the last three years. If an offensive lineman misses on a block no one may notice. If a linebacker misses his coverage the average fan will not have a clue that the open receiver who just scored a touchdown was his man. A defensive corner, however, lines up completely isolated, where every fan can see that if he gets beat it was his man.

Bubba was an easy scapegoat for the fans and certain coaches. Major made sure to blame Keane for everything he could. Claude Bassett and Hal Mumme jumped in to point the finger at Keane as well. When Mumme was making decisions to fire coaches at the end of the fourth season, he chose Keane to be one of the token ones. Mumme fired one of the best coaches in the country when he fired Bubba Keane. I felt that Keane's firing was simply an attempt by Mumme to pacify Major and place some of the public blame on Keane.

Keane spent four years as a loyal hard-worker who daily improved his players' technique and performance. At the time of this writing he is out of coaching. The profession of college football will sorely miss "Bubba."

Darrell Patterson, "All I Do Is Make 'Em Better"

If you can take your players and make them perform better you are a special coach. If you can take your players and make them perform dramatically better your are a great coach. Darrell Patterson took his players and made them perform dramatically better.

Tremayne Martin went from a part time role player to an All SEC safety. Willie Gary was named all SEC Freshman and freshman All-American. David Johnson was named First Team Freshman All-American and one of the top 10 freshmen in all of college football. Anthony Wajda was named All-SEC. All of these players had one thing in common: Patterson coached them.

In the spring of 1997 Patterson was the constant source of criticism and verbal barbs by Major. Many of these verbal strikes would come in the locker room in front of the other coaches. I was amazed at Major's indignity! I wondered if and how Patterson could continue to take his public attacks. Eventually Patterson confronted Major, and then like all bullies, Major had to find someone else to abuse in public. Patterson's next three years were much more comfortable than they would have been had Patterson not confronted Major.

Mumme needed assistant coaches to blame when our 2000 season went bad and we finished 2-9. Like Keane, Patterson was fired by Mumme and made to be a scapegoat. Patterson, very simply, had made all his players better. If all of us had improved our players as much as Darrell, we would have been SEC champs. Darrell is currently an Assistant Coach at Arkansas State where there is no doubt he will continue to be a positive influence on young athletes.

Sonny Dykes, "I Can Take All You Got"

The coach who made tight end James Whalen an All-American, by teaching him the techniques and tricks of the trade, was Sonny Dykes.

Sonny was born into a football family. His father is legendary former Texas Tech Head Coach Spike Dykes and his older brother Rick Dykes, is the current Offensive Coordinator for the University of Arizona. Some sons of famous coaches have a golden path paved for them in the coaching profession. Sonny was definitely not one of those. He worked his way up the coaching ladder starting in high school, then moving to junior college, and eventually becoming a graduate assistant at Kentucky. Sonny took a full-time coaching position at Northeast Louisiana after one year at Kentucky; however, in 1999 Sonny would once again be a Wildcat after the Head Coach at NE Louisiana was fired.

Mumme would find many occasions to verbally berate and publicly humiliate Sonny. In the two years Sonny coached at UK, I was astonished at the depth and intensity of the attacks on Sonny.

The college coaching profession is full of good people, but it is also well known for coaches who believe public humiliation is a tactic to use when dealing with assistant coaches. I never have, nor will I ever understand, how a grown man gets a thrill out of trying to degrade another grown man in front of his peers.

Sonny was able to overcome this constant barrage of criticism and verbal abuse to contribute heavily to the success of our program. Not only did Sonny do a marvelous job in coaching Whalen, he did a solid job in handling our punt team, kick-off returns, and extra point field goal teams. Some of the punt fakes and kick returns were the result of Sonny's coaching.

The 1999 Junior Varsity team went 3-2 with Sonny as the head coach. This performance showed he could coach every facet of the game. When Mike Leach was named head coach at Texas Tech University, Sonny was named his Wide Receivers Coach. I strongly believe Sonny will follow in the footsteps of his father and make a great Division I head coach. There is no doubt when Sonny becomes a head coach he will also follow in his father's footsteps as a good person. I guarantee you all graduate assistants will be treated with dignity and respect under Sonny. He will remember what not to do from the way he was treated by Mumme.

Dan Lounsbury, Having Your Priorities Straight

Dan Lounsbury and I definitely butted heads when he first came to Kentucky in December of 1999 to replace Dykes. Lounsbury was a longtime Division I assistant with significant background references. He would eventually become a valued mentor and friend, but we definitely had our rough spots in the beginning.

There wasn't an offensive playbook for the first three years of the Mumme Era. I learned the offense on a trip to BYU and Montana with Hatcher, and from sessions with Morriss. Hatcher and Leach tried to explain to me that nothing was definite and to expect constant change on a daily basis. My first year was very difficult because it was hard for me to adapt to that concept. I tried to explain to Lounsbury what Hatcher and Leach had done with me and Dan struggled with the concept also.

Lounsbury was able to convince Mumme that we needed a playbook, and we eventually made a written playbook and a video playbook. A point of reference actually existed now for all the coaches. The playbook was a great idea, but it was basically useless because the offense and its rules continued to fluctuate.

Dan was frustrated from day one. This style or philosophy of coaching was something he had never been around. There was no organized schedule of offensive meetings, no basic timetable to work or not to work and basically no real structure. Early on in his brief one year at Kentucky, Dan knew he needed to get out and find another job.

I grew to respect Dan when I watched him coach on the field, and I listened to his players praise his coaching expertise. There was no doubt Dan was knowledgeable and a skilled veteran. Derek Smith became a first team All-SEC performer under Dan's coaching. Dan's one pass play that we added to our offense became one of quarterback Jared Lorenzen's best plays for the year 2000.

Dan's best quality was that of a dedicated family man. His time at UK was made even tougher with the loss of his wife's father, who made his home with Dan and his wife Lee. Family priorities were top order and he taught me a valuable lesson in love and family when I watched him handle the death of a loved one in the middle of a season.

Dan was able to land a job coaching QB's at Texas Christian University before the last days of Hal Mumme's tenure at Kentucky. I'm sure that he'll continue to be a top quality coach and eventually will be an offensive coordinator again at the Division I level and with the right breaks he'll make a good Head Coach.

Mike Fanoga, Don't Take It Anymore

Mike Fanoga also took several verbal barrages from Major. Each day I wondered if he would explode and beat Major to within an inch of his life. I believe some of us would not have moved to help Major. Fanoga would have been justified in our eyes.

Having come to Kentucky with Mumme after coaching together at Valdosta State and Iowa Wesleyan, Fanoga had been a dedicated Mumme assistant. He relayed to me Major had treated him the same at Valdosta. I've always remembered a valuable childhood lesson about bullies: if you let them run you over they will never stop. Major never stopped verbally attacking Fanoga. Fanoga's loyalty to Mumme must have been incredibly strong because he put up with Major for many years.

Fanoga was one of the most popular coaches on our staff with the high school coaches. He would do anything to help a coach or a player. His players always played hard for him and after being taken off the field and made Director of Player Development by Mumme, Fanoga eventually decided to coach again. Jack Harbaugh of Western Kentucky University hired Mike as his Defensive Line Coach and Fanoga was one of the big reasons Western Kentucky University won the Ohio Valley Conference and advanced into the playoffs in the 2000 season.

Conclusion

Mumme was fortunate to have some quality assistants during his four years at Kentucky. Any success we had in our four years came as a direct result of these men's efforts.

LESSON #3—Leadership does not care who possesses it. There is not an age requirement or experience requirement to be a good leader. Our coaching staff possessed both young and older coaches. Some of our oldest were our worst leaders, while our youngest (Chris Hatcher) was probably our best leader. Hatcher's actions demanded respect and the players followed his lead.

CHAPTER 4

RECRUITING STORIES, "WHAT A BLAST"

LESSON 4—True friendship is based on caring and honesty. It will survive rough days and tumultuous times.

Success in college football can be achieved through a combination of good coaching, top-notch facilities, and strong alumni support. The most important factor in being successful, however, can be described in one word—Recruiting. You can be the greatest coach in the profession, but if you fail to get quality players you will not win. I thoroughly enjoyed recruiting because of the intriguing characters I met on each trip.

Charles Grant (We Were A Leak Away)

Charles Grant was one of the greatest high school football players in the history of Georgia. Most every college in America had Grant on its wish list and many had made the journey to Miller County, GA. Grant was a physical freak, standing 6'5" and weighing 250 pounds, while playing running back and linebacker. Most colleges had projected Grant as a future defensive end, but he was versatile enough to have tied Hershel Walker's touchdown record during his high school career.

My recruiting of Grant began late in the process because Hatcher, who was a native Georgian, had worked the phone calls with Grant since May of his junior season. Hatcher was a graduate assistant at the time and NCAA rules prohibited grad assistants from leaving campus to recruit. Bassett had already been to see Grant play and was in awe of his talent.

I went to Grant's home on one of the last weeks of the recruiting process. We were one of the finalist for his talents because of Hatcher's diligent phone work and because wide receiver Jimmy Robinson, also a Georgia native, had done a great recruiting job on Grant's official visit to

UK. Early in the day I located the small trailer where Grant and his mother were living and set up a time for visiting that night.

It was dark and there was no lighting as I sat in the driveway waiting, when suddenly there was a knock at my window. The knock by Grant's mother startled me. I rolled down my window and she told me to follow her to the laundromat where we could talk. I went to a poorly lit small building consisting of a few washers and dryers, where I met several of Grant's relatives, neighbors, and friends. I was badgered with questions and comments about Kentucky football and drilled as to why I thought Grant should even consider Kentucky. This was fun! My greatest joy came in those situations, and I could tell in the one-hour's time at the laundromat I had won over the local crowd.

We went back to the trailer where Charles met us and we began to discuss his future. I knew Hatcher had laid a solid foundation and Grant was close to deciding to be a Wildcat. Mumme and Bassett had done a good job in editing a 1997 highlight video and I knew the video could play a major role in closing Grant.

After an hour of casual talk about family, academics, and football, I decided it was time to play the video and move towards getting a verbal commitment. Grant put the video in and I waited for the start, but there was a problem. The video wouldn't play! Since I have no mechanical skills at all, I thought my video closing was dead. Charles saved the day when he went to the back of the trailer and came back with his tools, a q-tip and a jar of vaseline. Within five minutes he had the VCR up and running.

As the video played, I could tell it was working. When it finished, I asked Grant where he had his best visit.

He replied "Kentucky."

I asked him where he could play and help the team the fastest and he replied, "Kentucky."

My final question was "Charles, where does your heart tell you to go?" He replied, "Kentucky."

I stood up and shook his hand and said, "Congratulations, you're going to be a Wildcat."

He grinned and gave me a hug and his momma said, "Are you sure this is what you want?" Grant replied that he was sure.

Verbal commitments are wonderful, but they mean absolutely nothing. Grant's high school coaches had told me they thought he might choose Kentucky, but reminded me we had better not let it become public if he did. They were sure Georgia would put a full court press on if they found his intentions were to go to Kentucky.

I stopped on the side of the highway and made a phone call to Bassett to inform him of Grant's decision. I explained it was crucial we kept it quiet and he assured me he would. Within two days the *Lexington Herald-Leader* wrote an article stating Grant had committed to Kentucky. There was a leak! Grant's coaches called, and within a day we lost Grant to Georgia.

If the leak had not happened, I'm not sure we would have signed Grant, but I sure would like to have found out. Grant didn't academically qualify, but after attending Hargrave Military Academy and making his test scores, he returned to Georgia. Grant had a phenomenal freshman season as a defensive end and running back! After suffering a knee injury, Georgia stopped playing him at running back, but he is projected to be a top draft pick when he leaves Georgia.

Leaking information to the press concerning recruits became a common occurrence at Kentucky. Sometimes it helped and sometimes it hurt. It was a good learning experience for me because I learned not to tell anyone anything unless I wanted it printed.

David Johnson, "A Gem Hidden Under A Mess"

Bassett's desk was full of videotapes. They were strewn all over and in no certain order. It was November of 1997, and I had the habit of going in and searching for tapes that might have been misplaced or not looked at yet. There was a tape for a running back/defensive back lying under a pile of tapes. The tape was labeled David Johnson, Princess Anne High School, Virginia Beach, VA.

As I sat back in my office and began to watch the video I was amazed. Johnson wasn't a good player; he was a great player. Not only was he a top running back, but he was an outstanding defensive back as well. My excitement swelled the more I watched. When secondary Coach Tim Keane walked by I requested he stop and watch. In a few short minutes Keane was sold that Johnson could play in the SEC.

Johnson wasn't on any of the "so called" experts list with the exception of a Virginia player listing which put him in the top 50 players in Virginia. I had learned early in my recruiting experiences that most of recruiting gurus who made these list were inaccurate at best. You could find some hidden great players. All you had to do was look hard enough and long enough.

Keane had a great eye for talent and if he said they could play, they could play. The next step was to let Defensive Coordinator Mike Major see the video. Major gave the okay to begin recruiting Johnson, and I took off to Virginia to meet Johnson and his family.

Recruiting David Johnson was one of my favorite recruiting experiences in my four years at Kentucky. His parents were hard working and loving and his little brother Brandon and I became fast friends. My weekly visits would eventually include a fiercely contested ping pong match with Brandon.

A couple of Division I-AA schools were the only schools recruiting David when I began the recruiting process. Many Division I college coaches are insecure and afraid to recruit a player unless they know he is being recruited by other Division I schools. These coaches feel if the player ends up being a bust, they can use the excuse that other coaches were wrong about the player also. This type of college coach will also jump on a player when they find out that another Division I school just offered a scholarship to someone they had previously rejected. Very shortly after we offered David a scholarship, Georgia Tech, Michigan State, and Maryland all began to recruit David. We were able to convince David to come to Kentucky with the promise he would have a chance to play immediately.

David was one of the key reasons we were able to win seven games in 1998 and go to the Outback Bowl. He was recognized as one of the top 10 freshman football players in America by *The Sporting News*. These were top accomplishments for a young man who was not heavily recruited originally. I am thankful I searched Bassett's desk and found this gem of a player hiding under all the stacks of videos.

Brad Pyatt, "Rocky Mountain High"

The altitude was about to get to me. I thought I was going to have a heart attack as I pushed the truck up the slight incline on a quiet street in Arvada, Colorado. Brad Pyatt had called his mother Cathy earlier to tell her he had run out of gas, and Cathy and I were now pushing Brad and his truck up the hill as Brad steered it over to the side of the road. Pyatt was one of the top receivers in America. He had a rare combination of speed, strength, and size. Mumme had made the recruiting of Pyatt a top priority for me and, as I pushed that truck up the hill, I had begun to wonder if I was going to pay the ultimate price for his recruitment—my life.

Traveling to beautiful places was one of the fringe benefits of recruiting, and the Denver, Colorado, area was one of my favorite places. I never got tired of seeing the snow-capped Rocky Mountains each trip I made to the Denver area.

The highlight film on Pyatt was nearly as good as any other receiver video I had seen. Not only did Pyatt make the hard catches seem easy, but he was also a very effective runner after the catch. He also seemed to have a knack for making the big play in critical situations.

Pyatt had been heavily recruited by Colorado, Southern California, Oregon, Miami, and other top schools. Since we were throwing the ball 45-

50 times per game and we were in desperate need of top quality receivers, Brad was enticed to the point where we thought we could close him.

Mumme, Morriss, and I made a visit in late January to see Pyatt and Kip Sixberry. Sixberry was from Mullen Prep in Denver and would eventually sign with us and become the youngest starter in Division I football at 17 years of age.

Patience was not a strong virtue of Mumme's and he was getting impatient with Pyatt. He wanted him to commit and he wanted it to be done on Mumme's only visit. I had been working on Brad since the spring and had developed a trusting relationship with his parents.

You could never be sure how Mumme was going to do in a home visit. It would vary from incredibly caring and patient to obnoxious and rude. Since the head coach was only allowed one visit, his visit could potentially mean disaster and might cause you to lose someone that you had nurtured for months. I had prepared the Pyatts for the visit and when Mumme asked for my cell phone to call Brad before we arrived at their house, I was confident Brad would say the right things. The phone call went well as did the visit and Pyatt committed to be a Wildcat.

Brad started his career strong and caught over 20 passes the first six games of the season, including a spectacular touchdown catch at South Carolina. He would struggle with bunions on his feet and never reach his full potential the first two seasons. However, Brad, recently had surgery to solve his feet problems and seems to be on track to becoming the player he has the potential to become.

Bobby Blizzard, "Recruit A Player Find A Friend"

Recruiting a player will normally mean establishing a relationship with their coach. There are exceptions to this rule and the recruiting of Bobby Blizzard was definitely one of those exceptions.

Blizzard was on most of the recruiting gurus lists as one of the top tight ends in America. He played at Hampton High in Virginia, one of the top high school programs in America. His quarterback was Ronald Curry who was the greatest all-around high school athlete whom I have ever seen in person. Mike Smith was the head coach and had consistently produced a championship program.

I could tell on my first visit to Smith's office he was probably not going to be a coach who would be on my side in the recruiting process. There was a strong belief in Virginia that Smith encouraged his players to attend the University of Virginia. I would come to find this to be true. High school coaches have a tough job in trying to do what's best for their players and also in keeping local boosters happy by sending their top players to the state university. Smith was able to persuade many of his players over the years to understand where his loyalty was. I knew getting Blizzard out of Virginia was going to be tough.

Blizzard and I immediately hit it off and established a good rapport. I felt like we had a great chance to land Bobby because he wanted to catch the ball. A weekly letter writing campaign to Blizzard, in which I would draw up a new play each week showing him a touchdown catch against an SEC opponent, was the starting point for my recruiting strategy to obtain Bobby.

Early in the season I was sitting at a local pub having dinner. The University of Virginia was on a Thursday night ESPN game when the commentator made a startling announcement: Ronald Curry and Bobby Blizzard had verbally committed to play for the University of Virginia. I was shocked. Nothing had occurred to make me believe this was going to happen. When I talked to Bobby's father, who was a high school basketball coach at Phoebus High in Hampton, Virginia, he was also shocked. Coach Blizzard assured me he would be talking to Bobby and would let me know what happened.

My philosophy on a verbal commitment is to talk to the player and see how strong it is and ask why he made it. If the player is firm and wishes to be left alone and makes it clear he was not coerced, then I honor his decision and stop recruiting the player. Many times, however, a player gets swept up into the momentum of events when he is on a campus, makes a commitment, then he will express regret, and change his mind when he gets home. Bobby and Curry both got carried away with the pageantry of the ESPN game and the big crowd at Virginia and eventually changed their minds later. Bobby would eventually sign with Kentucky and Curry with North Carolina.

After his successful visit to the Kentucky vs. NE Louisiana game I felt very confident that we could eventually sign Blizzard. His high school team won another state championship and several top colleges were heavily recruiting Bobby. His goal was to catch the football and play early. Kentucky offered him those opportunities better than anyone else.

When it came time for Mumme to make his one in-home visit I felt certain Bobby was ready to commit. I informed Mumme before we entered the house that I was going to get a commitment that night. Mumme told me not to press it and to take it easy because he was afraid I would blow it and lose him. My many visits, talks, and letters gave me the confidence to press for a commitment.

Mumme did a solid job that evening, and with Bobby's family listening I asked Bobby some closing questions: "What do you want most out of college football?"

He answered, "Catch the football."

I then asked, "Where can you catch more balls in one year than all the other schools who are recruiting you combined?"

He answered, "Kentucky."

I said, "Congratulations you're going to be a Wildcat." I then stood up and shook his hand and gave him a hug. Bobby's mom Laverne Aikins and father David both asked Bobby if he was sure this was what he wanted. He replied that it was and Mumme stood up and shook hands with everyone.

Shortly after the congratulations were over, two Division I schools that were recruiting Bobby called, and Laverne informed them Bobby couldn't talk because he was going to Kentucky.

We withstood many more obstacles before getting Bobby to Kentucky. Obtaining a high school transcript from Hampton High proved to be challenging. Coach Blizzard had to be extremely persistent before even he, being Bobby's father, could get a copy. After examining the transcript, Bobby had to take several classes his second semester to have a chance to qualify academically. He came miraculously close, especially considering his late start, but failed to qualify and went to Hargrave Military Academy to finish his NCAA qualifications.

Bobby eventually joined us in January of 1999. He was weak and slow as a result of very little weight training in high school. With hard work he went from a 180-pound bench press to a 305 pound bench press in two seasons. He also increased his speed from 5.2 to 4.69 in the forty-yard dash. When Bobby reaches full strength in another season he could be a solid player with NFL possibilities. He decided in the spring of 2001 following a 21-catch season in 2000, to transfer to North Carolina where he believes his chances of reaching his goals could best be reached.

Recruiting opened the door to my meeting new people and new friends. One of my greatest treasures in recruiting was the friendship that I established with Laverne, Bobby's mother. She is one of those friends I will keep forever.

Derek Smith, "Let Me Cut Him"

Derek Smith was one of the greatest athletes to ever play in the history of Kentucky high school athletics. Not only was he one of the most heavily recruited football players in the state, but he was also a top basketball player receiving several basketball scholarship offers as well.

I was not involved in the early recruiting of Derek, as Bassett had been the primary recruiter on all of Ft. Thomas Highlands players. Bassett was getting impatient with Smith, however, because unlike his teammate, future

Kentucky quarterback Jared Lorenzen, Smith would not make an early commitment. Bassett was becoming increasingly irritated because Smith continued to talk about the possibility of playing basketball in college. Smith also was becoming close to Penn State Assistant Coach, Jay Paterno, and was beginning to lean toward attending PSU.

I had been recruiting Bo Scaife, a tight end from Mullen Prep in Denver as well as keeping the recruiting process going with Blizzard at Hargrave. Bassett called me into his office and informed me of his increasing impatience with Smith. He went on a tirade about Smith's disloyalty for not committing to Kentucky, and he told me he wanted me to take over Smith's recruitment.

I tried to explain to Bassett that growing up in Kentucky and loving Kentucky basketball was something you had to experience to understand. Smith was a great kid who was taking his time in the recruiting process because he was unsure. He was doing exactly what he should have done, and fortunately he had strong enough parents to allow him to withstand the intense pressure of Kentucky fans. This important decision would be made on his own time.

The last instructions I got from Bassett on the recruitment of Smith shocked me, even coming from Bassett. He informed me to move Smith's scheduled official visit back to the end of January instead of its earlier date. Bassett told me his intended purpose was so I could convince Bo Scaife to commit before Smith and then Bassett could have the pleasure of pulling Smith's scholarship offer out from under him.

I replied to Bassett we needed great players like Smith and I would not follow his orders, but instead I would work to keep him. The next three weeks would be used to establish a relationship with Smith and we hit it off immediately. He is a smart young man who knew what he wanted and was not going to be pressured into committing anywhere until he was ready.

My plan was to relay to Smith, in simple terms, what it meant to play football at Kentucky if you were from the state of Kentucky. Our relationship became trusting because I wanted what was best for Smith and we would explore this during our conversations. After three weeks of developing a relationship, Smith verbally committed to being a Wildcat. I went in to tell Bassett the next morning. He responded with an emotional outburst of anger. The fact that Kentucky had just landed one of the top players in the country wasn't important to him, he was seething because he had looked forward to calling Smith and cutting his scholarship offer.

I told Bassett to get over it, that we had just landed a great player and a great kid who also happened to be an in-state product. When I left his office, he was furious.

Later that morning I walked up the hallway in our football office complex and happened to witness an incredulous event. Bassett had stopped Mumme in the hallway to tell Mumme that he "Bassett" had talked to Smith and received a commitment. Mumme gave Bassett a hug and congratulated him on his great job recruiting Smith. As Bassett turned and walked away from Mumme he saw me looking at him and he knew I witnessed his "extraordinary story."

Derek Smith was first-team All SEC as a sophomore at Kentucky and will probably be a top draft pick one day in the NFL. He loves the University of Kentucky and passionately plays hard each week.

Not A Science

Recruiting in college football is the most important ingredient in determining success or failure. It is definitely not an exact science and everyone will make mistakes. I enjoyed this part of college coaching the most and definitely learned many lessons from my four years of recruiting for Kentucky.

LESSON #4—True friendship is based on truth and caring. It will stand the test of time and survive tough days and tumultuous moments. Bobby Blizzard was one of the most heavily recruited players whom we signed at Kentucky. His two-year career with the Wildcats didn't pan out to what he wished it would be or what we wished. Bobby's mother Laverne, and his father David, were consistent positive forces in his life before Kentucky, during Kentucky, and will continue after Kentucky. Even though Bobby never realized his dreams at Kentucky, the family and I remain close because we have an honest relationship with each other. I believe Bobby will continue his football career and reach all his goals, but I'm not certain. I am certain, however, the Blizzard family and Tony Franklin will remain true friends for years to come because our relationship is based on trust and honesty.

CHAPTER 5

GAMES TO REMEMBER

Lesson 5—All you can do is all you can do, but all you can do is enough.

Installation

A fast-paced installation period took place in the Spring of 1997. We put together a simple offense that was rapid fire and ready to go. Bill Curry left a good nucleus of talent which really fit into Mumme's style of offense. Tim Couch and Craig Yeast were obviously great players with talent anyone could see. Other players such as Kio Sanford, Anthony White, Jason Watts, John Schlarman, and Kevin Coleman could have lined up and played for any SEC team. If three other receivers had not lost their eligibility due to academic problems, we would have had as much talent as any SEC offense.

1997 Louisville

When I walked into Commonwealth Stadium for the opening game versus Louisville in 1997, a huge grin kept coming onto my face. My father had brought me to see Kentucky play since the early 1970s, and I was in a dream state when I began to watch the stadium fill. Friends of mine began to holler at me and fellow high school coaches waved and told me they were proud to see one of their own on the field at Commonwealth. The experience was memorable.

Hal Mumme showed a swagger of confidence that made him look as if he had been coaching at this level for years. The swagger was always one of his best qualities. Beaming with assuredness and cockiness that he was going to lead the team to victory, Mumme made everyone feel confident.

By the time we took the field the stadium was overflowing. There was a buzz in the air letting everyone know something special was going to take place. By the time of the opening kickoff the excitement was at an earthquake level. Mumme had given what would become a normal pre-game speech with very little fire and brimstone. His pre-game speeches usually consisted of "Well boys, let's go have some fun—remember no matter what happens, good or bad, just play the next play and Attack, Attack, Attack!"

Hal Mumme's first touchdown call as Kentucky's coach was "Ace Flip 617 Switch" and Tim Couch laid a perfect strike to wide receiver Lance Mickelsen near the left sideline in the Nicholasville Road end zone. The stadium went wild. Couch would go on to have what would become a normal Saturday afternoon with Mumme's offense throwing for 398 yards and four touchdowns.

Anthony White and Kio Sanford would both turn in electrifying open field runs after short throws in the flats. Sanford's 80-yard run after a catch on "Blue Open Z Randy" was a huge play as Louisville had mounted a comeback and was threatening to take Mumme's opening game victory away. Hustling from his center position, Jason Watts made a key block on Louisville's sideline and Sanford did the rest with pure speed.

The build up for the game had been a question of toughness, with Louisville coach Ron Cooper and the news media questioning Mumme's practice philosophy of no tackling or hitting below the waist. After finishing the game with a run pounding drive, Mumme made a point to tell the team about its toughness. The players believed he was right and you could see the confidence beaming from our team.

Being different was what helped Mumme obtain the job at Kentucky, and the opening game let fans see what they had yearned for. Throwing the football, gambling on fourth down, and punting to the sidelines would all become trademarks of the Mumme Era. A glimpse of hope was provided for the Kentucky fans that better things were on their way.

1997 Indiana

We traveled to Indiana to play the Hoosiers in Bloomington on September 20, 1997 for a critical game. The most important games in football are making sure you win all the games you should win and winning most of the games that you can win. Indiana was beginning a new era with coach Cam Cameron, who had been an NFL assistant as well as a Division I assistant. The most important aspect of this contest was we both desperately needed to win the game.

Mumme broke his calm pre-game speech routine and began to deliver an emotional, screaming discourse. He questioned whether the team was ready to play and became increasingly irritated as he described Cameron as a coach who thought he was better than Mumme. According to Mumme, Cameron said Mumme was "a little ol' Division II coach." As the years went on I heard a few of these speeches where the opposing coach had mysteriously said something about someone. After a few moments of ranting and cursing, he eventually decided to attack a drawing board. I looked around the room and saw the players' eyes and knew their reaction was similar to mine: what does Cam Cameron saying you're a Division II coach have to do with us beating Indiana? Jonas Liening, our junior left tackle, looked over at me and sarcastically said, "Wow, Coach Franklin, I'm really fired up now, how 'bout you?" He laughed and walked away.

Emotional outbursts were common for Mumme over his four seasons and there were more than I can remember. The players eventually learned to ignore them. They were unpredictable in their timing or their cause, but they were usually personal to whomever Mumme picked as his adversary. One thing was for certain, if his intention for his numerous outbursts were motivational, it didn't seem to work.

Indiana was unprepared for what was about to happen to them. Couch exploded for a seven-touchdown passing barrage and several players took part in the successful offensive eruption. Big plays came from Yeast, Sanford, Mickelsen, Anthony White and others, as we were unstoppable. The Hoosier defense was slow and not very talented and our match ups were perfect as we went on to a 49-7 victory.

Mumme seemed to believe after the game that his ranting and raving and chalkboard attack were the key reasons for victory. Match-ups, momentum, and talent normally decide college football games and Indiana was a great example of Kentucky taking advantage of all three. Couch was phenomenal and we matched up very favorably against the Hoosiers scheme and talent. Whatever the reasons, the 1997 victory was a big one because we should have won, and we did!

1997 Alabama

Alabama has one of most storied pasts in all of college football. Its SEC and national championships put it in a class where it doesn't take very long to inventory. When the Tide rolled into Commonwealth Stadium on October 4, 1997, they brought all their tradition and glory, but they didn't bring the talent they normally have. Mike DuBose had taken over a program still under NCAA sanctions for violations committed before his arrival as Alabama's Head Coach. The Tide had been forced to reduce their scholarships because of the sanctions, and, although they came to Commonwealth Stadium ranked in the Top 25, this was not a typical Alabama football team.

Night games at Commonwealth Stadium have a unique electricity to them and on this night there was a smell of something special was in the air. It was evident there was a chance to make this a memorable night because former NFL legend and Kentucky great George Blanda was in attendance and addressed the team. I'm not sure how special it was to our team, but I was thrilled to have one of the greatest players in all of professional football history to take part in this event. I remembered several of his dramatic victories as a quarterback and kicker for the Oakland Raiders.

There is a saying in football that the "magic eye in the sky doesn't lie," meaning the video recording reveals a team's strengths and weaknesses. It was obvious our talent matched up well with Alabama. The game proved to be an evenly matched game just as we had felt it would be. It would be a game for heroes! Several players would get their opportunity to make history and be the first Kentucky team to beat the Crimson Tide in 75 years!

Couch had his normal stellar performance, making several huge plays we eventually took for granted because they would become so common. Two plays stand out which the average fan may have taken for granted.

Derek Homer was Couch's fifth and final read on a swing pass that Homer caught and turned into a eye-popping 62-yard run, making four to five Bama players miss tackles as he crossed the right side of the field to the left side. Homer outran all of the Tide defenders with Yeast making the last block at the 5-yard line. Assistant equipment manager David Coogle made just as spectacular of a run down the sideline as he ran stride for stride with Homer into the end zone while carrying the next in play game ball! Coogle's spectacular run was caught on our season ending highlight film making him an important part of Kentucky history.

"35 Naked Smash" was the call when Couch faked to Homer and with a blitzer coming in his face Couch utilized his "get big" drill technique and launched a perfect strike to Kevin Coleman. Coleman's end zone catch put the Cats on top with a 27-17 score. Checking off at the line of scrimmage by Couch was another example of his legendary big-play ability.

The Wildcat defense came up with the biggest play of the evening when senior defensive end David Ginn leaped high and blocked a field goal attempt. Anwar Stewart picked up the loose ball and ran 68-yards into the end zone to make the score 34-31 with 6:34 remaining in the fourth quarter. Ginn was a factor of Mumme's off-season program, becoming an effective leader after Mumme put him in a leadership position during winter workouts. Mumme promised Ginn if he sacrificed and was a team player he would get a chance to make some big plays. Mumme had a unique ability to make a back-up player accept a role which would allow him to contribute and Ginn was a classic example of Mumme's off-season accomplishment.

When the game was tied at the end of regulation and went to overtime the atmosphere was exhilarating. The defense came up with another big play when Tremayne Martin made a bone jarring hit and freshman Jeremy Bowie came up with the ball. It was now up to the offense. All we had to do was kick a field goal and the game was over.

Mumme's practice habits included practicing an overtime script each Thursday in the stadium. Our players were confident when they took the field and on third and eleven, Couch called "Blue Flip 93 Y Delay." (See Insert B, below). Couch hit Yeast on a 13-yard curl and Yeast busted through two defenders for a 26-yard score and the winning touchdown as pandemonium broke loose.

Players and coaches jumped and screamed as thousands of Kentucky fans climbed over the fences and flooded the stadium field. Mike Major, the Defensive Coordinator, screamed, "Kentucky beat Alabama, we beat Alabama!" Mumme hugged everyone in sight and all the staff was outwardly ecstatic except for Mike Leach. Leach seldom showed any emotion and these fantastic circumstances were not going to be any different. I have no doubt he was happy, but Mike just never showed it.

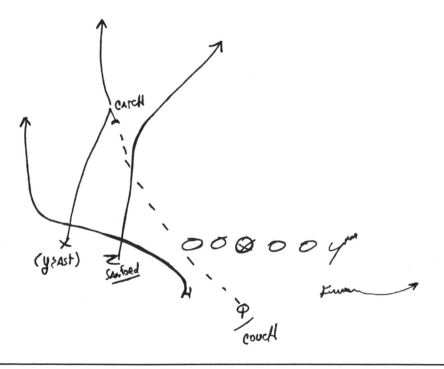

Insert B. "Blue Flip 93 Y Delay".

The Alabama victory gave Mumme and the UK football program exactly what it needed, national recognition and instant respectability! ESPN played the replay of the fans tearing down the goal posts many times over the following weeks and high school recruits began to stand up and take notice of Kentucky football. The victory over what turned out to be a losing Alabama football team would be a launching point for the Kentucky football program to become a top national program. All we now had to do was follow up with more victories, plus recruit, and coach with integrity. The next few years Kentucky fans could have the Top 25 team year in and year out they so desperately wanted and deserved.

1998 Preview

1998 provided several memorable games. Our talent level had improved with a couple of key freshman recruits on defense. We felt we were definitely a bowl quality team with Couch and most of the offense returning, and our eventual invitation to the Outback Bowl on January 1, 1999 proved our hunches to be right.

1998 Indiana

The September 19, 1998, rematch with Indiana was one of the biggest games in the Mumme Era. It was a game we were supposed to win! We had thoroughly whipped them 49-7 the previous year and we had them at home. To go to a bowl game, we had to win.

Indiana came into the game with a defensive game plan that included rushing only two to three defenders and dropping eight to nine to defend the pass. Couch was struggling with one of his worst games and Yeast was playing sub-par. We were down 27-10 in the third quarter and we needed a big play.

Mumme had already used fake punts in previous games and everybody was now preparing to defend them. Backed up on our own 22-yard line and facing fourth down and 17 yards to go, this was not a time any normal football coach would think about a fake punt, let alone call one. This was the situation on which Mumme thrived. He had an opportunity to do something most coaches would not even consider.

Indiana had to cooperate by lining up unsound. A potential receiver would have to be left uncovered, and then Mumme would undoubtedly call the fake. He scanned the defense to see if there was a leak in the defense. I watched him signal for the fake and, I walked down to the opposite end of the sideline to get a better look. Mumme had used a trick formation to make

Davis an eligible receiver, even though Davis lined up at left tackle. The left outside receiver stepped off the line of scrimmage and the right wide receiver stepped up. This movement made Davis an eligible receiver and nobody was covering him. Matt Mumme took the snap and Davis caught his pass, made one tackler miss, and went 78 yards for a touchdown. Mumme's call was brilliant and one of the gutsiest calls I've ever witnessed!

Commonwealth Stadium erupted as this was the spark we needed to mount a comeback win. Couch hit Anthony White for a 48-yard touchdown pass to allow Kentucky to complete a 35-31 come from behind victory.

1998 LSU

We traveled to LSU with a 4-2 record and a chance to beat a Top 25 LSU team on the road. Kentucky had not beaten a Top 25-SEC team on the road since 1977. This was a game that could make or break us as a bowl possible team. LSU was talented, but we felt we matched up well.

Fans had lined up and shouted at us as our bus drove into Tiger Stadium. Tiger families and friends had been playing, cooking, eating, and drinking hours before our arrival. Numerous fans gave up the patented "middle finger salute" as well as some showing their bare backsides. Our players loved it and Mumme was like Cool Hand Luke, showing no signs of nervousness or intimidation.

I made a pre-game call to Jimmy Harrell, an assistant coach at Murray High School in Murray, KY., who had been one of my first coaching mentors when I was a student teacher at Murray HS in 1979. Jimmy loved the Tigers and had told stories of famed Tiger Stadium on a weekly basis. So far his descriptions of the atmosphere had been accurate. This experience was one I wanted to share, and I promised Jimmy I would call him after our victory.

The game was a fan's delight with big plays on offence and a spectacular nail-biting finish. Tiger fans were wonderful, as they booed their own team and everything seemed in place for a big upset. Craig Yeast continued to get single coverage and Couch was blistering the Tiger defense, but when LSU stormed back from a 14-point deficit to tie the game, it looked as if we were headed for overtime.

With less than two minutes to play it looked as if we were going to run the clock, punt, and play for the overtime. On third down and 12 yards to go a time-out was called. Couch, Leach, other players, and I gathered around Mumme. Somewhere during the discussion, Kris Comstock our right tackle, said "Why don't we run the reverse to McCord we ran against South Carolina?"

Mumme responded, "Why not?"

The reverse to McCord worked perfectly and after a 38-yard gain we were almost in field goal position. Couch hit tight end Jimmy Haley with a perfect 14-yard toss after assistant coach Chris Hatcher had suggested to Mumme to run 'Blue Flip 94.' Freshman Seth Hanson stepped onto the field and drilled a 33-yard field goal for the victory.

An assistant coach and a player suggested two critical play calls! One of Mumme's strongest assets was that he listened to players and coaches in critical situations. One of his biggest inabilities was not giving credit when credit was due. The press played up the theory that the reverse had been a three-play plan and brilliant strategy decision by Mumme. In fact, it was a wonderful suggestion by a player. Regardless, the win at LSU was huge even if LSU went on to a losing season.

The Hot Dog Story

The LSU game had another interesting twist. Mumme told a story that he believed LSU Head Coach Gerry DiNardo was so uptight before games that he (Mumme) thought he could get into his head. Assistant Athletic Trainer Jeff Allen was told to buy a hot dog prior to Mumme's pre-game meeting and handshake with DiNardo. Allen was instructed to bring Mumme the hot dog and Mumme would then eat it in front of DiNardo. This was supposedly going to rattle DiNardo because Mumme was so cool he was eating hot dogs prior to kick off while DiNardo was supposedly sweating bullets. Mumme has told this story numerous times laughing loudly as to how he shook up DiNardo with his mental mastery.

1999 Preview

1999 was the first year without Couch as the quarterback for Mumme. Many of his critics had questioned whether Mumme's Air Raid offense would work without Couch. Dusty Bonner stepped in and with an inexperienced offensive line and inexperienced receivers, Bonner continued to work the miracles of Mumme's offense as he led us to the Music City Bowl.

1999 Arkansas

Arkansas entered Commonwealth Stadium on October 2, 1999 ranked 20th in the nation. They were a very physical team. We were coming off a home loss against Florida and needed a win against a Top 25 team to throw us into the bowl picture. Mumme's critics would have a hard time criticizing his offense if such a young team could go to a bowl. Beating the Razorbacks would certainly have us headed in the right direction.

Bonner and Hatcher had developed a great feel for each other. Hatcher had convinced Mumme to use a game plan with a lot of formation checks. Bonner would line the team up in a certain formation and let Hatcher scan the coverage. Hatcher would then signal to Mumme the best play. The plan worked perfectly as Bonner and Hatcher teamed together to call the perfect game. Quentin McCord came up with two big touchdown catches and Dougie Allen made a spectacular over the shoulder catch in the back corner of the end zone for another touchdown. Allen would unfortunately tear ligaments in his knee on the catch and have a season ending surgery.

The victory over Arkansas helped a young football team grow to believe they had what it takes to win against SEC competition. The victory propelled the 1999 post-Couch Era to a slot in the Music City Bowl and helped solidify the belief that Hal Mumme's offense could work without Couch.

Conclusion

There were other key victories in the Mumme Era with great plays and spectacular moments, but the preceding games were most memorable to me

.

LESSON #5—All you can do is all you can do, but all you can do is enough. In 1999 Dusty Bonner took over for the legendary Tim Couch as quarterback. Bonner wasn't tall enough, fast enough, couldn't throw far enough or hard enough for any of the football experts or critics. However, Bonner took a team with very little offensive experience and led the SEC in several passing categories. The under-appreciated Bonner took UK to six wins and a bowl game. No one in college football could have done any better. Bonner simply did all he could do to the best of his ability and led our team better than anyone in college football could have done at Kentucky in 1999.

CHAPTER 6

THE PRESS

Lesson 6—The public owes itself the responsibility to not blindly believe any facet of the press without legitimate questioning of the particular reporter's agenda. Read and watch the media daily with a skeptical eye, but be thankful they exist for they truly help prevent corruption and tyranny.

Thank God for the First Amendment to the Constitution and its guarantee for Freedom of the Press. Without the diligent and persistent work of the news media, dictators and tyrants would run our country. If not for the work of some diligent reporters many of the NCAA violations we now know occurred would have remained a mystery, until the NCAA eventually found them. The sanctions could have been delayed and possibly even tougher, if these reporters had not done a thorough job.

In my 20 years of coaching at the high school and college level I have had many opportunities to deal with various news media. I have come to one conclusion. They are human. Some members of the media will have an agenda or purpose when they begin to seek out information. When they are fair, their agenda will be placed aside if the truth is found to be different than their intentions. Although reporters are supposed to drop all their personal beliefs and feelings when covering a story, their human qualities make it an impossible task. If berated publicly and treated less than human, you can bet some will treat a story differently than if treated with respect.

I know there will be times in my life no matter what the truth is and no matter how I treat a media person, some will slant a story not in my favor, but it has only occurred on rare occasions. Most reporters have treated me fairly. I realize if I choose to make a living that involves public scrutiny, then I must learn to deal with those rare media people who seek unethical agendas.

The Honeymoon

Nearly every head coach who starts a new job will begin his first year in a "honeymoon" relationship with the media. The coverage will consist of telling stories, mostly inspiring, about the coach's past and the hope he will bring to the program. The new coach will normally have to do something to end the honeymoon. Some coaches are pretty good at messing it up, but Hal Mumme certainly enjoyed one of the longest honeymoons in SEC history before eventually ending on some really testy stories. I was amazed at how the media treated Mumme with "kid gloves" even after he began to treat some with disrespect. Smelling blood, several took their gloves off in the end of the Mumme era and some "final round knockouts" were written.

Guy Morriss is currently involved in his honeymoon with the media. There are two major differences in his approach to the media and Mumme's approach: (1.) Guy knows he is in a honeymoon and, unless he changes, is not going to be surprised when certain media members go after him or some phase of his program. (2.) Guy will treat each member with respect and dignity simply because that is how he treats most people. Guy's diverse football background has prepared him for brutal days ahead, and when they come he'll be much better prepared than Mumme.

Bob Watkins

Many of you may not know who Watkins is, but in several local newspapers throughout the state Watkins has his column appearing weekly. I read Watkins' commentary on Kentucky sports with interest each week. He is one reporter who is not afraid to give a strong opinion. I've grown to respect his articles, although I don't always agree with his opinions, because he seems to not favor any particular coach or program. One week he may say something positive about Tubby Smith and the next week he may criticize him for a particular decision. I think they call it true journalism.

Billy Reed

I've read Billy Reed's articles since I was a kid when he used to write for the Courier-Journal. There have been times when I've hated Reed for his negative articles on my beloved Wildcats or their coaches, and there have been times where I've loved him for his articles on my beloved Wildcats. Reed causes people to think. He starts arguments. He causes emotional outbursts. Reed, most of all, sells newspapers. The gift of clever writing is one not owned by all and Reed has mastered the art of controversy. Just as a coach, athletic director, or player thought Reed criticized everything they did, Reed would write something positive about them. He definitely "stirred the pot" and I, for one, will miss his biting columns as he recently retired from the *Lexington Herald-Leader*.

Chip Hutcheson

If anyone wanted to know the entire story of my press conference in February, 2001, all one had to do is read *The Times Leader* in Princeton, Kentucky. They wouldn't have missed a word. Chip Hutcheson has covered news in Princeton with incredible accuracy and fairness for more than 25 years. Chip did a marvelous job in reporting the facts to my hometown of diehard Kentucky fans. The stories Chip has written over the years have kept a small town well informed of important events, and Princeton is lucky to have kept him.

Rick Bozich and Pat Forde

Since Rick Bozich and Pat Forde write for the *Courier-Journal*, a Louisville based newspaper, which is the only state wide newspaper in Kentucky, they are sometimes perceived by UK fanatics to conspire to hurt Kentucky. Bozich and Forde can both be biting and controversial in their opinions, but they tend to even themselves out on articles which are negative or positive concerning all state university programs. Causing dialogue and stirring interest appears to be their forte! That's why they are columnists. Controversial topics and pushing the buttons of Kentucky or Louisville fans keep their readers in an uproar. Their articles always catch my interest because you never know what side of an issue they are going to take.

John Clay

If a badge of courage were awarded to a journalist for the four years I was coaching at Kentucky, it would have to go to Clay. Mumme occasionally berated Clay like an assistant coach. For the first three seasons, Clay was a beat writer who followed the daily practices of Kentucky football and reported daily during the season and once or twice weekly during the off-season. Since a beat writer must use the goodwill of the Kentucky coach and staff to accommodate him on a daily basis, he normally isn't as opinionated as a columnist. Clay spent three years reporting on the daily activities and listening to Mumme's occasional verbal lectures. When Chuck Culpepper left the Herald-Leader and Clay took over as columnist, he had a great insight into what was really going on and he wasted no time in writing gripping and biting stories that probably had Mumme squirming. I've found Clay to be consistently fair in his articles and not afraid to take a controversial topic head on. The public will be well served by his insight.

Rusty Hampton

Rusty Hampton stepped out of the normal beat writing mode when he wrote a lengthy and well researched article on the mistruths and falsehoods of Claude Bassett's background. Hampton was one of the reporters who called me regularly during the investigation of the Kentucky football program wrongdoings. I respected Rusty for his diligent effort and refusal to take no for an answer. Eventually he was one of the reporters who came to my home and wrote a brief article on my interpretations of the events over the previous four years. Similar to Clay, Hampton had to treat Mumme with "kid gloves" because of his role as a beat writer but he was not afraid to ask Mumme tough questions. He did some great investigative work that helped the *Courier-Journal* break the story of the $1400 money order sent to Tim Thompson by Bassett. Hampton is a knowledgeable football writer who does his reader's justice with his daily columns.

Chip Cosby

After John Clay moved into the columnist position, Chip Cosby took over his job as a beat writer. I didn't get to know Cosby that well during my last season at UK, but I've enjoyed reading his articles since my departure. The *Lexington Herald-Leader* looks to have found a good replacement for Clay, as Cosby seems to be a gifted writer.

Mark Story

Talking to Mark Story of the *Lexington Herald-Leader* was always fun. His frequent phone calls to my house were always entertaining during the investigation. Story had a way of hitting a nerve and getting me irritated at somebody by telling me something they had recently said about me. Several times, I almost lost it and came close to blurting out information before I would catch myself. My planned February press conference was getting tougher and tougher to wait for with Story's techniques beginning to affect me. Eventually his call to tell me about a Mike Major quote that he was printing, when Major had decided to tell the false story that Guy Morriss and I had conspired to get Mumme fired, enticed me to jump the gun and give him some quotes before I had planned. Story's humor in some of his articles had me holding my stomach from laughing so hard. I make a point to read his articles when I can. He is a good journalist who taught me some good techniques to use in my future.

Jim Adams

I met an investigative reporter named Jim Adams only one time in my life. A gruffy looking man showed up on my front porch one day covered in snow and showed me his business card as Jim Adams, Investigative Reporter for the *Courier-Journal*. I let him in and he stayed only a few minutes, but he made quite an impression. When he left my house, I told my wife that Adams would find something. You could tell his questioning was different than a sports journalist. Long-time personal assistant to five Kentucky Head Coaches, Janetta Owens later told me when a newspaper sends their investigative reporters in, you can bet if there is any dirt, they will find it. Adams eventually discovered several pieces of information that helped pin evidence against Bassett and Memphis Melrose Coach Thompson.

Larry Vaught

I've already mentioned Larry Vaught. In his dual writing role as the sports editor for *The Advocate Messenger* and *The Cats' Pause*, Vaught has established himself as a top sports writer. Versatility enables Larry to do a sparkling job covering all sports as well as producing issue-oriented commentaries. Vaught's is not afraid to go out on a limb and voice his opinion, even if it's unpopular. My good friend Sam Harp told me once that Vaught has written some critical articles over the years as he has followed his Danville football program, but Larry was always professional and fair. The Danville area is lucky to have kept Vaught through the years. His superb writing talent could have moved him to larger newspapers at anytime. I deeply respect Vaught's opinion as a sportswriter who knows sports, but more as a quality person whom I've been lucky to know.

The Voices of Kentucky Football

While growing up in Kentucky, some of my fondest memories are of listening to Cawood Ledford do the play by play of Kentucky sporting events. Following Cawood is similar to following Bear Bryant as the head coach of Alabama; nobody could ever be as good. The combination of Tom Leach and Jeff Van Note, however, became as good of 1-2 combination as there was in college football. Leach took over the football duties from Ralph Hacker, who had succeeded Cawood, and picked up right where Cawood left off. Van Note provided classic, good football information and was not afraid to second-guess the coaching decisions. His long-time NFL experience gave the listener some great insight that few color-men in broadcasting have. The Leach and Van Note team made a class act in their game day coverage. I've listened to their replays after our games were finished and felt like I was watching each play again from the sidelines. Van Note's recent retirement announcement will cause many Kentucky fans grief. Hopefully, a capable replacement is found, but it will be tough to find someone as skilled.

The Homers

The occasional media person, who seem to only represent UK athletics and their coaches' self interest make the job of the real journalists much more difficult. By printing the company line or asking soft questions, these writers, radio, and television media personnel make a mockery of the true media people who make a living trying to accurately report the news. I have no problem with someone representing the Kentucky Radio/Television Broadcast Team and spinning a story to cover Kentucky's butt, however, when they jump into another suit and pretend to be real newsmen reporting real news, they blow any credibility they might have.

Dave Baker is the most recent example of this. In my opinion, his live television interview of Bassett's confession of sending the $1,400 to Tim Thompson was one of the most unprofessional acts of sports journalism I've ever witnessed. Kentucky fans love Baker far and wide and he should be loved, as he is a die-hard Big Blue loyalist. When he changes hats, however, and gives the appearance of a real journalist and the subject is Kentucky sports, he should simply withdraw. It would be an act of professional courtesy to the media members who are attempting to report the entire story in a non-biased way.

Radio Talk Shows

When you enter the world of talk radio you enter into an unusual atmosphere. It's very similar to going on the Internet where anyone can use a fictitious name and immediately become a celebrity. Vicious attacks on coaches are relatively easy on talk radio because there is very little accountability. If you listen to the same call-in show weekly, you'll hear the same callers several times. I've often wondered if anybody else listened, but I've found out many of the shows have an extremely large audience. The main goal of the talk show host is to provide a subject that stirs emotion to entice callers to act. "Reliable source," a phrase used frequently on the Internet chat lines, is a favorite term used by callers and host alike. Amazingly, some people will quote an anonymous caller the following day as if this caller's word were the gospel truth!

Lexington is blessed with some interesting and thought-provoking shows. Larry Vaught, Sue Wiley, Larry Glover, and Tim Woodburn do a thorough job stirring the thought process on all sports and Tony Cruise from Louisville presents an interesting and thought-provoking program as well.

Television

All of the local TV stations in Lexington do a good job in following the Kentucky sports programs. I've especially enjoyed watching Krista Voda, Alan Cutler, and Ryan Lemond on Lexington's Channel 18. Their policies tend to be geared more toward reporting good stories about Kentucky sports than doing investigative work. Although Channel 18 made a mistake in reporting on my future, I still enjoy its coverage and respect their professionalism. My family and I were leaving our house for lunch in February, 2001 when Ryan Lemond announced it appeared I was returning to Kentucky as Guy Morriss' Offensive Coordinator. This, of course, was not true as Dr. Wethington blocked Morriss' attempt to rehire me as his Offensive Coordinator.

Dick Gabriel is one of the few media people who does a more than credible job wearing two hats. He was able to represent the UK Radio/ Broadcasting Team with insightful sideline reporting and later put on his journalism hat and ask coaches tough questions. I will always respect Gabriel's ability to support Kentucky, but also ask true journalistic questions. He gained my respect as well as most Kentuckians.

Conclusion

The news media carries a large burden in protecting our personal freedom in this country. I'm not naive enough to believe all of the media is ethical and moral. They are like any profession; they have some bad people who do bad things, yet they are an integral part of our society helping to keep people in power on their toes. People must understand however, that writers, broadcast-ers, and radio people are human, thus they will make mistakes. Don't ever believe all you read, hear, or see without first questioning it. If the source is unreliable or an "inside source," then be wary before believing the story. Another example of an "inside source" reported story having absolutely no closeness to the truth was in July 2001 when Oscar Combs reported in *The Cats' Pause* that I was possibly going to be hired back by the UK football program. I had to laugh when a reporter and several friends asked me if this was true. I assure you there is no one in power associated with Kentucky who would ever allow me to coach at Kentucky again.

It is important to remember all media people are hampered by deadlines, time, and space available. There may be a spectacular 6,000-word story a reporter wants to write, but the editor may give him 300 words of space. What you read is extremely limited as to the story reported. A TV newsman can interview someone for two hours and go back to the station and be given 30 seconds of airtime. The final account the viewer sees may only be the negative portion of the interview, especially if the station has its own agenda. I have no doubt some of these media personalities I've mentioned will attack me for writing this book. Some will legitimately question my intentions, while others will simply have their own private agenda. Readers must continue to understand all writers are human and will be influenced by human emotions and conditions.

LESSON #6—One of our most valuable freedoms is the freedom of the press. Many people in our country have died fighting to preserve that freedom. The press owes the public fair and honest reporting of what is taking place in our society. The public owes itself the responsibility to not blindly believe any facet of the press without legitimate questioning of the media person's agenda. Read and watch the media daily with a skeptical eye, but be thankful they exist, for they truly help to prevent tyranny.

CHAPTER 7

GOOD STAFF/GOOD PEOPLE

Lesson 7—Success can happen for any business, team, or government as long as you have determined and flexible people dedicated to a cause and selfless in their actions.

There are numerous people on a Division I football staff that are not coaches, but who play a major role in the success of the program. Our coaching staff was blessed with several good people in low profile positions who played a strategic role on a daily basis in making us successful.

Jack Fligg, "True Class"

If I could draw a picture of true class and elegance in the coaching profession, it would be Jack Fligg. Jack was the Director of Football Operations for Mumme's first two years. His guidance and nurturing were a vital part of our success, and his departure in 1999 was the beginning of the end for the Mumme Era.

Jack had the ability to give advice in a non-threatening way that most of us looked forward to when we were fortunate enough to get it. He kept the eventual chaos from erupting earlier by monitoring the daily activities of all of us, especially Bassett. Bassett had the unique ability to cut most everyone at some time or another, but he seemed especially aggressive towards Fligg. I believe Bassett knew if he could get Fligg out of the football affairs, then Bassett would be able to have a free reign in all of his activities.

As a long time Division I assistant, Fligg had developed a reputation as a top recruiter, having recruited Heisman Trophy winner George Rogers at South Carolina. However, he was best known in the profession as a true gentleman. His presence provided Mumme with a definite fixture of sound advice and class.

The college football profession definitely misses Jack Fligg as he and his beautiful wife Jonell, have retired to the great golf courses of Marietta, Georgia.

Janetta Owens, "The Ultimate Survivor"

Janetta Owens probably has the greatest book banked in her memory of any sports person in Kentucky athletics history. She served as Personal Assistant and confidant to Fran Curci, Jerry Claiborne, Bill Curry, Hal Mumme, and presently Guy Morriss. The class and elegance of Jack Fligg is also evident in Janetta Owens.

Moving to Lexington from Corbin in 1976, Janetta has worked her way into the hearts of many Kentucky players and coaches over the last four decades. She is well known for her sincere caring of every Kentucky player and coach as well as for her competency and professionalism. Many fans, alumni, and media people have come to recognize her as a permanent fixture in Kentucky football. After being named head coach, Morriss immediately requested to have her return to assist him. Mumme had given her a different position in his last year.

Janetta's beloved husband, Lewis, passed away in November 1999. The love and affection for the both of them was shown by the hundreds of people who lined up to express their condolences. Former head coaches Jerry Claiborne and Bill Curry were present with Curry flying in from Hawaii to pay special homage to the special couple.

When Hal Mumme was first hired, I advised him to keep two people: Jack Fligg and Janetta Owens. I think their presence during Mumme's time at UK was a valuable addition which contributed heavily to his early success.

Kwyn Jenkins, "Ready Beyond Her Years"

Kwyn Jenkins was an Office Aide for a brief time when we first arrived at Kentucky. As a part-time student and part-time office worker she quickly made herself an important part of the Mumme Era.

Kwyn is like myself, Janetta, and several others in the Kentucky family: a die-hard born and bred UK fan. Her father Bill had been a member of the "Thin Thirty" at Kentucky in the 1960s. Although only 19 when she started working at Kentucky, she showed some of the same qualities of leadership that Chris Hatcher had. Age was no factor when deciding who was most capable of getting the job done. Kwyn simply got things done and got them done right.

Showing maturity beyond her years, Kwyn became a favorite with coaches, alumni, and staff. Mumme would eventually feel confident enough in her to promote Owens to a player and parent liaison position and to have Kwyn take over as his personal assistant.

The greatest asset Kwyn demonstrated was in the job no one wanted, Summer Camp Coordinator. The best day of my coaching career was the day I was "fired" as Summer Camp Coordinator and Hatcher and Kwyn took over. Kwyn, Hatcher, and eventually Rob Manchester put together a model for college summer camps. Every high school coach looked to Kwyn for advice or help in solving problems during our successful summer camps.

My wife, children, and I recognize Kwyn as a part of our family. Her spunk and spirit are characteristics I hope my three daughters adopt.

When the ugliness began near the end of the Mumme Era and some within the UK family began to hide for cover and play "cover my butt at all costs," Kwyn decided she had seen enough and left before Mumme resigned. She learned some valuable lessons about friendship, ethics, and morality as the walls began to tumble. Those lessons will provide a great foundation for her as she moves on through life having an education in the real world well beyond her years.

Sandy Wiese, "Medal For Bravery"

Sandy Wiese deserves an Authentic Medal for Bravery. For four years she worked for one of the most obstinate, vulgar, and abusive men I have known. Her job was to make Bassett happy and do whatever he asked. Failure to comply with his wishes could certainly mean the end of her job.

Most every player and his parents got to know Wiese before he became a Wildcat. As Assistant to the Recruiting Coordinator, she supervised one of the grandest recruiting operations in all of football. She was responsible for making sure that each detail of a recruit's official visit worked to perfection, an impossible task of course.

No one loved Kentucky football, or Kentucky, period anymore than Sandy and her husband Phil. They included family and friends to insure every visit was a great experience for each family that came to Kentucky. Passion is necessary to be good at anything, and Sandy was passionate about helping recruits to truly understand what being a Kentucky Wildcat was all about. Successful recruiting in 1997-2000 was due in large part to her efforts.

An assistant coach on the road recruiting must have a good touch with the home base to constantly be updated on changes, flights, information, etc. Sandy was our home base, making our three to four months on the road much easier.

When the investigation into the NCAA violations began, I was told by Athletic Director Larry Ivy to inform Sandy if she told the truth nothing would be held against her and her job at Kentucky would be secure. Sandy trusted me and when asked questions by Ivy and Sandy Bell, she cooperated fully. Without her cooperation Kentucky would be in a bigger mess than you could ever imagine.

Sandy was rewarded for her cooperation with a breaking of Ivy's promise. Everyone in life has dirt somewhere in their lives or jobs. If someone decides to find dirt on you and dig deep enough, they will find it. Sandy was called over to meet with UK authorities where she was presented with the master copy of a newsletter. She had made copies and provided postage for the Lexington Bryan Station PTSA as part of a business co-op deal. Sandy freely told she had been providing this service, after asking for and receiving Bassett's approval. Sandy had been assisting various organizations at Bryan Station for eight years as an involved parent of two Bryan Station graduates. She believed since Bassett was her immediate supervisor, his approval was sufficient. She was notified she had broken university policy and sent home the following day.

Was it a strange coincidence the university decided to punish Sandy immediately after they were finished getting testimony from her? Even stranger, by the time she left her meeting at Memorial Coliseum and returned to Commonwealth Stadium, Bassett, although no longer employed by Kentucky, had called Mumme. The following day the Human Resources Department suspended Sandy. At the conclusion of the Human Resources meeting, Sandy was told it would be a good idea not to discuss these events with anyone. Mysteriously, three to four hours after Wiese's dismissal, a local media person close to Bassett had informed several Kentucky employees at a local restaurant of the events concerning Wiese's dismissal that day. A few days later, media asking for information about the NCAA violations bombarded Wiese. The inside sources had struck again!

The unethical dismissal of Sandy Wiese awakened me to something I should have already known, trust very few people associated with the Kentucky football program. In my opinion, Sandy was served up as a sacrificial lamb by certain University Officials to appease Mumme and Bassett. University officials can say they were just following policy, but I believe that is simply not true. I believe they selectively picked the people they would decide to eliminate and left several others, with their own dirt hanging around, to continue their employment.

My decision to write this book and to explore legal options against the wrongdoers was fueled when, in my opinion, certain UK officials abused Sandy Wiese. She deserved better and in the end, she will win. Amazingly her love for UK sports is still strong and she will be pulling for the Wildcats for years to come.

Sandy Bell, "An Ethical Coach's Best Friend"

One of the most difficult jobs in all of college athletics is that of a Compliance Officer. Their job is to make sure every coach, player, parent, fan and booster understands NCAA rules and doesn't break them. It is a totally impossible job. If you do it very well, someone is always going to be mad at you. The University of Kentucky is fortunate to have Sandy Bell as its Associate Athletic Director for Compliance.

Bell engineered one of the most thorough self-investigations in NCAA history during the end of the Mumme Era. Some disturbed fans will now despise her because they are convinced everyone cheats and Kentucky is the only one who turns themselves in. Winning without integrity isn't winning at all. The idea everyone cheats is an idea made up by losers. It simply isn't true.

Early in the Mumme Era, I believe Bell had strong suspicions concerning Bassett and his yearning to break NCAA rules. I also believe she was restrained by then Athletics Director, C.M. Newton and told to give Bassett some freedom. My suspicion is that a signal was sent to Sandy not to work hard to find wrong doings in the Mumme program. I detail my reasons for this suspicion in Chapter 20.

I know Bell to be a friend of coaches and a lover of Kentucky athletics. Most of the coaches deeply appreciate her attempt to make sure we are compliant. She is also a stand-up person who once, when one of her subordinates failed to admit a mistake, stood up and took responsibility with the NCAA. If UK comes out of this NCAA investigation and does not receive a near death penalty they will have Bell to thank. True fans of the university believe in winning with integrity, and Bell does an admirable job making sure Kentucky will do its best to enforce the rules.

Tom Kalinowski, "The Second Greatest Survivor"

The second hardest job in college football behind Compliance Officer is Head Football Equipment Manager. Tom Kalinowski has served in that capacity since Fran Curci was head coach in 1978. This thankless job goes beyond providing equipment for the players. An away trip is very similar to trying to move from one home to another in two short days. If you can imagine moving out of state five weeks every year, you might come close to feeling what Tom's job is on every away game.

A group of several student managers work closely with Tom all season long to keep the football program going smoothly. The area with all the Nike apparel is call "Fort Knox" and Tom and his assistants guard it just as closely as Fort Knox is guarded. Tom probably had his toughest time ever protecting "Fort Knox" during the Mumme Era. Major was notorious for "losing" Nike rain suits and needing a replacement. Bassett might enter on any moment's notice demanding hats,   t-shirts, etc. for someone. No matter whom he gives what, the equipment man is always going to make enemies. He cannot please everyone.

Kalinowski has done a wonderful job over the last 22 years taking care of players and coaches. He has been able to maintain a perfect balance between running a tight ship and keeping enough people happy to keep his job.

Rob Oviatt, "A Devastating Loss"

Twice voted SEC Strength Coach of the Year, Rob Oviatt's decision to leave the UK football program after our 1998 season was a devastating loss. Oviatt is the consummate professional and is a truly classy human being. The players had a deep respect for Oviatt that transpired into great dedication in his weight room. Oviatt possessed a dry sense of humor which I began to appreciate over time. He had a look of extreme seriousness that made you wonder if he ever smiled. He is truly one of the best people in this profession of college athletics.

After the '98 season, Oviatt was approached by then LSU head coach Gerry DiNardo, to take over the LSU strength program. Although he knew DiNardo had a chance to be fired the following season, Oviatt took an offer that nearly doubled his Kentucky salary. Mumme was furious Oviatt would even consider leaving and after offering Oviatt a less than comparable raise, he insisted that Oviatt stay. Rob left because he believed the opportunity to be worth the risk. He also believed DiNardo to be an honest, good man whom he would enjoy working for. He was not disappointed as DiNardo turned out to be the type of character Oviatt thought he would be.

Even though DiNardo was fired and Oviatt chose to move on, Oviatt was proud to have made the move to LSU. Rob is currently the Strength Coach at Washington State University and is working for a top notch head coach and cohesive staff.

I am proud to call Rob Oviatt a friend. He is truly one of the really genuine, good people in college sports.

Barb Deniston

Barb was the primary contact for the CATS academic program with the Kentucky football team. I know of few people who worked the hours to help young people the way that Barb did during my four years observing her at

Kentucky. She was tough and hard-nosed, but extremely caring. Many of the players excelled specifically because of her efforts and graduated from the University of Kentucky because of her hard work. Mumme supported Deniston in her efforts by occasionally taking players off the field when she reported academic problems with players. The CATS program started in 1981 by Bob Bradley, continues to thrive today without a speck of dirt because of the work of people like Barb Deniston.

LESSON #7—Success can happen for any business, team, or government as long as you have determined people dedicated to a cause and selfless in their actions. All organizations must have strong infrastructures of people who strongly believe in the cause and heavily contribute knowing their satisfaction will come from seeing the finished product. These sometimes relatively unknown people realize without their dedication, success will not happen.

CHAPTER 8

THE GREATEST FANS IN THE WORLD (LET ME DEFINE A FAN)

Lesson 8—There is an incredible strength in numbers. Every monumental movement has started with one person who is passionate about their beliefs . . .if you are truly committed and have a worthwhile idea, thousands will follow you.

Early Childhood Memory

They peeked their heads in and out of the room and ran back and forth up and down the hallway. They couldn't bear to watch the last minutes of the game. Would UK make those free throws or not. Could they hold on to win?

You would think grown men wouldn't act this way, but my father, Robert Franklin and his childhood friend, Billy Hobby, watched many games while ducking in and out of rooms. Their hearts pounded furiously as they tried to help Adolph Rupp and Joe B. Hall coach their last few minutes. I was only a small child, but I can remember them yelling into the radio or television and I wondered if they really believed the players and coaches could hear them.

True Fans

True fans live and die with each bit of news about their beloved teams. They take their teams victories and defeats personally. Their daily lives may not be the dramatic and exciting stories they had dreamed of as a child, but through their teams they find spirit, hope, and drama.

University of Kentucky football fans epitomize the classic definition of what a real fan is and should be. When Hal Mumme and I began to discuss his possibility of obtaining the UK Head Football Coaching job, I explained to him that UK football fans were the greatest in the world. More than 50,000 would show up each Saturday to watch the Wildcats play even though they were not winning. Hope, faith, and loyalty constantly defined the character of UK football fans.

The only way to drive the UK fan away is to demean them or degrade them. There had been seasons when the UK football fan gave up hope and quit coming to games because they felt hopeless. By the next season, however, fans would have convinced themselves this was going to be the great one, and on opening day the stands would be full.

A true fan doesn't want UK to win by cheating. They believe winning without integrity isn't really winning at all. Every excuse for not winning has been heard by the fan and some will believe the excuses. Knowingly, most fans, however, look around the country and see the Northwesterns, Kansas States, and Oregon States turning around traditional losing programs with less money, worse facilities, and less fan support than Kentucky without breaking NCAA rules.

Joe Pickens, "Don't Talk About My Wildcats"

77 year-old Joe Pickens lives in the small town of Princeton, Kentucky in Caldwell County. I have known Joe since 1972. When I think of a real UK fan, he always comes to my mind. Very few days pass when Joe doesn't have some discussion about the Wildcats. Local townspeople know they had better be careful if they decide to degrade a UK coach or player in Joe's presence. Hell hath no fury like a mad Joe Pickens when he feels someone is bad-mouthing the Wildcats.

Working most of his life in the strip mines of Western Kentucky, Joe and his wife Ann, put two daughters through college. Many years he would awaken at 3:30 AM to begin a drive to the coalfields of Webster and Muhlenburg Counties. Hard work and sacrifice were a daily habit. The reward was raising a successful family and turning on the radio or television on Saturdays to listen to the Wildcats.

There isn't a skybox that has been blessed with Joe's presence and over his lifetime he's only been able to see a few games in person. There haven't been $20,000 donation checks mailed from his house to C.M. Newton to help build the latest necessity for UK athletics. Like the majority of Kentuckians, Joe spent his hard earned money on his children and grandchildren.

The average UK fan doesn't donate thousands of dollars per season. Most of them can't. They are like Joe Pickens, they pay taxes, buy UK shirts and hats, and if lucky get to attend one game every five to ten years. They possess something that makes their lives enriched—passion for the Wildcats. Thank God for the Joe Pickens in the world!

Bobby Franklin, "I'll Be Yelling For The Cats Long After You're Gone"

I was told I could coach anywhere in the world, but if I showed up at the University of Tennessee or the University of Louisville I could expect no "good luck" calls. This warning came to me on numerous occasions from my brother Bobby Franklin during my four years coaching for Kentucky.

With a personality similar to Joe Pickens, my brother would follow the Cats anywhere. His social and family life over the years, has revolved around the Wildcats. There wasn't a prouder human being in the world than Bobby when his little brother was coaching for the University of Kentucky.

Bobby would travel on a moment's notice to go watch the Wildcats play if he was lucky enough to obtain a ticket. Our father whetted our appetites as kids by taking us to Freedom Hall a couple of times to watch Pete Maravich score 60 points in LSU's losing attempts against the Wildcats. We were both bred on UK football and basketball. Bobby even flew to Las Vegas when he was just out of high school to watch the Wildcats play in a Christmas tournament in the 1970s.

During my four years coaching for Kentucky, Bobby watched the Wildcats in person every Saturday home game. There was never a louder, more passionate fan in the stands of Commonwealth Stadium. After each game we had a family reunion in the parking lot and celebrated our victories or drowned our miseries.

Each Saturday, Bobby would remind any of the Kentucky coaches who would join our family party of a likely reality. He would tell us that one-day we would all leave for better jobs or be fired. The point was made that we would no longer live and die each Saturday with the Wildcat football program. Bobby reminded us that he, on the other hand, would continue to bleed blue and that each Saturday regardless of where we ended up coaching, he would be yelling and screaming for the Wildcats. Bobby too epitomizes a true blue Wildcat fan.

Not Good Enough

I had grown up a UK fan since birth. My memories of UK sports consisted of boyhood fantasies about one day being allowed to wear the blue and white. My football talent wasn't good enough to play for UK and I ended up playing for Murray State University. My first collegiate start came when we played at Morehead State in 1976, my freshman year. The team stayed in Lexington on Friday night before the game and went to a movie. When we got off the bus several young kids came running toward us asking us if we were UK players. Some of the best football ever played was being played at Kentucky in those years. I remembered thinking how special it would have been to run onto the field at Commonwealth Stadium and hear 50,000 screaming fans.

Following Pookie, "An Eye-Opening Experience"

Throughout my 16 years of coaching in Kentucky high schools, I followed UK sports from afar. Like most high school coaches, my main concerns were with who we played the next week, not UK. The opportunity to travel and watch a game very seldom presented itself until one of my former players, Pookie Jones, became the starting QB for the Wildcats. From 1990-1992 I made as many games, both home and away, as I possibly could. My fire for UK athletics was rekindled as I enjoyed my trips to Georgia, Mississippi State, Tennessee and Vanderbilt, as well as while making the four-hour trips to home games in Lexington.

When Pookie was the starting QB I got to see Kentucky fans from a totally different perspective. Pookie was as fine a person as I have ever known and we were very close as we still are today. Ninety-five percent of the fans were wonderful and supportive, but I also got to listen to the other five percent that were intellectually and socially lacking.

I got to watch Pookie experience racism from a front row seat. Being one of only a handful of African-American quarterbacks to ever play for Kentucky, Pookie was definitely the target of those few racist fans. There is still a group of people in society who believe African-Americans should play receiver or running back, not quarterback. Pookie and his family had to occasionally hear the remarks and boos which had nothing to do with performance, but sadly were race related.

As a fan, the experience of going to see SEC football and traveling to see places I had seen only on TV was a memorable experience. Sitting in the stands and listening to some select fans was a learning experience. My three years of following Pookie as a Kentucky fan and as a Pookie Jones fan helped prepare me for my eventual four year coaching experience at Kentucky. I knew there would be some things which would happen and would NOT be a positive experience. Because of my travels during Pookie's Kentucky career, I was better prepared.

A Real Fan's Power

Without paying fans, Division I college football wouldn't exist. The people who fill the stands each Saturday must understand the power they have. Those fans not fortunate enough to travel and see the games in person also possess power. The large donors are a necessary part of college athletics and many of them are quality people. They wish only for what's good in the program. Unfortunately, there are others who believe their donations entitle them to be involved in the decision-making process.

It is you, the average fan, who can make the most impact. When you see things happen, making you ashamed of your program, remember you do have power. Contact you legislator, stop buying Kentucky licensed products, and stop buying tickets to games. I promise you collectively your power is stronger than any one booster or donor. Money talks and the average fan holds the key to success. Don't be afraid to use it. They will listen when your collective voices hurt the pocketbooks. Don't accept anything less than winning with integrity. It can be done and it should be done.

Kentucky football fans are the best! In a state where basketball is supposedly the king, 68,000 fans show up most every Saturday to support the Wildcats football team. Hundreds of thousands more listen on the radio or watch on television. You deserve a program that wins and wins with integrity. Don't stop until you get it!

LESSON #8—There is an incredible strength in numbers. Every great movement has started with one person who is passionate about their beliefs. Don't set back and allow the limited few money donors to dominate or run an organization. Begin a movement that leads the masses. If you are truly committed and have a worthwhile idea, thousands will follow you. Average fans working collectively can take back college athletics from the money flashing booster and make a program do the right thing.

CHAPTER 9

PLAYERS TO REMEMBER

Lesson 9—Talent in some people is obvious, while you must dig deeply to uncover value in others. The digging, however, can provide phenomenal returns when you reach and unveil its worth.

The Warriors

College football is made possible by 17- to 23-year-old young men who make tremendous sacrifices to be a part of college athletics. Their weekly activities consist of 20 hours of football practice and weight lifting. Many spend countless hours in the training room for rehabilitation or injury prevention. Most spend a minimum of 10-20 hours in academic studies with tutors, as well as taking 12-18 hours of course study.

Living dangerously is an understatement for college football players. God didn't make our bodies to withstand full speed collisions by 200-pound obstacles. There is not a day that goes by that some part of their body doesn't ache. The summer heat occasionally takes the life of an athlete who is rigorously preparing for the upcoming season. Many of their study hours are done with an ice bag attached to some part of their body.

The reward for their sacrifice is a college education paid by the university as merit for their athletic excellence. Most scholarship athletes however would play for free and some do. Walking onto a college football field with 68,000 fans watching in person and millions watching on television provides a reward most players can't describe. Some would play if nobody showed up to watch, simply because they love to compete. The thrill of competition is what motivates most of the players.

Several players easily stand out and grab my attention from my four years of coaching running backs and receivers for the University of Kentucky. Spectacular plays, peculiar practice habits, memorable personalities, and other traits make certain players stick in my memory.

Anthony White, "Mr. Production"

Anthony White became the third player in the history of college football to rush and receive for more than 1500 yards each in a career. White was the perfect back for the Mumme offense because of his unique ability to be effective as a runner or as a receiver out of the backfield. Not one single defender in the SEC could cover White out of the backfield. He became Couch's favorite third down receiver because he was "money in the bank." White was durable and dependable, never missing a snap because of injury in his three years.

I loved coaching Anthony White because he was cool and calm and extremely football smart. He very seldom got excited and continued to make play after play. Anthony has made it into his second year in the NFL with the St. Louis Rams.

Derek Homer, "Comeback Kid" Role Model

Derek Homer was a significant contributor to Kentucky's success in all of his four years. Derek's career had tremendous highs and some occasional low points. Homer was a sometimes emotional player who would occasionally blurt out his feelings. We definitely had some clashes at different times in our careers. The admirable characteristic about Homer was he would always bounce back. If he was wrong, he would admit it and handle any repercussions like a man.

Homer and White had a good relationship based on mutual respect. While White was elusive and an open space make-you-miss runner, Homer was a speed back that would run over you. Their combination was an effective 1-2 punch for three years and they were both unselfish in helping each other. From 1997-1999 they combined for more yards from scrimmage, rushing, and receiving totaled, than any two back combination in the SEC.

Homer busted his butt as hard as any college student in Kentucky football. He rewarded himself with a college diploma in four years. I will always admire Homer for having the tenacity and work ethic I want my children to learn from. Hard work and overcoming adversity are traits that will make you a success no matter what path you choose to take. The example Homer set is one lesson I will never forget.

A.J. Simon, "The Leader"

A.J. Simon, walk-on fullback from Newport, Kentucky, is one of my all-time favorite players to have coached. I told A.J. he reminded me of myself;

slow and non-elusive. Memorable stories are made by people in life who do things they are not supposed to do. Simon should not have been able to play in the SEC. He was too stiff, too slow, and too short, but they couldn't measure the size of his heart.

A.J. provided several big plays with his fourth down fake punt runs and passes. His lead blocking led to many big runs for Homer and White. Many of the surprise special team plays A.J. not only participated in but also helped to create.

Simon's greatest talent was leadership. He was a player who loved competing and was a valuable asset off the field as much as on it. His artistic drawings on my meeting room board were so comical and so real that no player would dare erase them. Our 1998 Outback Bowl would not have been possible without his leadership.

Alex Herman, "The Greatest JV Player in History"

Alex Herman was the greatest junior varsity player in the history of Kentucky JV football. Herman was a walk-on receiver who dominated our junior varsity games with hopes that one day he might contribute in an SEC game. Every day for three years Herman would bust his butt on the scout team.

Herman's grit and determination was noticed by the coaching staff and he became an important part of our special teams, making some key plays in SEC competition. He was another classic example of not taking NO for an answer. Competing for the love of the game made Herman a memorable character.

Craig Yeast, "Spectacular"

Craig Yeast electrified Kentucky fans four years with big plays. Time after time Yeast would burst out of a crowd of defenders for a touchdown. The 1997 Alabama overtime touchdown catch and run was electrifying and will go down as one of the most memorable plays in UK history. My favorite Craig Yeast play occurred during the 1998 Mississippi State game. In a game that made us bowl eligible, it was his spectacular end zone catch made after a scrambling throw by Couch which enabled us to overcome a superior football team.

Yeast became a two-time All-SEC performer and in his senior season was voted to several All-American teams. The Cincinnati Bengals selected Yeast in the fourth round of the NFL draft. Amazingly, the first spring Mumme took over Yeast struggled with the new offense and the new coaches. Three wide receivers were competing for playing time with Yeast and he was listed behind them on the depth chart at various times during the 1997 spring. However, all three players had academic difficulties and Yeast took all of their playing time and made the best of it with an All-American career.

Kevin Coleman, "Football Is Fun"

Kevin Coleman made several big catches for Couch during the 1997 and 1998 seasons. He was deceptively fast, although Mumme liked to tell everyone how slow he was. Coleman eventually ran 4.56 (in the 40-yard dash) for the NFL scouts. His ability to lean a defender one way and break the opposite direction allowed Coleman to get open often.

The greatest gift Coleman possessed was his ability to make everyone laugh. Not a day went by when he didn't crack us up. Mumme's practice philosophy demanded you score after every catch. Coleman had the unique ability to catch any pass and take one step and be out of bounds. He would then slide back behind the players on the sideline and spark someone into laughter. I don't remember a day where Coleman didn't have fun!

Kio Sanford, "Special Plays"

Kio Sanford made some of the greatest runs after catches ever seen at Commonwealth Stadium. If not for a nagging injury his senior season he easily could have been an All-American. His run after a catch against Tennessee was spectacular. He must have had every player on Tennessee's defense touch him at least one time before he scored. The catch-run took so long Couch was 30 yards downfield making a block after completing the pass.

Chad Scott, "A Future Great"

Chad Scott has a burst of speed on game day unlike few players I've seen. When I began recruiting him I thought he was going to be a special player with game breaking ability. After a solid freshman season and several spectacular bursts, I believe that if he stays healthy, and holds off quality backs Artose Pinner and Martez Johnson from taking his job he will remind Kentucky fans of former running back Mark Higgs from the Jerry Claiborne Era.

Jeremy Davis, "Nasty Attitude"

Jeremy Davis had a short career, lasting only one season at Kentucky. Davis had been recruited as a linebacker, but was moved to blocking back after Major decided he couldn't play defense. Davis loved football and knocking the snot out of people as much as anyone. He provided some devastating blocks in a short playing career.

Some players hit because it is part of the game, but a very special breed gets a glaze in their eyes because they love it. Davis was one of those. I hope he regains his eligibility one day because he has a passion for the game.

James Whalen, "From Nowhere To All-American"

James Whalen was one of the most confusing players during the early morning off-season workouts in 1998. He seemed to be in horrible physical shape and he would sometimes lie on the workout mats and whine that he couldn't go anymore. Whalen's actions would make his whole group repeat and some of the players considered giving him a good butt whipping.

As a walk-on wide receiver from Oregon, after a year in a California junior college, Whalen would eventually become known to some as simply "Number 85." Offensive Coordinator Mike Leach disliked Whalen so much he refused to call him by name, and mostly referred to him by number. Whalen played only sparingly as a wide receiver in 1997, but he was fast becoming a favorite of Mumme.

In 1998 Mumme moved Whalen to tight end and at 215 pounds he was definitely one of the smallest tight ends in America. His playing time increased, as did his production, but he still split time with Jimmy Haley and Kevin Coleman.

By the start of the 1999 season, Whalen was up to 225 pounds. He had become a more physical player, while still possessing decent speed and great athletic talent. Whalen became Bonner's favorite receiver and broke the NCAA reception record for tight ends with 90 receptions. The Tampa Bay Buccaneers drafted Whalen after he had finished a storybook career at Kentucky from walk-on to All-American and he currently plays for the Dallas Cowboys.

Mumme was the only coach to believe in Whalen. The rest of us would have been happy if we had run him off. Mumme saw something special in him the rest of us missed and Whalen rewarded him with a tremendous season. Whalen proved that if your belief and conviction are strong enough and you work hard enough, someone may believe in you and give you an opportunity. Whalen certainly took advantage of his opportunity.

Jason Watts, "Fun And Furious"

LSU's Anthony "Bugger" McFarland was one of the top defensive linemen in the SEC, eventually being selected high in the NFL draft. Our key to beating LSU in 1998 was to have our center, Jason Watts, block

McFarland and keep him off Couch. No one else in the SEC had been able to do this, but when the game ended with a UK victory, Couch was untouched by McFarland and Watts should have been the Most Valuable Player of the game.

Watts was one of my favorite people to be around. He was a fun-loving, alligator-wrestling, young man who always seemed to have a smile and a good word to say. If a defensive player was caught not paying attention and found himself waking up after being knocked silly, it was probably Watts who had rung his bell. He loved the game of football!

Nasty, aggressive, and violent action played by fun-loving brutes make the game of football unique. Watts played the game the way it was meant to be played. There have been few SEC centers who made as many blocks 15-20 yards downfield as Watts did.

Mike Webster, "Take No Crap"

Offensive lineman Mike Webster was a former defensive lineman converted to offense. Offensive Line Coach Guy Morriss helped make him a good enough player to be signed by the NFL and play in Europe. Webster shared playing time his first offensive season in 1997, and eventually was a major contributor on the 1998 Outback Bowl season. You definitely wanted Webster on your side in a bar room brawl because he had the glaze in his eye like Jeremy Davis. He liked to battle and enjoyed the combat part of football. Webster took no crap from anyone and was a classic warrior.

John Schlarman, "Not Big Enough—Just Good Enough"

At 6'1 and 260 pounds John Schlarman was too small to be a good player in the OVC. There is no way he should've played in the SEC. Somebody forgot to tell Schlarman! With proper technique and brute strength, John became an All-SEC offensive lineman. The same tenacity will make him a competent college coach with Kentucky—he currently helps Morriss with the offensive line.

Bamidele Ali, "Making The Best Of It"

Bamidele Ali was definitely not thrilled to be moved from defensive linebacker to defensive end. He was only 207-212 pounds depending on what day you weighed him. Although it wasn't his natural position and not where he wanted to be, he worked hard enough to become one of the top sack artists in the SEC during the 1997 season.

As each practice ended most everyone would begin walking off the field, everyone except Ali. I would see Ali by himself taking several extra repetitions to improve his pass rush techniques. Ali took an unwelcome change in his football career and made it a positive through hard work and determination.

Mark Jacobs, "A True Defensive Lineman"

Mumme began to scream, curse, and threaten. Mark Jacobs had done it again! Running by Couch in a full speed bandit drill, no one was allowed to touch Couch. It was basically an impossible task for the defensive pass rushers. Their job was to rush full speed, defeat the blocker, and stop at a moment's notice without touching the QB who was moving in the pocket. As Mumme continued to curse Jacobs, Jacobs ran by Mumme and fired a verbal jab. That was Mark Jacobs, he didn't care who it was if he thought he was right, he wasn't going to take any crap.

Jacobs played football with total reckless abandonment. When we had Jacobs on defense we had one of the meanest and nastiest players in all of college football. I absolutely loved watching him play the game. His leadership on defense was one of the major reasons we went to a New Year's Day bowl game after the 1998 season.

Marvin Majors—See "Mark Jacobs" Above

If you took the preceding two paragraphs and changed the name to Marvin Majors you would come close to describing Jacobs' teammate and fellow defensive tackle. Majors provided the same leadership and tenacity that Jacobs did in the 1998 bowl season.

Jeff Snedegar, "I Hated Him, Wished We Had 10 More Like Him"

I hated Jeff Snedegar every practice! There was no telling what running back or receiver was going to be decleated by Snedegar during our supposed "non-contact" skelly period. My brother Bobby loved Snedegar. Bobby reminded me football was a violent, nasty, physical game and Snedegar played it the way it was meant to be played!

Stopping the run is crucial to winning in the SEC and Snedegar was the best we had. He belonged in the era of NFL linebackers of Dick Butkus, Tommy Nobis, and Jack Lambert. Possessing a snarl and game day face which struck fear into opponents, I was glad he was on my team. His departure in 2000 hurt our defense more than most would realize.

Marlon McCree, "All I Do Is Make Big Plays"

Big play defensive players have a knack for the ball. Someway or another they constantly find themselves around the football. Marlon McCree went from being a player whom some of the coaches wanted to run off to being one of the all time big play makers in Kentucky football history.

A 5'11", 195 pound football player in the SEC is supposed to play corner or safety, not linebacker. McCree found a way to slither between huge offensive lineman to make big play after big play. Being drafted by the Jacksonville Jaguars was his reward.

David Johnson," True Courage"

Being honored as one of the Top 10 Freshman football players by *The Sporting News* in 1998 is quite a feat. Coming back from shattering your eyeball socket on a tackle and still having the desire to play in the SEC is courageous! David Johnson made spectacular plays for us in 1998 to help get us to the Outback Bowl. He started the season in 1999 with a bone shattering tackle that caused a fumble against Louisville in the opening game. The collision shattered his eyeball socket.

Courage means to do something when you are afraid. Anyone who has been physically hurt knows how difficult it is to use that part of your body again without some reservation. David Johnson went through an entire season and off-season not knowing if his vision would be okay. Now he is playing football again. Few players have performed the courageous accomplishments that David has by returning to compete. I hope the fans appreciate him, I know I do.

Conclusion

There are hundreds of other players who contributed and are special in my memories. These few just give you a glimpse of some of the special players involved in the Mumme Era of football.

LESSON #9—Talent in some people is obvious, while you must dig deeply to uncover it in others. When you find this hidden gem, it may shock you with its worth. The only coach to believe in James Whalen was Hal Mumme. Mumme saw a possible goldmine in Whalen that the rest of us missed. We simply didn't look deeply enough.

CHAPTER 10

COACHING IN THE BIG TIME (HIGH SCHOOL VS. COLLEGE)

Lesson 10—Don't ever love a job or a position more than you believe in doing the right thing. Right is right and wrong is wrong. Don't be blinded by your ambition in your quest for self-promotion.

Some genuinely good people coach college football. I have met some rare friends, many of whom I believe will still be friends 20 years from now. On the other hand, some of the most arrogant and obnoxious people I have met are college coaches. When I coached high school football, several of the college coaches I met had an arrogance that was offensive in nature. Many had never coached high school and had no understanding of what it meant to teach five hours a day and then go coach football. Only a few made a positive impression and several demonstrated a feeling of superiority.

There is a feeling by some coaches and by most fans that the most capable and best football coaches are professional and college coaches. Many Division I coaches feel they are the best and look at a pecking order that would go from NFL to Division I to IAA, II, III, and then high school coaches. This is the farthest thing from the truth. A quality coach is a quality coach no matter what level he coaches. The only difference in a Division I college coach and a high school coach is opportunity and luck. Most jobs in college are obtained by knowing the right person at the right time.

As soon as Hal Mumme was dismissed as Kentucky's Head Football Coach amidst a fiery scandal, many critics immediately jumped on the bandwagon belief he had failed because he was "just a Division II coach," with limited Division I experience. That had very little to do with his downfall. Mumme just happened to be a one in a million lucky Division II coach who got an unusual opportunity. Other Division II coaches may have bettered Mumme's initial success and probably would not have blown the opportunity. It's a shame because very few Division I A.D.s will give another Division II coach the opportunity Mumme had.

Hal Mumme vs. Mike Holcomb

I will always believe Mumme was a special offensive football coach. He had the ability to eventually figure out a defensive scheme and attack the weaknesses. His greatest talent during his most successful coaching stints was remaining very simple in his scheme. The practice method and system he used was ingenious. Mumme also used the talent to the best of their ability. It wasn't unusual for him to roll 8-10 receivers and 4 to 5 running backs in and out of a game based on their ability to do one thing better than somebody else.

National recognition was given to Mumme for his offensive genius. After coaching with him for four years and watching his teams for several years before, I believe he was definitely a top-notch offensive coach. He was almost as good as Mike Holcomb, but not quite.

Breathitt County High School began throwing the ball before throwing was cool in Kentucky. Head Coach Mike Holcomb is a pure genius in the passing game. As I traveled around the country and watched the teaching and coaching of the passing game, I saw the gurus of BYU, Louisiana Tech, Purdue, and Montana. None of these premier passing teams have anything on Mike Holcomb.

High school coaches must take the talent they have coming in each year and line up and play. There is no recruiting except in the hallways and gymnasiums of the school. Holcomb has taken average athletes at best and year in and year out put up dazzling displays of aerial mastery. It would pay for a smart college coach to fly to Breathitt County to sit down with Mike to seek out his teaching secrets. They never will, of course, because it would take some courage to admit to your colleagues you had gone to the mountains of Eastern Kentucky to a small high school to learn some football.

Craig Clayton of Hopkinsville High, KY; Bob Redman of Louisville Male, KY; Bob Sphire of Lexington Catholic, KY; and Curtis Higgins of Trigg County, KY, are a few of the coaches in the commonwealth of Kentucky who are passing game gurus. I strongly believe given the same opportunity Mumme was given at UK, Holcomb, Redman, Clayton, Sphire, and Higgins could have been just as productive as Mumme's offenses were. The only difference in my opinion would have been a better defense and more wins than Mumme's teams at Kentucky produced.

Steve Spurrier vs. Rush Propst

I never took the opportunity to meet Steve Spurrier. When his name is mentioned around the country it normally will bring a strong opinion from someone. Florida Gator fans absolutely love Spurrier's perceived cockiness, arrogance, and honesty. Outside the Gator fans you will not find as many lovers of Spurrier. Within the coaching circles of college football, you will find some coaches who dislike Spurrier for various reasons. Most have no personal relationship with Spurrier, they dislike him because he tells the truth without sugarcoating it and he beats their butts most of the time.

Spurrier is one of my favorite coaches because of his pure honesty! I don't agree with some of his methods, but I love his direct honesty and the fact that he wins without cheating. Some coaches, fans, and media wanted to make comparisons of Mumme to Spurrier. I believe the only thing they had in common was their fondness for throwing the football.

Spurrier's critics like to attack his perceived arrogance and ego, just as Mumme's critics attacked him. The difference is huge. Spurrier's competitive desire to win led him to realize that until he had a championship defense he wouldn't win a national championship. He realized you couldn't outscore everyone so he made the recruiting and coaching changes necessary to accomplish his goal. I can't imagine Spurrier going on a radio show to defend his best friend and defensive coordinator if he weren't getting the job done, as Mumme did when telling a radio call in fan he and Major were a "package deal."

When you win and win big, you will make enemies. Envious fans and coaches would like to discredit Spurrier's success by pointing to the phenomenal high school talent in Florida. Spurrier's building of the Florida program into a yearly national championship contender is no doubt aided by the fertile Florida recruits, but his winning at Duke University was an even greater accomplishment. Spurrier is no doubt one of the top coaches in America, almost as good as Rush Propst of Hoover High School in Alabama.

The state of Alabama is one of the top high school football states in America. There is a pure passion for the game. Some of the nation's top high school coaches practice their profession in Alabama. Robert Higginbotham of Tuscaloosa County; Terry Curtis of UMS Wright, Jack Wood of Hewitt Trussville, Spence McCracken of Opeleika, and Rodney Bivens, former Head Coach of Anniston, are just a few of the premier coaches in Alabama. Propst has learned from all of these great coaches and has evolved as the best.

Propst, just as Spurrier, stirs emotions when his name is mentioned. Fans and opposing coaches either love him or hate him, but they all respect his ability to coach. He has won at various levels of Alabama football and has been selected "Coach of the Year" on more than one occasion.

The best characteristic of Propst coaching is his ability to adjust. Most of his career he had a defensive mentality and believed in smash mouth football. In 1999 Propst took the job at Hoover High knowing he would have to throw the football to win. He made a commitment to learn the Kentucky passing offense and practice methods. For two years he studied every aspect of the UK offense and in the 2000 season was rewarded with a 6A State Championship. His offense broke several Alabama state records.

Hoover High's coaching staff works as many hours, if not more hours, than most college staffs. His accomplishments at each level and his ability to adjust his philosophy to fit his talent makes Propst at least as good as Spurrier. Colleges have made a mistake in not hiring him or going to see him to steal his secrets.

Similar to Spurrier, Propst realized the importance of defense and adjusted the Kentucky practice philosophy to help the defense. Spurrier and Propst are very similar in their coaching successes. Most of you reading this book just haven't heard of Propst. Like Holcomb, Propst could have done as well as Mumme with the offense at Kentucky. He probably would have won more games, however.

Sam Harp and Chuck Smith vs. Tommy Tuberville

Tommy Tuberville is my favorite Division I head college coach. I've only personally been around him twice, once at lunch in a Montgomery, Alabama, hotel and once during spring practice at Auburn University. Running Backs and Special Teams Coach Eddie Gran and Offensive Coordinator Noel Mazzone had become friends of mine, and I've also been around several of his other assistants. Each assistant coach has one common theme when discussing Tuberville—Tuberville's loyalty to his staff and their loyalty in return to him.

Any employee of any operation wishes for the same thing: to be treated with respect and to have his best interest looked after. Tuberville is known for treating his assistants with respect and dignity and they in return are incredibly loyal to him. Assistant coaches have camaraderie at every level of coaching and all share their feelings about their bosses. Auburn's assistants share a type of reverence for their boss that is uncommon in today's world.

Tuberville is headed towards a National Championship destination at Auburn. He has put together a quality staff and has won over the state of Alabama with his and his staff's treatment and respect of high school coaches. You've got to be secure in your ego to give responsibility and credit to assistants and that's exactly what Tuberville has done. Those qualities make him almost as good a coach as Sam Harp and Chuck Smith.

Danville, Kentucky, is home to two of the nation's best football coaches, Harp of Danville High School and Smith of Boyle County High School. Together, they have made Danville the city of champions with both teams winning state championships in the 2000 season. Smith built the Boyle County program from traditional loser to a dynasty. Harp took over a traditional powerhouse and made it better, winning five State Championships and dominating class A and AA football for the decade of the '90s.

Harp is similar to Tuberville in the loyalty his assistant coaches have for him. He has consistently done things to publicly praise his assistant coaches while privately doing anything he can to help them in their careers and family lives.

It takes a strong person to hire assistant coaches which may be as qualified as you or may even be better coaches than you. Harp has consistently hired quality assistant coaches who were former successful head coaches. Many head coaches are uncomfortable hiring strong personalities. They fear they may give up some of the glory if their assistants are perceived to be stronger than them. Not Harp. He has hired former successful head coaches Jerry Perry and Marty Jaggers and has allowed them the freedom to coach, plus he's given them public and private credit for their work.

Sam Harp and Chuck Smith are fierce rivals. They both know how to build football programs and establish and maintain winning traditions. Both coaches have fiercely loyal assistants because they allow them to work independently and they give them credit for their success. Ronald Reagan said anyone can achieve success as long as they don't care who gets the credit. Harp, Smith, and Tuberville are great examples of unselfish head coaches who have built successful programs with staff loyalty. Just as Holcomb and Propst, there is no doubt Harp and Smith could have achieved great success in Division I college football, however, the opportunity never presented itself.

Bob Stoops vs. Mike Yeagle and Dale Mueller

Bob Stoops gained a reputation as a defensive genius when he was the Defensive Coordinator for the University of Florida during their national championship season in 1996. He comes from a family of coaches and has been raised in a coaching atmosphere. Unlike some other successful head coaches, when Stoops became the head coach at the University of Oklahoma in 1999, he didn't continue as a coordinator. Stoops hired two coaches as co-defensive coordinators and hired Mike Leach from Kentucky to be his Offensive Coordinator.

There is an art to being a successful head coach. Many great coordinators are unable to master that art, but Stoops has evidently taken his family history of coaching and built a solid foundation for success as a head coach. He won the 2001 national championship game by being solid in the kicking game, offense, defense, and establishing player and staff morale.

When Leach left to become Head Coach at Texas Tech, Stoops promoted Offensive Line Coach Mark Mangino to fill the position. The move was positive for staff morale and Mangino rewarded Stoops for his loyalty with an offense that helped win a national championship.

Stoops has an opportunity to build a dynasty at Oklahoma, if he decides to stay and continues with his same work ethic and consistency. He would have to stay a long time, however, to come close to the dynasties of Dale Mueller and Mike Yeagle. Mueller and Yeagle are the Head Football Coaches of Fort Thomas Highlands and Beechwood in northern Kentucky, across the Ohio River from Cincinnati. They have both built or continued dynasties with the same characteristics of Stoops. Both programs excel at each phase of football: offense, defense, kicking game, and player and staff morale.

When I visited Mueller during the spring of 2000, I was amazed at what he was able to demand from his players. The off-season program at Ft. Thomas Highlands is second to none. Many people will discuss the tremendous athletes at Highlands, and it's true they have had several Division I players. However, it is Mueller's demanding off-season workouts and his precise knowledge of the game that has allowed him to continue Highlands' great tradition.

Yeagle and Mueller are a notch above Bob Stoops at this time, with their 11 state championships between the two of them. If Stoops stays at Oklahoma for another 30 years and continues to grow as a coach, he may one day match their success.

Bill Taylor & Paul Leahy vs. Joe Lee Dunn and Woody Widenhofer

"Offense sells tickets and builds momentum. Defense wins championships." This was Hal Mumme's written philosophy he sent on his resume to the University of Kentucky. It's a great philosophy. It would have been even better if he actually had practiced it.

I have always been more of an offensive minded football coach, even though I coached defense many years as a high school coach. Early in my coaching career I learned that you must be sound on defense to have the chance to win a championship.

Vanderbilt's Woody Widenhofer and Mississippi State's Joe Lee Dunn were the most troublesome defensive coaches during my four years in the SEC. It was fun to watch their defenses on video. They were both creative coaches who presented the offense with a variety of alignments, schemes, and blitzes each week. Woody's 1997 Vandy defense was the best we faced in our four years at UK and Dunn's 1999 defense was a close second.

Both of these coaches presented problems to their opponents because of what seemed to be numerous fronts, blitzes, and stunts. There is a perception there are more defenders on the field, coming from every direction, than you can block. Offensive coaches were utterly confused and many times would change entire game plans to compensate for their confusion.

Both Woody and Joe Lee also had a unique ability to make their players play hard and with emotion on every snap. Their combination of strategy and player relations made them almost as good at coaching defense as Bill Taylor and Paul Leahy.

Bill Taylor coached at Daviess County High School in Owensboro, Kentucky, for over 20 years. His teams were always known for their fierce aggressiveness and their confusion-making defensive alignments and blitzes. Taylor had the unique ability to make young men want to play hard. Several players would have died for him. His emotional intensity was unlike any coach I have ever seen. Taylor and I coached together in the early 1980s and he was one of my valued mentors. He demanded intensity and emotion each day from his players. Bill's ability to make his defensive players play above their potential was second to none, not even Woody or Joe Lee.

Paul Leahy was Jack Morris' assistant coach for more than 20 years at Mayfield High School in Mayfield, Kentucky before taking the head job from Morris in 1993. Following a legend is never easy and Leahy was following the Coach of the Decade for the 1970s and 1980s. Morris was one of the greatest coaches in the history of high school football and Leahy had been his defensive coordinator for many of those years.

The defenses at Mayfield High School were notorious for being hard-nosed, aggressive, and sound. Leahy had that unique ability to get the emotional and physical best out of his players each week. His defenses could line up in one front for two to three weeks and beat most everyone, but when they played a superior offense you could expect to see multiple fronts, blitzes, and coverages.

Leahy took his defensive knowledge and passed it on to David Morris in 1993, Leahy's first year as head coach. With a struggling offense, Defensive Coordinator Morris was able to continue Leahy's defensive tradition and win a state championship in Leahy's first year as head coach. In 1995 that gave Leahy another state championship duplicating the stellar defense with Morris continuing the defensive tradition of excellence.

Woody and Joe Lee are nationally known for their defensive expertise. Taylor and Leahy were just as good if not better. The only difference is more people got to watch Woody and Joe Lee than Taylor or Leahy.

Richard McFee vs. Bobby Bowden

Bobby Bowden has given many players second chances during his tenure as the Head Coach at Florida State University. The media has taken turns in bashing Bowden for running a loose ship. Some of those players have rewarded Bowden for his second chances by turning their lives around and making a positive difference in the world. Others have let Bowden down and gone on to commit worse acts which made Bowden look foolish for giving them another chance.

Nobody but Bowden knows what the purpose was, or is, when he gives players a second chance. I want to believe he does it because he is caring and genuinely concerned if he gives up on them, they have no hope. The bottom line is Bowden is willing to take the criticism and some of his second chances have proven successful.

Richard McFee is well known in Virginia as the Head Football Coach of Huguenot High in Richmond. Outside of Virginia, fewer people may have heard of McFee, but his success in changing lives of young men is second to none. He has taken inner city kids and positively produced opportunity after opportunity for them.

McFee believes in tough discipline and is well known for his rigorous practices. He also believes in second chances. Others may have given up on several of his players where McFee sees something special worth fighting for. I've never seen a high school coach work as hard as McFee to help get his players into college. He worked with their academics, as well as their football skills. McFee provides other coaches with a model of how to positively change young people's lives.

Tough decisions were made many times by Bowden. He has taken criticism for giving a player another chance when it would have been easier and more politically correct to immediately give up and dismiss the player. Bowden, I believe is similar to McFee. Both see a higher calling in their profession and will continue to positively change lives because of their willingness to take criticism. McFee and Bowden could teach several coaches about the higher call of coaching.

My Mentor And A Lesson

The best all-around football coach I had the privilege of coaching with was Billy Mitchell. Mitchell was one of the last signees of Bear Bryant during his final recruiting season at Kentucky. Billy played for Kentucky and eventually would coach with Jerry Claiborne at Virginia Tech before coaching with Fran Curci at Kentucky for eight years.

I met Billy in 1981 after he was fired from Curci's staff and landed as the Head Coach at Daviess County High in Owensboro. We coached together for two years before Billy left to start football at Kentucky Wesleyan College. We coached together again at Calloway County High in Murray, Kentucky in the early 1990s.

There wasn't a phase of football in which Billy didn't excel, and he was the perfect mentor for me. After I left Calloway County, Billy turned Calloway into a consistent winner. Even after his retirement, he continues to coach part-time and help that program thrive.

Billy had prepared me for what to expect in college coaching. I had no unrealistic expectations of the quality of coaches or the quality of people I would meet in college because of Billy's advice. I knew some coaches would be really sharp and that others would be dull. Some would be good people and some would not.

One lesson Billy taught me was invaluable. He told me many Division I college coaches would do anything to keep their jobs. The difference of integrity levels between high school coaches and Division I college coaches would be large. High school coaches work for an extra $2000 or so at most schools, whereas Division I college coaches make $60,000 to $2 million per year for coaching. A high school coach will more readily stand for a principle and fight for what is right, no matter what his coaching job risk is. A Division I college coach will more likely break from any moral responsibility which might cost him his job because he knows if he loses the Division I opportunity, he may not ever get it again.

Mitchell's advice was right. I found out early and often numerous Division I coaches wouldn't risk their jobs for a principle. If you're going to be in a foxhole with a friend for your final fight, you have a better chance of finding a high school coach to jump in with you. Many of them fight for what's right no matter the cost.

Conclusion

There are many quality people and outstanding coaches in Division I college football. However, they tend to be put on a pedestal and are perceived to be superior to high school coaches. My experience in both high school and college gave me insight that strongly suggests this perception to be wrong.

All of the high school coaches I previously mentioned could easily be top Division I college coaches along with hundreds more if only given the opportunity.

LESSON #10—Don't ever love a job or a position more than you believe in doing the right thing. Right is right and wrong is wrong. Don't be blinded by your ambition. The biggest difference in high school coaches and Division I college coaches is a sense of morality. Many high school coaches will refuse to do something against their standards, even if it costs them their coaching jobs. Division I college coaches perceive their risk to be higher and are much less likely to risk their high profile career or job to stand up for principles.

PART II
THE BAD AND THE UGLY . . .

CHAPTER 11

HEY BIG MAN!

Lesson 11—Good and evil are constantly warring with each other. Take notice of this conflict and fight to prevent evil from winning this war. Strong ethical leadership can promote the good in a person and eradicate the evil.

Claude Bassett welcomed most everyone he coached with at one time or another with, "Hey Big Man!" Coaches and office workers sometimes referred to Bassett as the "Big Man." His penchant for eating good Mexican food had driven Bassett's weight to over 300 pounds on his six foot frame during his last days at Kentucky. The "Big Man" would come to mean several things to several people. He was full of "hot air" to some and a stand up guy, who served as a martyr for the UK football program, to others.

First Impressions

In January of 1997, I had my first meeting with one of the most mind-boggling people whom I have ever known. There was a recruiting meeting for all the coaches who had been hired by Mumme. Mumme had requested I come to the meeting even though I had not been officially hired.

Recruiting Coordinator Bassett was conducting the meeting and his mannerisms seemed to indicate he was making sure everyone knew who was in charge. My first impression was this guy was definitely a horse's butt. Over the next four years, I would find this impression to be true. I also found him to be one of the most brilliant men that I've known and at times, a genuinely caring man.

Bassett had many personalities and if you were around him for an entire day, there was a good chance you would get to see all of them. Early in the day he may be laughing and joking with everyone in sight, and later in the day he would be yelling and cursing with someone on the phone. Bassett could be extremely rude to people. If someone walked in he didn't like or didn't know he could be short and belligerent.

One of the first days I was at Kentucky, Fligg was addressing Mumme on a complaint he had received concerning Bassett. The complainer had called Fligg to tell him Bassett was driving on New Circle Road and trying to dial his cell phone. According to the complainer, Bassett had run him off the road and nearly caused a wreck. Bassett was denying the event ever took place, and I didn't think anything about it for several months.

I would eventually come to realize the caller was probably right. Bassett driving down the road with his cell phone is a tragedy waiting to happen. I would eventually find a reason not to ride with Bassett for fear of dying in an accident with him at the wheel.

Hardest Worker in College Football (Not!)

When I first began coaching for Kentucky, I became quite fond of Bassett. He could be incredibly charming and extremely funny. I became fond of his children after they moved to Kentucky following our first season. Although I saw his display of temper and moodiness on numerous occasions, I also saw an incredibly gifted and talented man. He had the ability to work a crowd as well as anybody I've known. Several of his speaking engagements would leave a crowd enthralled and wanting more. Intriguing was an understatement when looking for ways to describe him.

The first year Bassett was at Kentucky his family remained in Texas. Bassett worked long hours daily and demanded that the staff do the same. He wanted all the coaches to make their recruiting calls from the office and many of my days would go from 6:00 AM to 11:00 PM. Since this was my first college job, I assumed all colleges must call from their offices rather than at home.

Over the four years Bassett was at Kentucky, he became known as one of the hardest working recruiting coordinators in college football. This was a correct assessment for the first year, but from the moment his family arrived from Texas, Bassett's office policy and office hours dramatically changed. Coaches were no longer required to call from the office and Bassett would leave most nights several hours prior to his year one nightly schedule. By the time we reached the third and fourth seasons, Bassett occasionally moved his office to other locations. One of his favorite work spots was the UK baseball stadium. During the spring, you could bet if there was a home baseball game and Bassett was in town you could find him giving the UK baseball team his verbal and emotional support.

I called him once on his cell phone during recruiting season to talk about a recruit when I heard his children yelling for him in the background. I asked him when he got back to Lexington and he replied he was in Dallas. When I asked him what his children were doing in Dallas, he told me he didn't know what I was talking about. I told him I could hear his children yelling for him. Bassett informed me it was his television set. Mike Leach once told me he had a similar experience, where Bassett was at a professional baseball game during recruiting season and told Leach he was at a high school. Leach said he could hear the major league P.A. announcer and crowd in the background.

No one would have begrudged Bassett for his time off at work if he had not so ruthlessly cut the throats of all the coaches concerning their recruiting. "Don't throw stones if you live in a glass house," would have been a good lesson for Bassett to learn. Unfortunately for him, he never realized he was living in a glass house.

Ripping Of Comrades

Bassett, at one time or another, ripped every coach. It was mostly done to another staff member and after years of repeating the cuts, we all knew he had cut us at one time or another.

I learned his attacks on the coaches were not personal. Claude seemed to believe most everyone was inferior to him and he seemed to need to reinforce it by telling somebody. If I walked into his office for the first two and a half years , there was a better than 50/50 chance he was going to rip on another coach. No one was sacred and the number one target of his ripping was usually Hal Mumme.

During the four years at Kentucky, Bassett went full circle with Mumme and Major. Bassett told me at least 10 times of his intentions to quit because of his inability to get things done with Mumme. Eventually I even had a local booster from Western Kentucky ask me what had happened between Bassett and Mumme. I replied, "Why?" and he said because Bassett had really ripped on Mumme to him. I laughed and told him that was "just Bassett" and when the booster left the room Bassett would be ripping him.

The most hilarious relationship of Bassett's was the one with Major. Guy Morriss once told me Bassett and Major had been close friends for years before coming to Kentucky. According to Morriss, Major had called Bassett for advice before several big games Major had coached.

Their friendship would be tested at Kentucky, as the egos of Major and Bassett clashed early and often. Bassett was supposed to be the king of recruiting, but Major made all the final decisions concerning the recruiting of defensive players despite his inability and unwillingness to pick good defensive players. Bassett genuinely had a good football mind. He understood defensive strategy and could have helped Major if the two had consistently worked together. His assistance would increase during the disastrous 2000 season when Major seemingly lost control of the defensive strategy making.

There were times during the four years at Kentucky where Bassett and Major would be joined at the hip, and other times when they were unable to stand each other's presence. The end of the last season was classic Basset-Major. I believe Bassett had begun a campaign with Mumme to position himself to become the next defensive coordinator. He was playing Mumme and Major like a banjo. He would show concern and caring for his little buddy Major to his face, while going back to Mumme and questioning Major's coaching ability.

After Mumme's futile attempt to become a defensive coach against Florida, he turned to Bassett to take more control in planning the defense. Bassett was in absolute heaven. Not only was he Recruiting Coordinator and Director of Football Operations, he was now acting as a top consultant to the Defensive Coordinator. His power was growing daily and he was savoring every moment.

I strongly believe Mumme wanted to make Bassett the Defensive Coordinator after Major resigned. However, it is my belief that Athletic Director Larry Ivy would not allow it. I also believe Major was told he was finished as Defensive Coordinator midway through the season, not on his resignation date prior to the Tennessee game.

Franklin VS. Bassett (The Beginning of My End)

In 1999, *Border Wars* recruiting analyst Tom Culpepper, named me one of the Top 10 recruiters in the South. Culpepper was one of the few recruiting analysts whom I actually respected, and I was honored with this recognition. He and his partner Jamie Newberg had a strong eye for talent and if they told you a player could play you could take it to the bank. Culpepper found several top players who were not on the "so called experts" lists and helped many colleges to boost their recruiting.

Normally the type of recognition I received would be nothing but positive; however, I would come to find out it was the beginning of the end with Bassett. Our relationship had already begun to deteriorate because of my refusal to be totally compliant to all of his requests. This recognition pushed his attacks on me over the edge.

One of my fellow assistant coaches told me Bassett had gone on a tirade for several minutes blasting me more than normal. Usually I wouldn't have been concerned because Bassett blasted everybody. However, I had recently noticed Mumme had been very cold towards me and I had an associate tell me about some off-the-cuff comments Bassett had made about my recent recognition by *Border Wars*.

My time had come to confront Bassett. I entered his office, shut the door, and pulled a chair up directly to his. He asked me what I needed. I pulled out a yellow notepad and drew a line down the middle. On one side I wrote "Coaching", and on the other side I wrote "Recruiting." I handed him the notebook and said, "Evidently, you don't think I can do either of these, so I'm hear for you to tell me to my face what you're telling others behind my back."

Bassett responded, "I don't know what you are talking about."

I replied, "Yes, you do and I'm sick of it. I walk in this office everyday and when I see you I want to hit you in the mouth. I'm not going to continue to work in this environment. Since you are the master of coaching and recruiting, I'm here to learn from the master. Now tell me."

Bassett replied, "I don't know what you are talking about. Who told you this?"

"Several coaches and others," I said. "It doesn't matter. You and I both know its true. I just want you to understand I'm aware of what you are doing. Now, when I walk out of this office, I'm forgetting everything and starting new with you. I hope we understand each other."

I then stood up and walked out of his office. Bassett was more careful over the next few months to which people he spoke to about me. However, when my ending with Mumme came after the 2000 LSU game, Bassett would come back with a vengeance.

The Rejection of Tim Couch

Bassett had decided there was only one quarterback we needed to follow Tim Couch and he was Jared Lorenzen of Ft. Thomas Highlands. Although other QB's were on our recruiting board, it had become obvious Lorenzen was his man.

It had been widely reported over the years that Bassett had recruited Heisman Trophy winner Ty Detmer at BYU. Anything that related to winning football games at Kentucky, from evaluating players to strategies, would always have something to do with BYU, according to Bassett.

Hatcher and I both felt like we needed to recruit another QB along with Lorenzen. I told Hatcher I thought Bassett would sabotage any effort to bring in a new QB besides Lorenzen. We decided to have some fun and find out. Hatcher had the highlight film of Couch's senior season at Leslie County. It was a phenomenal display of what many experts called the greatest high school quarterback to every play. There was no mention of what teams were playing and the color was off so there was no way to tell whom this high school player was.

We entered Bassett's office and Hatcher announced he had found an unknown QB from a small town in Georgia, named "Ty Warren." Hatcher told Bassett he thought Warren was really good, but he wanted Bassett's opinion. Bassett told us he would look, but we already had Lorenzen committed and two other quarterbacks on the board that were great ones.

Hatcher put the Couch video in and we both stood in silence as we listened to Bassett pick apart the flaws of "Ty Warren." Every comment had some explanation that related to many of the former BYU quarterbacks Bassett had seen. When the tape was over Hatcher said, "What do you think?" Bassett replied the QB was pretty good, but not as good as Lorenzen or the other QB's we had on the board. Those other QB's were A.J. Suggs, who signed at Tennessee and later transferred to Georgia Tech, and Chris Stephens, who signed at Florida, and later transferred to North Carolina. Hatcher and I thanked Bassett for his time and left his office. Bassett never knew he had just rejected Couch!

This was not the first great player I had seen Bassett reject. My first month as a coach at Kentucky, I found a receiver in Virginia whom I thought was incredible. Excitedly, I rushed up to Bassett's office to show him this player. Bassett proceeded to question every facet of this player's ability. I walked out of his office dejected thinking I sure had a lot to learn about college football. Later I would realize my eye for talent was actually better than Bassett's, Mumme's, and Major's eyes collectively. In the beginning, however, I was shocked by how difficult it was for a "reputable" recruiter like Bassett to judge talent.

I later went back to Bassett again to discuss the same receiver and showed him he was on an All-American list. Bassett decided to watch again and we eventually offered him a scholarship. This receiver was David Terrell who went on to Michigan to become an All-American and the first receiver picked in the 2001 NFL draft.

I don't believe Bassett rejected David Terrell or Tim Couch because he couldn't spot talent. He rejected them because he wanted to show his power. Eventually I would learn how to work Bassett and get him to approve most of the recruits I liked. Several times Bassett would fight for one of my recruits to get Mumme and Major to offer a scholarship after their initial rejection of the recruit.

In Defense of Bassett (Mumme & Major Were Horrible)

Hal Mumme had to be a nightmare for Bassett to work for. One day Bassett might be told we were not going to sign any wide receivers, and the next week Mumme would say to sign four. Bassett might have Mumme lined up to call a top recruit and Mumme may have forgotten or just left a message on the recruit's recorder. The recruit might go a week without talking to a Kentucky coach, which could cause you to lose the player.

Bassett was chosen by Mumme to play the bad guy role. If there was a recruit whose scholarship offer Mumme wanted to pull, Bassett would usually be the bearer of bad news. Mumme didn't seem to enjoy recruiting and he didn't work at it very hard. When I traveled in Virginia during the recruiting month of May, I always bumped into Frank Beamer, the head coach of Virginia Tech. Kentucky's head coach might spend part of the month in the Caribbean Islands vacationing. If Bobby Bowden practiced this recruiting philosophy I could understand, but UK wasn't quite a national powerhouse yet. Mumme certainly wasn't making Bassett's job any easier.

The Good Side

If it was Halloween time, the only coach who would remember everyone's kids was Bassett. He knew each and every coach's child by name and knew something about him or her. Mumme, on the other hand, has walked past my children on numerous occasions and never acknowledged their presence, whereas Bassett would make each child feel special.

If your son or daughter had a big baseball game, Bassett might call to wish them luck or he might even show up for support. I've never known if he did it for show or if he genuinely cared. Irregardless, it didn't really matter because he was good at making your family feel special during times when they needed it.

My hometown had several people who absolutely loved Bassett and some still do. He made the summer coaches outing a special trip and he always stopped by to visit the good people at "Jewell's Bar-B-Que." When my Dad's good friend Jack Pedley had a heart attack, Bassett would make a get well call, and when the wife of Red Salyers, another one of my father's best friends, passed away, Bassett made sure to pass on his condolences.

There were times when I felt there were two completely different men named Claude Bassett. There was the brilliant, compassionate and caring Bassett and there was the ruthless, backstabbing and self-promoting Bassett. It was a shame the good Bassett couldn't win out over the evil Bassett. An incredibly talented man wasted great gifts by choosing to not consistently use his potential for good.

LESSON #11—Good and evil are constantly at war with each other. Take notice of this conflict and fight to prevent evil from wining the war. Strong moral leadership can bring out the good in a person and eradicate the evil. I strongly believe Claude Bassett was talented and full of good. I also believe if Hal Mumme had exercised strong leadership skills, he could have coached Bassett into more good and exorcised any evil.

CHAPTER 12

STEPPING OUT OF BOUNDS

Lesson 12—Beware of the man with the silver tongue, for he can make you believe events you saw with your own eyes disappear as if they never happened.

Do What He Says

On more than one occasion Hal Mumme entered into a meeting and instructed the coaches to "...do what Claude Bassett tells you." In the beginning, I wasn't clear what he was talking about. By the end of the fourth year, I was clear about what Mumme's instructions meant.

Bassett needed to be in control and he had a strong need to show his power. Major and Leach had not worked with Bassett, but had been with Mumme for six years or more. There was a definite friction between them from the first days the staff was assembled.

Mumme needed to remind Leach and Major that Bassett had his power in recruiting. As the years went by, many on our staff had conflicts concerning recruiting with Bassett, and Mumme reminded them Basssett was in control and they had better follow his orders.

Trouble With the Truth

Hal Mumme introduced Bassett numerous times to crowds of alumni, boosters, and fans. Several of those announcements would include the supposed fact that Bassett had a master degree in Constitutional Law from Harvard. I remember how impressed I was when I heard these credentials and Bassett reiterated them to me on numerous occasions. It has now been well documented by the media Bassett never attended Harvard University, let alone earned a master degree from the institution.

Bassett had done a remarkable job at McAllen (TX) Memorial High School as their Head Football Coach. He had turned around a losing program and gone 10-1 in his second season. However, his third season the program fell back into the losing category with a 2-8 record. That record didn't stop Bassett from giving a group of coaches from the Western Kentucky Football Coaches Association a detailed blow by blow description of how he led McAllen Memorial into the play-offs at the Alamo Dome in San Antonio his final season. That statement of course was not true, as Texas teams with 2-8 records don't make the play-offs.

A newspaper reporter told me a story about Bassett giving a vivid description of how loud the Arkansas Razorback Stadium was. He described a game in which Arkansas had played BYU during Bassett's coaching days at BYU. According to the reporter, Bassett gave a thorough and colorful explanation of how the game ended and how the crowd was not that loud. This reporter suspected Bassett might be telling a lie and when he went back to his office he got on his computer and checked. Arkansas and BYU had never played! Another classic Bassett fabrication.

Some of the letters Bassett had written to recruits were misleading. One of my all time favorite letters was the one he wrote to defensive recruits, describing how defensive coaches from Nebraska and the NFL had come to learn from the UK football program. Mumme had paid secondary coach Charlie Darlington from Nebraska to come to Kentucky and help Major with a new defensive scheme. Bassett's letter implied to the recruits it was Nebraska traveling to Kentucky seeking knowledge from our perennially near last place SEC defense and its Defensive Coordinator, Major.

Bassett was a compelling storyteller. He could keep a room of high school coaches on the edge of their seats as he told recruiting stories from BYU or high school coaching stories from Texas. Major told me early in my career the compelling thing about listening to a Bassett story was when you heard it the second or third time it would be just as good, because he made so much of it up he would forget what he had told people previously. Major was right, I had heard some of Bassett's "true stories" ten to twenty times. They were always fun to hear and the facts were very seldom the same.

Super Dave, Professional Film Evaluator

David Emerick is the son of June Mumme's sister. He worked in the UK football office from the beginning of the Hal Mumme Era until the end. He was a favorite of the coaching staff, one of whom fondly nick-named him "Super Dave." His official title would eventually be a Student Intern, however, his basic job description was Bassett's "go-for." Emerick did everything from picking up recruits at hotels and airports to writing letters to recruits in Mumme's name. As the years went by, Emerick's role with Bassett continued to increase. The final two seasons, when Bassett had assumed the job of kicking coach, Emerick was his on-the-field ball shagger.

The most unusual job Emerick possessed was that of Talent Evaluator. Although Emerick was not a coach, and to my knowledge, had no background of even playing high school football, he became Bassett's talent evaluator the last season. Emerick would be given videos of recruits and told to watch them and come back to Bassett with the high school players Emerick thought could play for UK.

Kentucky football coaches never watched hundreds upon hundreds of videotapes that were sent to Kentucky over the last three years. Bassett became more of a "list" recruiter his last two seasons. If a kid was not on someone's list as a top recruit, then there was a good chance no Kentucky coach would ever see the video. I had to give specific instructions to Emerick and recruiting assistant Josh Bullock to bring me all tapes from Kentucky, Virginia, Alabama, and Colorado, as well as those of any offensive player that was not a lineman or a quarterback. I also would go into Bassett's office and search for tapes on the floor or on the long table where they could be thrown under something. This was the only way that I could be sure to see tapes from most of the areas I recruited and of the positions I recruited.

Emerick was a good young man whom the players enjoyed and he did a good job handling recruiting visits. I'm not sure he was qualified to evaluate Division I talent. However, I would wager $10,000 Emerick watched more video on high school recruits than Bassett did during the fourth season.

Are You From Texas?

If a recruit was fortunate enough to be rated as one of the top 5,000 seniors in the state of Texas, there was a solid chance he would be offered a scholarship from the University of Kentucky. Although that is an exaggeration, my point is from November 1996 to February 2001 a Texas high school football player could be a lesser quality player than one from Kentucky, Florida, or Alabama, and still have a great chance to receive a scholarship offer from Kentucky.

Kentucky coaches Mumme, Bassett, Major, Adams, Patterson, Lounsbury, Highsmith, and Morriss all had Texas ties through family, playing, or coaching. In my opinion there were two strong reasons why UK recruited Texas so hard: (1.) The opportunity for UK coaches to visit family and friends. (2.) The misconception that Texas high school football players were better than anywhere else. I strongly believe better players from the state of Kentucky could have replaced 80% or more of the players we signed from Texas!

High school football is king in Texas. A young man who plays in 4A or 5A Texas high school football will be coached by top quality high school coaches who may be better coaches than many of their college peers. When a young man comes from the state of Texas, he better be ready to play from day one because he has probably come close to reaching his peak. He will have been through rigorous off-season programs that have him closing in on his potential and he may not get much better.

There are hundreds of good high school seniors in Texas every year, but after Texas A&M, Texas, Texas Tech, Houston, Rice, TCU, Baylor, SMU, Oklahoma, Arkansas, and other closer schools than Kentucky get their pick, the talent level drops considerably. Kentucky made a strategic mistake in recruiting Texas more heavily than Kentucky and other southern states with SEC ties. A player from these states may not have been as polished, and wouldn't have been through the off-seasons like a Texas player, but their upside potential was usually much greater.

"BATS"

The University of Kentucky is nationally known for its academic tutorial system for athletes known as C.A.T.S (Center for Academics and Tutorial Services). The previous success and national reputation of C.A.T.S. would not be enough to satisfy Mumme. He eventually would seek the help of his "Harvard Degreed" assistant Bassett, to assist in the academic progress of selected players. This actually worked on some players because they hated being in Bassett's office so much they actually would improve just to get away from him. This program would eventually become known as BATS (Bassett's Academic Tutorial System), or as Mumme liked to refer to it as "Bassett's !@#$ kicking tutorial service."

BATS worked wonders for some players until someone began to question the amazing work of a few athletes who seemed to have complete vocabulary transformations in a matter of days under Bassett's tutelage. It was obvious to anyone who took time to notice there was more than tutoring going on for some of the players. The UK compliance office eventually investigated and found wrongdoings they turned into the NCAA. It took the University of Minnesota getting wrapped up in a NCAA scandal concerning academic irregularities before Newton, according to Mumme, became nervous and called a halt to BATS. UK officials, to my knowledge, never officially looked into BATS irregularities until the investigation of other NCAA violations by the UK compliance office in late 2000.

Bob Bradley and Barb Deniston of C.A.T.S. have a national reputation for excellence. Colleges from all over America have come to UK to study their program. The history of C.A.T.S. is one of total integrity and the implementation of BATS did nothing to hurt that reputation as C.A.T.S. had nothing to do with academic irregularities that occurred under Bassett.

I'll Whip His !@#$

Claude Bassett could stir up emotions in people as quickly as anyone I have ever known. There were people who loved to hang around Bassett and listen to his stories daily. His recruiting of Alvis Johnson, father of Dennis and Derek, and Bob Redman, coach of former Louisville Male players Chris Demaree, Richard Hardin, and Montrell Jones, was classic. He befriended Alvis and Bob and worked them steadily for years to reap the fruits of their players. Both men seemed to have genuinely enjoyed Bassett's company, friendship, and storytelling.

There were other parents and adults whose reaction to him was quite the opposite. Some would be simply frustrated with his overbearing personality, while others were offended to the point of telling me to keep him out of their sight. I was helping recruit a top defensive lineman in the Midwest that the defensive coaches felt could have helped us immediately. During my conversations with his father, I told his dad Bassett and I would be coming back the following week. The father told me, "If you bring that man out here, my son will definitely not go to UK, and I will personally whip his !@#$." The father went on to tell me that Bassett's rudeness, brashness, and overbearing personality were too much to take. Needless to say, we did not sign that defensive lineman.

Strong women seemed to be a problem for Bassett and two current UK players have mothers you would definitely want on your side in battle. They were tough, opinionated, and asked good questions; they were exactly the type of mothers they should have been when helping their sons decide what college to attend. Bassett so strongly disliked one mother they engaged in a shouting match at one point of their relationship. The mother relayed the story to me and by her accounts Bassett had really met his match. During the shouting match, according to the mother, Bassett screamed at her, "You don't want to mess with me!"

She replied, "No, you don't want to !@#$ with me," as she pointed her finger at his chest. Bassett kept his distance from her throughout the remainder of his stay at Kentucky. The other mother was also offended by Bassett. During my recruiting of her son, she informed me of her extreme disdain for him and told me that if he ever offended her again in a specific way, she would "…whip his !@#$." I firmly believe she could have.

The Golf Cart—Power On Wheels

If you were lucky enough to ride the golf cart during a UK practice, you knew you had made it BIG. Bassett was probably the only full-time assistant coach in NCAA Division I who spent much of his practice time riding in a golf cart around the practice field. Dignitaries as high as President Charles Wethington and Newton got high priority rides when they would enter the practice area.

The golf cart was the ultimate power symbol for Bassett. Bassett, Mumme and Major discussed some key issues in that golf cart. There was always a bumping order in the golf cart rides. You might think you were a big shot riding around the field, when out of nowhere, someone more powerful in Bassett's daily pecking order would show up and you would be bumped out of his cart. Bassett got a three-row seated golf cart in his final year and it was a pure symbol as to how much power he had obtained.

The final days of practice for the 2000 season showed the ultimate power of Claude Bassett's days as a coach at UK. Major had already resigned and Bassett was without a doubt Mumme's true number one man. As they rode around the practice field and seemed to evaluate the coaches and players, several of us knew that Bassett had achieved consummate authority. Little did Mumme and Bassett know it would only be a few short days before their "tires" were going to be deflated and their power depleted.

The 2000 Louisville Fiasco

Bassett had the ability, similar to Mumme, to make himself believe anything he wanted to believe. Going into the 1999 season, Bassett had become the Kicking Coach and the kickers had gone through one of the most rigorous training regimens of any group in America. He took great pride in coaching the kickers, and in 1999 Andy Smith and Mark Samuels did quality jobs in punting and kicking. Going into the 2000 season, Seth Hanson was returning from a red shirt season after his freshman season had brought him pre-season All-SEC honors for 2000. Bassett didn't want Hanson to be the kicker!

Hanson was one of the truly good people on our football team. He was one of the leaders of the Fellowship of Christian Athletes, and he had a strong conviction in his beliefs. Bassett was not thrilled with Hanson's FCA beliefs as he told me on numerous occasions about "that FCA !@#$" that Hanson was in. Bassett professed to be of Mormon belief, but I'm not sure if the Mormon Church would want him to be their spokesperson.

Before the first game in 2000, Bassett began to explain to Mumme why Hanson couldn't kick both field goals and punts. He finally convinced Mumme to use senior walk-on Brandon Sanders as the extra point and field goal kicker while Hanson would only handle the punting. Some of the assistant coaches were nervous because Hanson had won games under pressure in 1998, whereas Sanders had no SEC game experience.

The opening game of 2000 dramatically ended in regulation with Sanders having a short, 18-yard field goal blocked by Louisville, and Louisville going on to win in over-time. I don't know if Hanson's kick would not have also been blocked. Louisville did a superb job and Sanders was *definitely not* the reason we lost the game. What is important is what the reasons were behind Sanders being chosen for the kick.

After the game, Mumme told me, "Don't ever let me listen to Claude Bassett again if it concerns a football personnel decision." Mumme knew he had made a choice that would haunt him for a long time. He made Hanson the kicker for the remainder of the season. Sanders was given the role of scapegoat, which he *definitely did not* deserve.

I don't know if Bassett made the Seth Hanson/Brandon Sanders decision based on kicking or personal favoritism. Only Bassett knows for sure, and by now he has convinced himself he made it because Hanson requested it. At least that's what he later told me.

Bassett's Spies

For each of the four seasons there were two to three games we would get "incredible" secret information about our opponent from some "unknown spies." Mumme would go to the board in front of the coaches and players and draw some "secret" information that Mumme would refer to as "Bassett's spies" information. In four years, to my knowledge, none of these supposed secrets proved to be valuable or even correct. Besides the fact that spying on an opponent is unethical and likely against SEC rules, it is a waste of time since each team has hours of videotape of each other.

One of the best spy stories came from the 1999 Indiana game in Bloomington. Bassett had driven up the day before the game with Josh Bullock, his Recruiting Assistant and they arrived at the IU parking lot to drive around and watch what part of IU's practice they could. Bassett told in vivid detail the IU punt block they were practicing for the game on Saturday. Mumme immediately began to prepare the team for this secret information. The following day, we beat IU and have not yet seen this "secret punt block." Bullock would later tell some of us they were circling the parking lot at 30 m.p.h. and that you couldn't see anything but specks, let alone a formation. Amazingly, Mumme always seemed to believe Bassett's spy information.

Cell Phone
(I'm Sorry, I'll Make Sure It's Higher Next Spring)

One of the most discussed topics concerning Bassett was the use of his cellular telephone. With Bassett's monthly bills at times being more than

$5,000, Kentucky probably set records for cell phone usage and costs. It was a story that almost became legendary about how hard Bassett worked the phone. Almost everyone believed when they watched practice and Bassett was on his cell phone he was talking to a recruit or a coach. It would be interesting to know exactly the breakdown of those calls for four years.

Bassett and Mumme told a story how Ivy called Bassett in after the first May recruiting period to question a several thousand dollar phone bill for all the coaches' cellular usage. This bill was supposedly as high as the previous staff's entire year. Bassett apologized to Ivy and said, "This is embarrassing! Our phone bill should have been at least $25,000 in May. My coaches aren't calling enough, but I promise they will call more next May."

Ivy was supposedly shocked by Bassett's answer and over the next four years high cellular bills would become common for Bassett and Ivy would tolerate it.

Mumme used to say Bassett "...wasn't happy unless there was a crisis and if there is not a crisis, he'll create one." I believe Mumme was right. I've seen Bassett coaching kickers on the field with his cell phone in hand, while screaming at someone on the other end about anything imaginable. His cell phone was definitely a crisis management center.

Cheating—When, Why, & How

I will detail some of the Memphis cheating in a later chapter, but much of it has already been discussed in detail by several newspapers. Hal Mumme, C.M. Newton, Larry Ivy, and Dr. Charles Wethington, in my opinion, would like for all of you to believe the UK Compliance report to the NCAA was all there was and with thorough investigative techniques and detailed research they have found the cheating and ended it as well as reported all of it. If you believe that I have some oceanfront property I'll sell you in Nevada.

I told Rob Oviatt, our 1997-1998 Strength Coach, at dinner one night prior to the 1999 Outback Bowl that Bassett wanted to be a martyr. I said, "One day Bassett will stand up in front of the world and tell everyone that he alone is responsible and that he alone should be punished for NCAA violations." Two years later this exact scenario would take place.

Bassett had occasionally bragged to me about the supposed cheating at BYU he had accomplished. He was also especially proud of one of his closest friends who had been banned from college athletics for his role in the SMU "death penalty" case of the late 1980s. He loved to talk about cheating and how he could lie his way out of anything with the NCAA. Thus, I began to believe he loved the limelight so much he actually would one day get so sloppy in his cheating he would get caught and play the role of martyr.

Any coach or administrator close to UK athletics who tells you they didn't strongly suspect the fact that Claude Bassett was cheating is, in my opinion, lying. Did they know the details? Some did, some didn't. Did they want to know the details and catch him to turn him in? Absolutely not!

Some cheating began in the first year. I knew college players were occasionally bought, but I was surprised at how coaches and boosters could be so flagrantly abusive and not come under the scrutiny of their own investigative compliance group

From day one, Bassett was concerned about UK's Assistant Athletic Director for Compliance, Sandy Bell. She was, I believe, suspicious of Bassett and closely watched him until, according to Bassett, he got Newton to tell her to back off. He had a relatively free hand from that point on. Bassett's meeting with Newton is discussed in Chapter 20.

In 1997, a Kentucky high school coach told me we had to be the dumbest cheaters in the world. I asked why and he said, "You've got the father of a recruit in front of Commonwealth Stadium before the Florida game selling tickets that Bassett gave him." Another coach later told me the same thing.

I had been at Kentucky less than one year when I got a phone call from a close friend. He told me he was worried we had "gone back to the ways of the '70s." I asked what he meant and he told me some boosters in west Kentucky were being asked by Bassett to gather up money to buy an auto for a top recruit. Bassett later had me in his office with this recruit and his father and I listened as Bassett called a banker and asked him to approve a loan for this player's dad. Bassett reminded the banker who he, Bassett, was and the fact that this player was very important to the University of Kentucky. The amazing thing was Bassett held this conversation on speakerphone with his door open and Mumme's office right next door. Anyone could have heard this conversation!

A few days later I got enough courage to call Bassett down to my office and confront him. I told him, "Too many people know what you are doing and you are going to get caught. You are going to embarrass this university, and I remember what happened to Kentucky in the 1970s. Please stop! We've got a good thing going and we don't have to cheat." Bassett's face turned red and he said nothing as he walked out of my office.

Bassett questioned me when another assistant coach said something to Mumme about the rumor we were buying an automobile for this recruit. Eventually, the recruit went to another school after refusing to commit to Mumme when he pressured him to make a verbal commitment or have his scholarship offer revoked. I believe Mumme got nervous when the UK assistant coach questioned him about the recruit and the automobile rumors and then decided to try to get out of the situation.

Conclusion

Hal Mumme told assistant coach Dan Lounsbury and me in the summer of 2000 that 50% of what came out of Claude's mouth was a lie. I corrected Mumme and told him it would be closer to 90%. The amazing thing is Mumme knew, but he simply didn't do anything about it, no matter how bad Bassett's lies hurt other people. The more he lied the more he was promoted with titles and pay raises.

LESSON #12—Beware of the man with the silver tongue for he can make you believe events you saw with your own eyes disappear as if they never happened. Claude Bassett is one of the greatest talkers of all time. During my first few months at UK I believed some of his stories, advice, and anecdotes. He was so good at lying that I now believe he eventually thought truth of his own lies. When men of this ability to persuade others enter into a power position we had better go on full alert! If they are good, they can motivate the world and all around them to do better things and accomplish good for all humanity. If they are bad, beware for the silver tongue can lead many followers to their own destructions.

CHAPTER 13

THE SHARK, NO DEFENSE!

Lesson 13—Be careful with whom you choose to associate, because we all become similar to those we work with, live with, and are friends with. Pick your friends with meticulous care. They could be your final downfall.

What Is A Shark?

Chris Hatcher and Sonny Dykes have both been credited for the nickname "The Shark." The nickname became a commonly used term to let someone know Defensive Coordinator and long-time Mumme friend Mike Major was coming. It was a common occurrence for someone to walk in after an "attack" and talk about how choppy the waters were. Warning signals would go out through the office just like a siren going off on a sunny beach warning swimmers of a nearby shark.

The theme from Jaws became a common tune hummed daily. Current UK Head Coach Guy Morriss' wife, Jackie went as far as buying "shark resistant" socks to help protect Hatcher from a possible attack. Hatcher also bought a device for his desk that, when pulled, a plastic shark would start to swallow a plastic man.

Just as a shark swims around in search of prey, so it seemed would Major. There were very few days when someone didn't "get bitten" by the Shark. Sometimes it was a little bite and other times it would be a full-scale attack. One thing was for sure, you had better be prepared because you never knew when the Shark would attack, and if you were not careful, you might get hurt.

The Shark was the perfect term. It was all in fun, but if we had not learned to occasionally laugh about a seemingly insecure little bully, we would have all gone crazy. Most of us prepared ourselves daily for the potential shark attack that might take place. However, the defensive assistants needed more shark repellent than the rest of us so Lori Hatcher, Chris' wife, bought blue "gummy sharks" for Hatcher to hand out to the defensive assistants as they passed by his office on the way to enter "the tank." It was a total family affair to protect each other from the potential shark attacks!

I've Never Seen these Players Before

Mumme told the defensive coaches to leave the room and go into their own meeting room and make a decision. He then walked back towards the conference table, faced me, and started to scream, "You are the only !@#$ coach on offense that I let recruit defensive players and it is your job to make Mike Major happy! You had better do a better job or I'll fire your !@#$ because Mike is definitely not happy!"

I calmly looked at Mumme and said, "Mike Major is a liar. He watched those kids videos in my office and approved both of them and he said he wanted them on official visits and would probably offer them scholarships."

Mumme replied, "I don't care, he's not happy, and its your job to make him happy." All of the offensive coaches sat silently as did Bassett, who knew Major had approved the players. He knew Major was lying, but he never said a word.

I walked out and proceeded to begin climbing the Commonwealth Stadium stairs trying to cool myself down before I decided what to do. My choices were to go to Major's office, physically beat him, confront Mumme and tell him what to do with this job, or to realize this was just another day in the life of Hal and Mike and continue to work with the hope I could get another job after the season and leave those two men behind one day. I came back from walking the steps and sat down in my office, a few moments later Mumme entered my office. He said, "I'm sorry, I shouldn't have done that, but you know how Mike is."

I replied, "Mike Major is a liar. He stood in this office and watched both of those players and was genuinely excited about my bringing them in on official visits. When he said he had never seen them before he was telling a blatant lie because he just watched them yesterday."

Mumme replied, "Well, you know how Mike is."

I then told Mumme, "Don't ever threaten me again. If you don't like the job that I'm doing then fire me, but don't threaten me. I don't take to threats or intimidation. That's not how you treat me."

Mumme responded, "!@#$, that's why I'm here to tell you I'm sorry."

I reiterated, "Don't threaten me anymore."

Major had just pulled off another classic Mike Major routine. He had blatantly lied in front of the entire staff and put another coach in jeopardy. I wasn't surprised, as I had already seen him dodge responsibility numerous times to place blame on another coach.

The two players Major had rejected on video that day came on their official visits that weekend. He told one recruit he could have a scholarship if he would agree to play defensive tackle instead of defensive end. That player was shocked. He really liked Kentucky and had already been offered scholarships by several of the top 20 colleges in America. His high school coach later told me he thought we would have had a great chance to sign him if we had offered him as a defensive end. He was 6'3" 245 pounds and ran a legitimate 4.5 forty and played high school running back and defensive end. His name is Nathaniel Adibi from Phoebus High School in Hampton, Virginia. Adibi would become a starter for one of the most respected defenses in America, Virginia Tech, as a red shirt freshman playing, of course, defensive end. The other player was Keith Willis, who also signed at Virginia Tech and is playing tight end.

Never Get On His Bad Side

In the summer of 1997, Mumme and I were driving across the Commonwealth Stadium parking lot when he blurted, "Mike Major likes you and that's a good thing. Don't ever cross him or get on his bad side because he will always win." I laughed and Mumme said, "I'm not kidding."

Mumme and Major's story of friendship has been told numerous times by reporters who reported their early high school coaching days were filled with late night video sessions, watching 16 mm film on the side of a refrigerator. Those stories are heart warming, but I believe that it has very little to do with Mumme's close relationship to Major. Their relationship deserves a closer look, but the next Athletic Director who hires Mumme can do that because I don't believe anyone in Kentucky cares anymore.

The Bully

The easiest and most accurate way to describe Major is that of a classic bully. Bullies will abuse those weaker than them until someone steps up and forces them to stop. There were only a few times that Major was forced to stop.

In my first spring at Kentucky, I got to see Major in his true bully form. Leach had told me he would be interested in my observations of Major after our first spring. I had noticed Leach and Major simply did not communicate at all with each other, and I had asked Leach to give me his thoughts on Major. Leach smiled and said, "I'll wait and let you make your own observations."

Eventually, I would come to find out Leach hated Major, but that Major simply didn't mess with Leach because Leach would not take any grief from Major. Their relationship was basically non-existent and when Leach also became alienated with Bassett, he would receive the ultimate gift; a strong recommendation from Mumme to leave and take the Offensive Coordinator job at Oklahoma.

Major's first spring was a show of his power. Several of Curry's players who were still around would be moved to a different position. Whatever Major couldn't blame on Curry he was going to blame on assistant coaches Darrell Patterson and Mike Fanoga. Patterson and Fanoga, as mentioned earlier, would be a target of Major's attacks for the spring of 1997, until Patterson decided he had enough.

At the end of a practice, Major entered the coaches' locker room and pursued Patterson. Major berated Patterson in front of the entire staff just as he had done on previous days. His comments were belligerent and accusatory in nature. Until Patterson turned to Major and explicitly and firmly told Major if he was going to talk to him then treat him with respect and like a man. Major began to start again on Patterson when Patterson firmly reiterated to Major to back off. Major did back off and Patterson's next three and half years were much more pleasant than they would have been had he not stood up for himself.

Fanoga and Major had coached together for three of the five years Mumme was the Head Coach at Valdosta State. Major would continue to verbally abuse Fanoga in front of coaches, players, fans, and anyone else within earshot. I later asked Fanoga why he took it (the abuse), and he said if he had ever confronted Major, Mumme would have fired him and he thought Mumme and Major would have tried to prevent him front getting another job.

The college coaching profession is a funny profession. Many assistant coaches spend hours on the phone every week staying in contact with other job possibilities. Most assistant coaches live in fear if their head coach decides to "black-ball" them in the profession, then they may never get another job. It is a good idea to stay on the head coach's good side if you want to remain in the profession.

They Can't Play For Me

To judge the talent of high school football players you have to actually work at it. The Division II mentality in recruiting is totally different than Division I. When coaching at Valdosta State, Major and Mumme could take recruits in January that had just been rejected by a Division I school and bring them to Valdosta State and many of those were great players. Division I recruiting worked differently. You must be able to judge players potential off junior film and many times make early offers by May of their junior season. This takes hard work, effort, and an eye for talent. In my opinion, Major had none of those characteristics.

Major didn't want to watch recruiting videos and he had trouble making a decision. He wanted to wait and see senior film. Bassett had to constantly press Mumme to force Major to watch video and make some sort of recruiting decision. Many times, Bassett would go ahead and offer a player whom Mumme and Major had rejected, knowing one week later they might change their minds.

The players Major rejected in some fashion in his four years at Kentucky read like a Who's Who In College Football. They included:

1. Marvin Constant—starting LB, Alabama as red shirt freshman on '99 Sugar Bowl Team

2. Kenny King—DE '99 All SEC freshman at Alabama, projected high NFL draft pick

3. Saleem Rasheed—'99-'00 starting LB Alabama, projected first round NFL draft pick

4. Nathaniel Adibi—2000 DE Virginia Tech, starter as red shirt freshman, projected high NFL draft pick

5. Jake Housewright—2000 starting LB Virginia Tech

6. Rob Reynolds—2000 Ohio State letterman as LB freshman season

7. Will Overstreet—'98-'99-'00 DL Tennessee, projected high NFL draft pick

8. Edward Kendrick—2000 starting DL Tennessee

9. Jeffrey Womble—2000 starting DT Florida State

10. Alonzo Jackson—2000 starting DE Florida State

11. Kendrell Bell— '99-'00 starting LB Georgia, 2nd round NFL draft pick 2001

There are three reasons I believe Major rejected great players: (1.) He couldn't tell what a good player was because he hadn't watched enough film to compare one player against another. (2.) The person who brought the film to Major was on his "bad list" and Major wouldn't have accepted

Lawrence Taylor if a "bad list" coach brought him a tape. (3.) Major consistently had to let everyone know he had the power.

Saleem Rasheed

Saleem Rasheed was a classic example of Major not having the right person bring the tape into him for review. Coach Robert Higginbotham is one of the most respected coaches in Alabama. He told me that Rasheed was the "real deal," he played like Superman, and he had a great academic and family background. Rasheed was the perfect college prospect and he was open to leaving the state of Alabama. Kentucky had caught his eye with our 1997 defeat of Alabama.

I brought Rasheed's highlight tape to Bassett and he agreed Rasheed was the real deal. Major then watched the video and decided Rasheed wasn't good enough to play for Kentucky. I had already offered Rasheed verbally by phone because I knew he wasn't just good, he was spectacular. Several months later Bassett would take the exact same video to Major and not tell him where he was from and Major loved the same player he had rejected months earlier watching the exact same video. By that time, Rasheed had knocked Kentucky off his list.

Marvin Constant

Marvin Constant had committed to the University of Alabama, but being from Tuscaloosa, he really wanted to get away from home. I was able to develop a good relationship with Marvin and persuade him to cancel his commitment to Alabama. He was excited about his official visit to Kentucky when Bassett came in to tell me some bad news. Major had rejected Constant, and Bassett wanted me to call and cancel his visit. I was embarrassed to have to tell Marvin, but I was sure Alabama would still take him. Constant was disappointed, but went on to Alabama where he was a starting linebacker as a redshirt freshman in their 1999 Sugar Bowl season before having a career ending knee injury in the 2000 season.

Kendrell Bell

Hatcher was excited when he entered my office in the spring of 1999. Since only recently being hired full time, Hatcher was excited about finally getting to recruit off campus. He was holding a video of a junior college linebacker that a friend of his had sent and told him the player had some interest in attending Kentucky. As Hatcher put the video in he had a thrill in his eyes, like I had in 1997, when I was first hired and still believed all of our staff was dedicated to winning. The player, Kendrell Bell, was absolutely phenomenal. He could do anything! He was big, fast, strong, and mean and made plays all over the field and was 6'3", 245 pounds. Bell could play any position for any team.

After the video was done Hatcher looked at me and said, "Major can't reject this kid, no way."

I laughed and said, "Wanna bet?"

We took off down the hallway and found Major in his office. Hatcher asked if Major had time to watch the video and Major said he did. After watching the 15-minute tape, Major told Hatcher, "I don't know where he can play for us."

Hatcher replied, "Linebacker, Defensive End, Defensive Tackle, Safety, anywhere on the field."

Major said, "I don't think he is better than anyone we already have at LB, I'll pass on him."

We left his office and Hatcher looked at me and said, "Unbelievable."

I replied, "Told ya."

Hatcher and I both would eventually stop trying to recruit defensive players. It was a frustrating experience and I got to the point where I couldn't honestly tell a defensive recruit's parents Kentucky was a good place for their child to come where he would be treated fairly and with respect.

Robert Reynolds

In the spring of 1999, I visited Bowling Green HS in Kentucky. Robert Reynolds was one of the best linebackers in America. Miami of Florida and Michigan had already sent their defensive coordinators to Bowling Green to offer him a scholarship. Kevin Wallace was Reynolds' high school coach and an old pal of mine. Kevin asked me why two of the top programs in the nation had already offered Robert and UK was dragging its feet. I couldn't give him a good answer.

Reynolds was 6'4", 210 pounds, mean, and could run. Mumme and Major watched his video and both came to the conclusion they didn't want him. However, Robert was going to be a top-recruit nationally so they devised a plan so Kentucky would have officially offered him a scholarship. This was a good political move because they could always tell the alumni and UK fans Reynolds was disloyal and had rejected their offer.

When Reynolds came for a visit to our spring practice, Mumme broke the news to Reynolds that his 210-pound frame could come to Kentucky and play defensive line. Coach Wallace later called me and told me we must be crazy if we thought Robert would play defensive line. Reynolds would eventually go to Ohio Sate and play enough to letter as a freshman, at linebacker of course. I saw Robert at a wedding in June of 2001, and he asked me why we didn't want him. After explaining the situation with Major, Robert laughed and said it was a shame, because he had been excited about playing for Kentucky.

The UK defense was consistently among the worst in the SEC from 1997 to 2000, and Major blamed everyone but who the blame should have gone to—himself!

The Storyteller

Major was speaking in front of a large gathering of coaches at the 1998 Nike Coaches Clinic in Louisville. Major was describing a tackling drill when he mentioned the year he worked with Bum Phillips at the Houston Oilers. I turned my head for a double take because I couldn't believe what I had heard. Major, of course, doesn't make any reference to his being an assistant coach working for the Houston Oilers or Bum Phillips in the UK media guide. Some NFL teams sometimes allow high school and college coaches to serve apprenticeships or help break down film, but this didn't seem to be his inference. I later asked a Kentucky defensive assistant if he knew about Major's claim to have worked with Bum Phillips. The assistant laughed and told me Major had made the same claim to him on other occasions.

Major was not nearly as eloquent a storyteller as Bassett, but he had similar trouble with the truth. According to a defensive assistant, he once told a group of high school coaches in his office about winning a state championship as the Head Coach of Dimmitt HS in Texas. This of course, was not true; his head-coaching record was 6-4. The same group of high school coaches also got to listen to Major describe a type of linebacker technique to use against a lead blocker called, "spill technique." Major gave an example of how he used this technique when playing at Arkansas while taking on legendary Texas running back Earl Campbell. There is no Mike Major listed in the rosters or letterman for the University of Arkansas so Major must have "spilled" Campbell with an anonymous name.

Major's fabrications on the field with his players were also memorable. He would bark out a defensive call loud enough for everyone on the field to hear and then after the call didn't work he would scream at his players and tell them he didn't call that defense. During games, Major would react to Mumme's yelling at him by telling Mumme it's "Tim Keane's fault." He wasn't exactly the stand up leader you would imagine taking you into battle.

Another example of Major skewing the truth was provided in a story released by the *Lexington Herald Leader* on February 2, 2001[1]. According to the story, Major had solicited donations from several boosters, explaining to them the donations would by used to help pay certain camper's registration fees. This would have been a flagrant NCAA rule violation. However, these donations weren't used for registration fees, they were used to supplement his camp stipend, as he was paid $12,000, or more, for his camp work in the 2000 summer camp, whereas his defensive assistants made less than $5,000.

The Package Deal

Mumme's response to the radio caller went something like this: "If you want to get rid of him, you're getting rid of me boy. We are a package deal." Call-in shows normally receive calls from a few quacks and flakes who get a thrill from being able to get under a coach's skin. Mumme was easy to get because he was extremely sensitive to criticism, and he had to answer weekly questions about why Kentucky couldn't play any defense.

That "package deal" would eventually be broken, as Mumme's fourth season was becoming the worse one yet on defense. The spring of 2000 had seen QB Dusty Bonner rip the first team Kentucky defense to shreds. The general feelings among Morriss and myself were that this might be the worse defense yet. With the loss of Snedegar there was not a nasty run stopper on defense and with Bonner at the helm, we had slashed the defense throwing and running. It was not a good sign.

During practice the week of our game against South Florida on September 9, 2000, an incident occurred which would be a turning point in the relationship of Mumme and Major. The first team offense would run several scout team plays against the first defense. One of South Florida's favorite plays was a quarterback draw, and the one player not accounted for when a team plays man coverage every snap is the quarterback. Kentucky freshman QB Shane Boyd took the snap and took three steps back as if he were going to pass, then ran the QB draw. No defensive player was anywhere around. Mumme told the scouts in the huddle to run it again. The result was the same. Mumme yelled at Major to line up again and explain to him how he was going to stop the play. Major lined up the defense and blamed linebacker Chris Gayton for not making the play. Gayton responded that he was in man coverage on the running back who had run a swing route out of the backfield (see Insert C, page 120).

It doesn't take a football expert to realize that a linebacker cannot cover a back on a route and make the play on a quarterback draw. Major tried to explain to Mumme and Gayton how this was going to work and both men

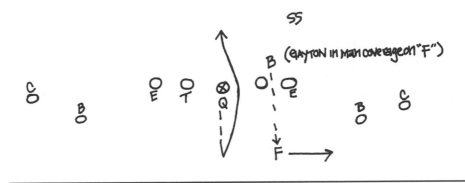

Insert C. Gayton in man coverage on running back.

looked at him as if he was crazy. Gayton argued with Major as Major again tried to place the blame on Gayton.

Mumme had seen enough. After nine seasons with Major as his Defensive Coordinator, Mumme seemed to have a light come on in his brain and he finally saw what some players and assistant coaches had thought for years. Mumme seemed to be thinking, "This guy doesn't have a clue what he is doing." Mumme brought the offensive team together in a huddle and said, "We've got to score 50 points because those guys won't stop anyone all year." There was a sigh of relief from the offense and they got excited because they now felt like there was hope. It was as if Mumme had finally figured it out and now maybe he would do something about it. The package deal was about to be broken.

You Take The Offense—I'm Coaching Defense

Mumme walked into my office the Sunday before we played Florida in 2000, and announced to me "Make a game plan for Florida. I'm going to coach defense this week and I won't be around until team period at the end of practice." He went on to say, "I had no idea that it was that bad on defense. I've got to do something."

I replied, "I'm glad you are going to do something, it's been that way for a long time."

After Mumme gave me some guidelines about the offensive game plan, he left. I finally thought to myself, "Maybe he'll finally fire Major and hire a real defensive coordinator so we will have a chance to win!" Mumme coached defense that week and we gave up our normal 50 plus points versus Florida.

During half-time Mumme decided after giving up 38 points at half he owed the defense an apology. After the game, however, Mumme found out that Major had not called the defenses Mumme had requested. Mumme had gone to the other defensive assistants and found out Major had not practiced Mumme's defenses when Mumme would leave the defensive field to go to offensive practice. Mumme was furious and eventually Major would "resign".

After the Florida fiasco, Mumme had a perfect opportunity to turn the defense over to Tim Keane and Darrell Patterson. Not only were both men capable of being effective defensive coordinators, but they were also capable leaders. The defensive players would have rallied around them and I believe we could have won three to five more games in 2000. Instead, Mumme gave Bassett a stronger role in helping the defense and nothing changed. Bassett finished the year with a defensive headset on during the final games. He cut Major's throat behind his back while pretending to defend him to his face. They had gone full circle with each other and were now back as "solid friends" just as they had started out in the Mumme era in 1996.

Major and the Press

I'll have to give Major credit for one thing, he was smart with the news media. Unlike Mumme, who had a habit of talking sarcastically to the media at times, Major treated the media with respect and they in turn never really went after him. Several members of the media continued to buy all of Major's excuses as to why the defense was consistently near the bottom of the SEC. He did a remarkable job of convincing these potential "sharks" that he was sincere and caring. I'll have to take my hat off to him in this area. He was good.

Conclusion

Mike Major would eventually write several of the coaches on our staff "love notes" near the end of the season (see Insert D, page 122).

This was typical Mumme/Major/Bassett style. Verbally abuse you, degrade you in public, cut your throat behind your back, and then be nice to you, give you a raise, or write you a "love note" and hope you would forget. Major and I barely spoke to each other my last season at Kentucky and his "love note" was an absolute joke. Morriss and I got a good laugh from our "love notes."

Later Major falsely told Mark Story of the *Lexington Herald-Leader* that Guy Morriss and I had plotted Hal Mumme's downfall and that Major had listened into our behind closed door plotting. With Major as Hal

WHAT IT TAKES TO BE NUMBER 1

Winning is not a sometime thing; it's an all the time thing. You don't win once in a while; you don't do things right once in a while; you do them right all the time. Winning is a habit. Unfortunately, so is losing.

There is no room for second place. There is only one place in my game, and that's first place. I have finished second twice in my time at Green Bay, and I don't ever want to finish second again. There is a second place bowl game, but it is a game for losers played by losers. It is and always has been an American zeal to be first in anything we do, and to win, and to win, and to win.

Every time a football player goes to ply his trade he's got to play from the ground up – from the soles of his feet right up to his head. Every inch of him has to play. Some guys play with their heads. That's O.K. You've got to be smart to be number one in any business. But more importantly, you've got to play with your heart, with every fiber of your body. If you're lucky enough to find a guy with a lot of head and a lot of heart, he's never going to come off the field second.

Running a football team is no different than running any other kind of organization – an army, a political party or a business. The principles are the same. The object is to win – to beat the other guy. Maybe that sounds hard or cruel. I don't think it is.

It is a reality of life that men are competitive and the most competitive games draw the most competitive men. That's why they are there – to compete. To know the rules and objectives when they get in the game. The object is to win fairly, squarely, by the rules – but to win.

And in truth, I've never known a man worth his salt who in the long run, deep down in his heart, didn't appreciate the grind, the discipline. There is something in good men that really yearns for discipline and the harsh reality of head to head combat.

I don't say these things because I believe in the "brute" nature of man or that men must be brutalized to be combative. I believe in God, and I believe in human decency. But I firmly believe that any man's finest hour – his greatest fulfillment to all he holds dear – is that moment when he has to work his heart out in a good cause and he's exhausted on the field of battle – victorious.

—Vincent Lombardi

Tony –

You ARE DOiNg A gREAT Job juST AS you Always have done. Keep on doing the job. I Know sometimes I don't tell you guys WHAT A great job you do AND for this please forgive. THANKS for doing what you do and for your friendship.

Coach Maj

Insert D.   Mike Majors "love note."

Mumme's defensive coordinator and Bassett as his recruiting coordinator, and the two of them Mumme's closest friends, there was no need to plot Hal Mumme's demise. He had chosen his own downfall and his own method of destruction by giving the two of them power.

LESSON #13—Be careful with whom you choose to associate because we all eventually become like those we work with, live with, and are friends with. Although no one may ever know all the facts from the Mumme Era, we can all be sure by choosing Mike Major and Claude Bassett to be in power and to be his friends, Hal Mumme truly became one of them, or maybe they became like him. Either way, they all ended up together with each other. Pick your friends with great care. They could be your final downfall.

CHAPTER 14

A MAD DOG, A HIGH FIVE, AND A YOUNG HEROINE

Lesson 14—Yes men will get you fired. Hire people who will tell you the truth, not what you want to hear. Hire people who want to be better than you and when they surpass you, hire someone else better than them. Success comes to a team or business when no one cares who gets the credit. A true friend tells you the painful truth every time, not just when it's convenient for him.

Mad Dog (Trainer/Psychologist)

Tennessee was beating us the normal 30 to 50 point margin when QB Jared Lorenzen scrambled for a 10 to 15-yard gain. Mumme, his headset dangling around his neck and not over his ears, began to scream, "Yes, Yes!" He turned and looked for Jim Madaleno, his trainer since his days at Valdosta State and said, "Do you believe that some of these stupid players actually had enough nerve to tell me they wanted Shane Boyd at QB?"

Madaleno, or Mad Dog as Mumme and Major sometimes called him replied, "That's why you are so good, you've got so much class, you're so much a better man than all these assistants and players, Hal you're just too good of a man."

I was standing at the opposite end of the field watching Tennessee's coverages and Mumme thought, since his headset was off, no one could hear him. He failed to realize the microphone was right in front of his mouth.

Madaleno's comments made me want to throw up, but I wasn't surprised. He was the most absolutely perfect assistant Mumme ever could have had. Mad Dog knew Mumme as well as anyone, and he thought he had a lifetime career as long as he kissed Mumme's butt and he was incredibly gifted at that job!

I would doubt any trainer in the history of Division I football had as much power as Madaleno. Not only was Madaleno a trainer, he also was an "amateur psychologist" and a Mumme-proclaimed expert on knowing and judging the character of players. God forbid if you were a player that got on his bad list because you could be assured Mumme would begin to question your character, desire, and heart.

He's Squirrelly

One of the best young men I've ever coached unfortunately got the tag of being "squirrelly" from Madaleno. Mumme said something to me about the player during the player's first season. I laughed at Mumme's comment that Madaleno had called the kid squirrelly and also at Mumme's implication that the kid couldn't be trusted. I said, "He's from one of the best families you'll ever meet, he's an honor student who says "'yes sir and no sir,'" and he's one of the most competitive kids I've ever seen. If that makes you squirrelly, than I guess he is."

If Madaleno's professional opinion was that the player wasn't hurt as badly as he proclaimed, he would get the label of "soft" by Mumme and Major. A disgusting thing in all of college sports is to have "non-players" making judgments about a player's courage or pain tolerance. Nobody knows how badly someone hurts except the person who is hurting, and 95% of Division I college players want to be on the field not in the training room.

The Trainer/Psychologist

One of Madaleno's most important jobs was to tell Mumme if the team was mentally ready to play or not. If Madaleno told Mumme the team was not ready, then the team and coaches could expect a rousing speech from Mumme based on Madaleno's expert evaluation and testimony.

There is no doubt in my mind Madaleno played a strong part in Lorenzen being named the quarterback over Bonner after Bonner had won the job. When Mumme wanted a strong YES to back up his belief then he knew exactly which coaches and staff to approach. I also believe, when Mumme was considering moving Boyd into the starting job before the 2000 Georgia game, Madaleno played an influential role in stopping this move.

Madaleno was an overall good athletic trainer whom most of the players liked and respected. He was a great help to the coaches' children or spouses when they received injuries and needed care or therapy. On more than one occasion he helped my children through injuries. It is regretful that his loyalty to Mumme went out of bounds on occasions to the point of hurting people.

A Trainer Out Of Bounds

During the last few weeks of Mumme's job as Head Coach at the University of Kentucky, Madaleno went too far. During a meeting with Mumme and another staff member, Madaleno wrongly began to tell Mumme about how Morriss and I had plotted the overthrow of Mumme. Madaleno was evidently repeating Mumme's comments that had become common in the weeks following my departure. Jim jumped in with both feet to help spread the conspiracy rumor. I wish I could say I was disappointed, but he did exactly what I thought he would do. He blindly followed Mumme.

I know Morriss is going into his head-coaching job at UK with the knowledge of Madaleno's role with Mumme. I believe he will keep his job simple, that as an athletic trainer. Hopefully, Guy can make Jim do what he can do well—provide medical assistance and keep his nose out of everything else.

High-Five

He walked around the weight room and gave high fives, low fives, middle fives, and side way fives to everyone he met. For weeks as anyone passed him in the hallway he gave a high five. It was very obvious that Coach Scott Highsmith had possibly earned his new nickname "High Five" faster than any coach in college football history! Players, coaches, and office staff might look for an alternate route if they saw him coming, just to bypass having to give up a high five.

For two seasons at UK ('99-00) Highsmith coached with his old college roommate, Mumme. It was one of the strangest hires I've ever witnessed. Scott had been a career assistant high school coach who told me he had kept only a casual relationship with Mumme throughout the years since their roommate days. I asked him if he had spent the years studying Mumme's offense, going to watch his teams play, or any other indication of why Mumme would have selected to hire him but his answers were "no." He told me he and Mumme had occasionally seen each other at clinics, but had no special coaching relationship.

A Strange Hire

The thing that made this hire so strange was a statement Mumme had made to me my first year at UK. It was the first time Mumme got sharp with his tongue towards me. I had seen Tim Thompson, Head Coach at Memphis Melrose High School, speaking at a coaching clinic. A high school coach was talking about Thompson and the rumor that Thompson was trying to get a college coaching job by shopping his top players that season as a package deal, with Thompson included. I suggested to Mumme he talk to Thompson about the defensive line coaching opening since he was committed to hiring a minority and Thompson had several top Division I prospects on his team.

Mumme exploded, "That would be really stupid Franklin. If I'm going to hire another high school coach, I'm going to hire a Kentucky high school coach, not a coach from another state!"

I thought to myself this guy Mumme is really sharp, what a stupid question I had just asked. Now, in 1999, Mumme had hired a career assistant Texas high school coach, who had no Kentucky ties, and in November of 2000 he would try to hire guess who? Tim Thompson of Memphis Melrose, with, of course, no Kentucky ties! By 2000 I had learned that Mumme's word was inconsistent at best. Harp was still sitting 40 miles down the road in Danville waiting for his phone to ring from the numerous times Mumme had promised him he was going to be his next hire.

Adjustment Time

Highsmith coached wide receivers his first season and switched to running backs his second season. He professed to being a deeply religious man and his office was full of biblical references. His players were in for quite a shock as his personality would be the total opposite of Mike Leach, whom Highsmith was replacing. Highsmith wouldn't allow any profanity by his players during his meetings or on the field. This would have been okay, if not for the fact that every other coach on the staff allowed it, and most participated in it, especially Hal Mumme. Leach had been one of the players' favorite coaches because of his casual style and his loose meetings and Highsmith was going to be the total opposite. Some of the players would struggle with Highsmith's personality and style of coaching as well as his religious mixing of football and life.

I have no problem with someone being proud of their religious faith, but I have a strong problem with someone exposing those beliefs in an educational or athletic environment. It has also been my experience that the most truly, good, God fearing people don't worry about how they look or what religious affiliation they represent. No, most truly, good, God fearing men live good lives and teach by example. They fight for principles based on what is right and not whether or not their jobs might be in jeopardy if they don't agree with everything which the boss says and does.

Take Responsibility

Mumme began to curse a running back during the 2000 spring practice session and the back turned to Highsmith as Highsmith repeated Mumme's correction to the back. The back later came to me and told that it had happened again, Highsmith had told the backs in a meeting to run the play one way and now Mumme had cursed them for doing it. A good coach will *always* and *immediately* step up and take responsibility when it is his fault and not his player's fault. After practice I stopped Scott and told him I wanted to talk to him privately. "Scott, you are losing your players," I said. "You've got to stand up for them when you make a mistake or else they will never trust you. Go ahead and take your butt-chewing from Mumme and move on, but stand up for your players."

Highsmith replied that he appreciated my advice and I actually saw him once take the blame, but after a good Mumme butt chewing it would be the last time I heard Scott protect his players. In turn, some would never respect him.

Can We Go Home Yet?

When I went to Kentucky as a coach, I spent nearly everyday from 6:00 AM to 12:00 midnight studying Valdosta State video to learn the offense. I watched recruiting videos and bugged every coach in sight to learn. Having been a head coach at three separate high schools, I certainly didn't need to have someone tell me what to do or when to be at work. I could have worked 24 hours a day, 7 days a week and still never been prepared enough for our opponents or seen all the recruiting tapes available.

Highsmith must have been incredibly smarter than me. He was able to stroll into work at 8:00-8:30 AM and go home many nights at 6:00 PM. He must have asked me 100 times, "Do we have anything to do or can we go home?" I've never figured how anyone could do all the work needed to be done and wonder if there was anything else to do.

Scott would walk up and down the hallway 20-30 times in a day. Mumme would normally be out of the office by 5:00-6:00 PM in the off-season, and Highsmith seemed to be a nervous wreck as he would walk by Mumme's office to see if he had left. Within five-minutes of Mumme leaving, Highsmith would walk by and say "Anything else?" and be gone.

Do Unto Others

Highsmith strolled up to me and said, "I'm going to take _____ (a top recruit) out to Jerry's restaurant for breakfast in the morning."

I looked at him as if he was crazy and said, "You're what?"

He repeated, "I'm taking _____ to breakfast in the morning."

I said, "Scott, who told you to do that?"

"Bassett" he replied.

"No, you're not going to do that Scott. That's a big-time NCAA violation and taking the most well-known visible player in the _____ out to a popular restaurant during the middle of the summer will get you fired."

Highsmith replied, "Claude told me it was okay, he wouldn't lie to me."

I laughed and told Scott, "Don't ever do anything he tells you without asking me first or you will break NCAA rules and you will be his scapegoat."

Highsmith said, "What will I tell Claude?"

"Tell him I told you not to do it and it's an NCAA violation," I replied.

Highsmith told Bassett and Bassett was furious with me, but by this time in our relationship, I didn't care. Scott seemed naive and didn't know better. Mumme had probably instructed him to do what Bassett said and he was intending to do what was requested.

Highsmith later came to me when Bassett told him to go back to a high school for the second time in the regular season, which was a clear NCAA violation. I told him not to go, and I put Sandy Bell on speakerphone so Highsmith could hear with his own ears Bassett was wrong about the rule. Highsmith told Bassett he had been told not to go to the school a second time, and Bassett was furious again! He called Sandy Bell on speakerphone and tried to get her to tell Highsmith that he could go. Of course she told Bassett the second visit was not possible.

Highsmith was the perfect hire for Mumme. He was so grateful and seemingly surprised to be coaching in Division I football in the SEC, he would probably never leave Mumme and would always be loyal. Even though Mumme probably told Highsmith to do what Bassett told him, and Bassett would attempt to trick or deceive Highsmith into breaking NCAA rules, Highsmith would continue to be loyal. After I left Kentucky I never got a phone call from Highsmith to show his sincere concern about my family or his appreciation for my preventing him from breaking NCAA rules. No, he must have been too afraid he might lose his job if he talked to me, or maybe he was simply too busy reading scripture. He probably is waiting for the right time. I wonder when the right time is?

Highsmith was a congenial and respectful man who was thrown into a situation where he didn't belong. I don't believe he intentionally wanted to hurt anyone. He simply didn't have the courage to stand up and do the right thing. When editing this book I struggled with whether or not to include this section about Highsmith or not. My final decision to include it was based upon my belief that people must always look through the appearances of people and see what they really stand for. If you are going to market yourself as a devout Christian, then your actions must always speak louder than your words. People are what they do, not what they say they do. Christ was willing to stand alone and a self-professed devout Christian should be willing to follow his lead

A Young Heroine

It was a crucial time in the Mumme Era. The team was losing, the fans were complaining, a new athletic director wanted answers, and Mumme's self-appointed quarterback was struggling. That quarterback had miraculously overcome a horrendous thumb injury on his throwing hand, but the team was ready to rally around his understudy, a true freshman quarterback.

The script read like a movie. All it was missing was a beautiful heroine to come save the day. Well guess what, she was there and ready to help at Mumme's request. Jodi Gillespie had worked for several years as one of Tom Kalinowski's student equipment managers and was now working toward a masters degree in speech therapy. What more credentials would a coach want to advise you on who your quarterback should be versus Georgia?

Gillespie relayed this story to me on Friday before the 2000 Georgia game. Mumme had appointed Gillespie as freshman quarterback Jared Lorenzen's advisor. Lorenzen was struggling and Mumme told Gillespie it was her job to advise him and then report to Mumme what she thought his mental condition was.

A high level meeting had taken place and Mumme had called in some of his top advisors: Scott Highsmith, Mike Major, and Jodi Gillespie. On Friday afternoon at the front receptionist desk at Commonwealth Stadium, where Gillespie had taken her additional position of answering the telephone, she gave me the details of this meeting. She told me Mumme implored her, "Tell Mike and Scott what you think Jared's mental condition is and if you think he's mentally ready to play against Georgia." Gillespie gave Mumme her answer and Major and Highsmith would take her lead and agree with her opinion on which QB should be the starter versus the Georgia Bulldogs. All three agreed that Shane Boyd should start, and Mumme left the meeting to go talk to Jim Madaleno. Something funny happened because Mumme's visit to Madaleno would lead him to change his mind again. When Mumme left, Boyd was his starter, but by the time Mumme returned from his meeting with

Madaleno he had changed his mind. Gillespie said she didn't know what had happened to change Mumme's mind.

I liked Gillespie. She is a smart young lady and believe it or not, I would have trusted her football judgment a lot more than I would have Major's. Regardless, if you are a head football coach in the SEC making $800,000 a year and you are considering making QB decisions based on the recommendation of a 23-year-old college student's psychological evaluations, you definitely have a potential problem.

Gillespie eventually became Mumme's personal administrative assistant a few weeks before his dismissal as UK's Head Coach. She had helped run his Quarterback Camp in the summer of 2000 and was also in charge of computerizing practice and game scripts. There is no doubt she was capable of all those duties and performed them to Mumme's satisfaction. The role of advisor to the quarterback is, however, at the very least a good subject for debate.

LESSON #14—Yes Men will get you fired. Hire people who will tell you the truth, not what you want to hear. Hire people who want to be better than you and when they surpass you, hire someone else better than them. Success comes to a team or business when no one cares who gets the credit. A real, true friend tells you the painful truth every time, not just when it's convenient for them.

CHAPTER 15

THE QUARTERBACKS AND THE DECISIONS

Lesson 15—Many things in life will happen to you over which you have no control. You can't change these events, but you do have complete and total control over how you respond to what happens to you. Your responses to what happens to you in life will determine the quality of life you lead. Control your responses.

Couch and Haskins

I told Mumme Billy Jack Haskins was the leader of the 1996 football Wildcats and he needed to be careful about how he handled the quarterback decision. This was December 1996 and Mumme had just been hired by Kentucky. He assured me he would research the situation and make sure he handled the situation with class, dignity, and respect. I had no reason to think he was not sincere at the time, but I would later find out sincerity was not one of Mumme's best qualities.

Mumme would bring in Billy Jack and tell him there was a flaw in his throwing motion and it couldn't be corrected in time. He reportedly told Haskins he would not get a chance to compete for the starting QB position and he would need to switch positions. Haskins was in shock he would not get the opportunity to compete with Couch for the job. He transferred to Rhode Island University and played his final semester of football at the Division I-AA level.

I had known Billy Jack since he was in the seventh grade when his father, Jack, hired me as an Assistant Coach at Calloway County in 1988. Billy Jack eventually would be "Mr. Football" in the state of Kentucky while playing at Paducah Tilghman HS where he transferred his freshmen year in high school. His mother Linda and his two sisters, Amy and Kelli, were good to my wife and family. Mumme's first major decision at Kentucky was to take family friends of mine and rip their hearts out! The family would not have been devastated by this decision if it had come on the field, but

Mumme had made the decision without ever giving Billy Jack a snap at QB under his system.

Several of the news media would applaud Mumme's decision as bold and brilliant. Any average fan could see Couch was the most stunning QB prospect in the history of UK football. Finally, Couch would be given the chance to shine after suffering in Curry's option offense as a freshman. Sure, Billy Jack was hurt, but who cared, Kentucky was going to be fun and gun now.

The rest is history. Couch took UK to 5-6 and 7-5 records and left after his junior season to enter the NFL draft where he was the number one player selected. Mumme was a genius. He had made the decision to award Couch the QB job without a competition from Haskins and it had paid off. Nobody doubted Mumme had made the right decision, or did they?

I was eating dinner with Couch in Cleveland while recruiting in the spring of 2000. Couch had a new running buddy in Cleveland whom we both knew—Billy Jack Haskins. During our discussion I asked Couch how he felt about Haskins. Couch said, "I don't blame Billy Jack at all, I would have transferred too." He went on to add, "We should have had a competition on the field. That's the way football is played." Couch said that he and Haskins could joke about it now, but it was definitely an uncomfortable situation at the time.

There is no doubt Couch was a much better NFL prospect than Haskins, but does that mean that he won any more games than Haskins would have if Haskins had played in Mumme's system? Billy Jack Haskins had a live arm, he was a tough competitor, and he knew how to win. In Mumme's system, he could have been just as effective as Couch was if he had beaten Couch out in the spring of 1997. However, he never was given that opportunity. After the Jared Lorenzen/Dusty Bonner competition in the spring of 2000 we would come to find out why Mumme didn't like QB competitions.

Whoa Franklin! You are crazy! You just wrote that Billy Jack Haskins could have been as effective as Couch in Mumme's system. You have lost your mind! Now, wait a minute. My definition of effectiveness in football is producing wins, not yards passing. Haskins *could* have won as many games, if not more, but we'll never know. There was not a quarterback competition.

Tim Couch

Couch was one of the greatest quarterbacks in the history of college football. He had it all: quick pocket feet, good arm, phenomenal touch, and incredible toughness. Any average fan could watch Couch and come away knowing they had just witnessed something spectacular.

The greatest attributes Couch possessed was not his arm or physical talents, however, it was incredible passion for the game of football and the game of life. He was paid millions of dollars to play QB for the Cleveland Browns, but Couch's greatness came from the fact he would have played for free! He simply loves the game of football, and, although God blessed him with amazing talent, there are very few quarterbacks in the history of football who have worked as hard as Couch to make themselves spectacular.

Mumme had the tendency to blame receivers for any ball that was not caught, but Couch would stand up and always protect the receivers and take the blame, even if it was not his fault. He never yelled at the offensive line or receivers. He was a stand up player for whom the players would have died for because they realized he was the leader.

Real leaders are always quick to pass the praise to others when good things happen and to step up and take the blame when something bad happens. Couch could have taught Hal Mumme, Mike Major, and Scott Highsmith lessons in leadership. I know he taught me a valuable lesson in passion and leadership. Tim Couch is a TRUE LEADER.

Bonner—Harp—Scipione, Who Gets To Carry The Torch?

No one wants to follow a legend, especially if that legend is a home-grown product like Tim Couch. Dusty Bonner, Chase Harp, and Mike Scipione were the three candidates vying to follow Couch after the 1998 Outback Bowl season. Scipione had the softest touch and at 6'6" he seemed to be Mumme's favorite to win the job. Harp had the strongest arm and was definitely tough. Bonner was the least likely candidate being only 6'0" and having an average arm at best. The competition would last for three-weeks and the long shot Bonner would eventually be named the starting QB.

Harp was the first to be disqualified in the competition and was ex-tremely upset about the repetitions that he had received. His immediate reaction was he would transfer and go play QB elsewhere. I met with Chase and his father, Sam, after they drove to my home in Harrodsburg. We discussed all of Chase's options and his future as a QB versus changing positions to tight end or defense. I told Sam and Chase I felt Bonner was the best QB and would win the job. Chase eventually decided to stay at UK and move to tight end where, when healthy, he has had a good career. If he stays healthy, Harp could be a future NFL tight end.

After Mumme's decision to take Harp out of the QB competitions he came to my office before practice the next day. He knew Sam and I were close, and of course he couldn't forget the number of times he had promised

Sam a coaching job. Mumme asked me if I had talked to Sam and I responded that I had. He asked me what Sam thought, and I replied that Sam felt Chase hadn't been given enough repetitions to know whether he could be the QB or not. Mumme exploded, "!@#$ Sam Harp and !@#$ you and all of you dumb Kentucky !@#$" I'm tired of worrying about Sam Harp. I offered him Jack Fligg's job (Director of Football Operations) and he didn't take it. Franklin, you are more loyal to Sam Harp than to me!"

I responded, "Coach, Sam is a coach and a parent. He may just be like you have been with your son, sometimes blinded by the fact that he's your son. We're all like that with our kids, but he is also a good coach and he respects your decision."

Mumme exploded again, "Don't ever bring up my son. He's had a harder time than anyone. He's never even got to be a starting quarterback in high school."

Mumme stormed out and left for the practice field. I stopped Mumme after practice and asked him back to my office. I told him, "I don't deserve your calling me disloyal because of my relationship to Harp. I did nothing to deserve that. All I've done is listen to the both of you. Because of the unique relationship among the three of us, I think I was right."

Mumme disagreed and left. The next day he walked into my office with his arm around Chase smiling and said, "Coach Franklin, how do you like our new tight end?"

There's no doubt Mumme felt intense pressure because of how he had treated Sam Harp. He once told Sam he had handled not getting a job at UK with great class. I've often wondered how many people Hal Mumme had promised jobs over his lifetime. Whatever the reason, Mumme had made it clear that Sam Harp was not in his coaching plans, ever.

Scipione and Bonner continued the QB competition for another two weeks and although in my opinion Mumme wanted Scippione to win, it became clear to everyone Bonner was the QB to replace Tim Couch. Scipione would eventually decide to transfer after a 1999 season that saw him not take one snap in a game and very few in practice.

Mumme had risen above himself and although Bonner was not the QB he wanted, he was the best and Mumme honored the competition. Unlike the Couch/Haskins QB decision, the competition was won on the field.

Dusty Bonner

He led a young inexperienced offensive team to a 6-5 record and a bid to the Music City Bowl. He led the SEC in several categories. He won the respect of his teammates and opposing coaches and he eventually won the job for the starting QB in 2000 by holding off the challenge of Jared Lorenzen. Dusty Bonner could have done a lot more to make his mark as a great QB at the University of Kentucky, but he was robbed of that opportunity by a head coach who never seemed to believe he was pretty enough when winning.

Dusty was like the ugly girl nobody wanted to take to the prom. He couldn't throw like Tim Couch or Jared Lorenzen, he couldn't be tall like Tim or Jared, and he wasn't from Kentucky like Tim and Jared. No, all Bonner knew how to do was win ball games. That's what Mike O'Brien and the Valdosta High football program have been doing for years. O'Brien, the head coach at Valdosta High School, and his staff of quality coaches had taught Bonner how to win and how to compete with class, dignity, and professionalism.

Couch and Bonner had a deep respect for each other. Bonner could get under Couch's skin as quickly as anyone and Couch appreciated the fact that Bonner was not in awe of him. Bonner watched every move Couch made for two years, and although he couldn't make some of the throws Couch made, he could follow Couch's leadership, toughness, and field generalship. Bonner was the perfect man to follow a legend because his ego was intact and he didn't need fan adulation, which would be hard to come by from the Kentucky fans still in mourning from Couch's early departure to the pros.

Bonner worked incredibly hard in the off-season following the Music City 1999 Bowl game. His arm strength had increased noticeably and there was no doubt that he had made a big jump in QB skills in one year. I felt with Bonner leading our team, we would have our best offense thus far. The first thing would be to hold off the challenge of Jared Lorenzen. Bonner knew that Mumme wanted Lorenzen to dethrone him, but he was more than ready for the challenge.

Bonner VS. Lorenzen (Spring 2000)

Guy Morriss and I discussed the need to make a QB decision immediately. After two weeks of spring practice, Bonner had continuously decimated our first team defense for touchdown after touchdown, while Lorenzen had struggled to lead the first offense to only one score. Morriss and I decided to approach Mumme together, and we both suggested Mumme end the QB competition so we could begin to focus on preparing for the upcoming 2000 season. Mumme agreed the competition wasn't close and decided to immediately make Bonner the starter. Guy and I were pleased Mumme had been able to overcome his own personal feelings and give the job to the best player, although Mumme had obviously tried in every way possible to make sure

Lorenzen could win the job. Obvious to everyone, including Mumme, Jared just wasn't ready yet, and Bonner had improved so much it looked as if he might turn into a special "Couch-like" player.

Bonner did turn into a "Couch-like" player. He threw for more than 50 touchdowns and led his team to a 10-1 regular season record. At the season's end he was named the best player in college football. The only problem was none of this happened at UK. Bonner won 10 games and the Harlon Hill Trophy for Valdosta State University and Head Coach Chris Hatcher. You see, Hal Mumme changed his mind after school was out and spring practice was over.

We Can't Stretch The Field

Jared Lorenzen entered the spring game in the fourth quarter. Eight thousand Kentucky fans went berserk, as I looked into Hal Mumme's eyes and his flush face, I said a silent, "Oh no" to myself. Then I regained my senses and remembered that even though Mumme was the most thin-skinned coach I had ever known, he wouldn't make a crowd based decision when it was such an obvious choice that Bonner had won the job by a landslide.

The fourth quarter of the 2000 spring game proved to be a life changing quarter for many people as Lorenzen lit up the second and third team defense for 300-plus yards. I still felt confident that Mumme wouldn't let the crowd influence him. I have no idea why I had so much confidence in this man. I should have known better.

A few days later I was sitting in my office when a giddy Hal Mumme walked in. I had been recruiting and had just returned to discover Mumme had made a startling decision. He told me nervously that he was going to make a change at quarterback. I couldn't believe what he said and I asked, "You're going to do what?"

He repeated that he was going to make Jared Lorenzen the QB based upon the supposed fact that Student Assistant Randy Garver had gone back with a stopwatch and timed the release of Bonner vs. Lorenzen. Garver's watch said Lorenzen could get the ball to the receivers faster and Mumme said he could stretch the field to throw the deep ball.

I told Mumme, "We had a competition for QB and Bonner won it. It wasn't even close."

Mumme said the two-week competition wasn't fair and that he didn't give Lorenzen a real chance. He went on to say we couldn't ever win against Florida or Tennessee with Bonner as a QB because of his lack of arm strength.

I reminded Mumme the best QB he had ever coached was a 5'10" 165-pound average arm player named Chris Hatcher. Mumme didn't want to hear any of my facts. I eventually asked him who he had talked to about this and he said, "C.M. Newton thinks this is the right decision." I knew then it was over!

If C.M. Newton told Mumme playing 320-pound defensive lineman Derrick Johnson at QB was the best thing to do, then that's what Mumme would do. According to Mumme, Major also strongly believed Lorenzen was tougher to defend than Bonner. I told Mumme that was funny considering Bonner had shredded Major's defense in every scrimmage, whereas Lorenzen had struggled versus the same Major defense.

I asked Mumme if he had talked to Morriss and he replied that Morriss was "wishy-washy" and never said anything strong either way. Mumme would later talk to Inside Receiver Coach Dan Lounsbury, who would strongly suggest to Mumme that not only was it a bad decision, but it could tear our team apart.

Lounsbury's and my comments were not what Mumme wanted to hear. We both had to be careful about how we approached Mumme on this touchy subject or we might be fired before the 2000 season even started.

During this first conversation with Mumme I asked him when he planned on telling Bonner about his demotion. Mumme told me he was going to wait until August and give Bonner the decision after three-a-day practices. I was shocked he wasn't planning to tell Bonner immediately, giving him an opportunity to transfer.

I told Mumme, "You've got to tell him now. You can't wait. He'll want to transfer."

Mumme replied, "I can't do that. I'm not 100% sure Lorenzen is going to be academically eligible and I would look like a fool if Bonner transferred and Lorenzen wasn't eligible. Can you imagine what the press would do to me?"

I replied, "Coach, you've got to tell Bonner if you are 100% sure this is what you're going to do. Jared will get eligible!"

Mumme was adamant he was not going to tell Bonner.

A few days later Mumme was told Lorenzen had passed a class from his first summer at Kentucky which now made him eligible. Mumme told me he was now going to tell Bonner. Many of the press would eventually praise Mumme for having the "class" to tell Bonner early in the summer about his decision, never knowing Mumme made the decision only because he found out about Lorenzen's eligibility status. Mumme would even tell reporters it was the right thing to do and that was why he was telling Bonner in the summer.

I called Mumme at his house on Sunday after coming back from recruiting. He had decided to tell Bonner the coming week, and I thought I'd give it one more try. After spending a Saturday going back over the spring videos, I had come away more convinced that Bonner was easily the best QB for 2000. Mumme answered the phone and it took only a few seconds to realize I had called him at a bad time. He was recovering from a minor surgery and was in no mood to talk, but I was running out of time. So I proceeded, "Coach, I went back and watched the scrimmages against the number one defense and charted Bonner and Lorenzen again, just to make sure that I didn't make a mistake. Bonner was better than even I remembered! He decimated the defense and Jared really struggled."

"Tony," Mumme said, "I've made my mind up! I don't care! Don't bring it up again!"

I told him I understood and hung up.

I would later tell Mumme he was the head coach and that it was my job to support his decisions and I would now support his decision to start Lorenzen, even though I disagreed. I would spend the summer talking to booster groups, alumni, high school coaches, etc. telling them why Mumme had made his decision and why it was right. That's what assistant coaches are supposed to do: speak up and state your opinion, especially if you disagree, and then support the head coach's decision when it is obvious that it is final. That's exactly what I did.

Bonner's Shock

I can only imagine the shock, disgust, and anger that Bonner must have felt when Mumme told him he was not going to be the QB at Kentucky. No one will ever know but him. Two nights prior to his press conference to announce his transfer to Valdosta State, we discussed all his feelings, as well as his options while we sat on my screened in back porch until 2:00 a.m.

The hardest thing for Bonner was trying to find a way that would make sense to tell his mother, Janice Studstill. There wasn't any rational explanation that would hold up. Bonner was a model student, a perfect gentleman, and had no problems on or off the football field, plus the same man who now decided to change his mind had earlier named him the starting QB. Bonner's mother was stunned! She immediately jumped in a car and headed to Lexington to ask Mumme what was going on. She and Dusty met Mumme at Mumme's home. During their conversation Mumme lit a cigar and began to puff away. Mumme sometimes smoked cigars after big victories at our Sunday meetings. I thought it was his ultimate sign of arrogance and confidence, and I always thought the cigar was his way of putting on his victory face. He had Newton's and Major's support, so there was no need to worry about respecting the mother of what was soon to be a former player.

Mumme gave his explanation to Janice and it made as much sense to her as it did to anyone else in the know. At one point Mumme tried to compare Dusty's newfound hardship with that of Mumme's own son Matt. This made Janice furious because there was absolutely no comparison between what Bonner had done at Kentucky and what Matt Mumme had done in his previous playing career. There simply was not a rational explanation.

Bonner's press conference was a great reflection of the differences between a real leader and an appointed leader. Facing the media and thanking his teammates, the fans, and his family, Bonner refused to take the easy shots at Mumme he could have. We had discussed three possible scenarios that he might use during his press conference and he had chosen the one with the most class and dignity. Later in his career, Mumme would get the same opportunity as Bonner: the opportunity to face the media and answer questions after his dismissal. Mumme would choose to take another route, the one where he faced no one.

Mumme took his $1 million buyout and left hundreds of unanswered questions. Mumme was an appointed leader. Bonner earned his leadership. Bonner's stand up style was the reason he turned around Valdosta State's previously morbid offense into one of the most explosive in college football. Mumme's appointed leadership was based on a title. When Mumme's chance to face the media and his critics came around, he did exactly what I expected. He took the easy way out for himself.

Mysterious Ways

Many times I've been told that God works in mysterious ways. There is no explanation for some horrible things that happen to people in their lives. Dusty Bonner could have never anticipated the events during May-June 2000 would have happened, but they did. You can't control everything that happens to you, but you can control how you respond. The response of Dusty Bonner was to turn a bad situation into a great one. His grit and tenacity inspired me and I am sure countless others to learn by his example.

Jared Lorenzen

The person most affected and most hurt besides Bonner in the Bonner/Lorenzen fiasco was in fact Jared Lorenzen. One of the most talented and unique athletes to ever come out of Kentucky, Lorenzen was thought by the Kentucky fans to be the next Tim Couch. Most of the fans welcomed his unexpected rise to the job as starting quarterback in 2000 as another brilliant and bold strategic decision by Mumme. They believed he had it all: size 6'4," 270-plus pounds, arm strength, he could throw a ball 75 yards or further, toughness, he could take any hit thrown at him. What the fans didn't want to think about was the fact that in a competition in the 2000 spring against Bonner, Lorenzen had not won the job.

In Couch's first year as a quarterback in the SEC he had 1 touchdown, 1 interception, and completed 38% of his passes. Critics have said he was in the wrong offense while some of Curry's staff has said he simply was not ready. You can argue for either side, but the bottom line is those few SEC appearances by Couch in his freshman year did give him some valuable experience in SEC game competition. Bonner was able to sit for two years and soak up Couch's experiences, and he probably was not ready to play until his third season, when he got his opportunity and took the Wildcats to the Music City Bowl. Lorenzen needed another year, minimal, to be ready to lead the Wildcats as their starting quarterback. He very simply was not ready to be the starter.

Three distinct disadvantages were given to Lorenzen that he unfairly was burdened with:

1. Mumme gave him the starting job after losing the competition to Bonner in a very public arena. He knew it, the players knew it, and most of the assistants knew it.

2. He would be the only Kentucky Mumme directed quarterback to not be coached by Chris Hatcher, who had moved onto Valdosta State. Instead, Mumme would directly coach Lorenzen on his fundamentals when he was available, and Student Assistant Randy Garver, who was a former offensive lineman with no quarterback playing or coaching experience, would handle Lorenzen's fundamental work when Mumme wasn't available.

3. Lorenzen was not mentally or physically ready for the Couch-like comparisons that were to inevitably take place by UK media and fans.

Lorenzen would be the quarterback in the 2000 Wildcats 2-9 season with no wins in the SEC. The season would be full of a series of distractions from the early season fiasco of Major losing his power as Defensive Coordinator to the total destruction of any cohesiveness between Mumme, myself, and other staff members. Offensive players also would grow weary of hearing Mumme blame them for the dismal offensive point production while giving Lorenzen very little of the blame.

The 2000 season ended with Lorenzen leading the SEC in several passing categories, as well as setting a couple of NCAA passing records for a freshman. His future is bright if he can hold off the emerging Shane Boyd and retain his job as QB. One thing is for sure; if Lorenzen is the starting QB at Kentucky in the 2001 season it will be because he won the job over Shane Boyd. Morriss will not give him the job. I believe Lorenzen could benefit from the departure of Mumme simply because of the new respect he could win from his team-mates. If he wins the job at Kentucky, he will become a solid NFL draft pick in the future with an opportunity to continue playing football for a living.

Conclusion

Playing QB at Kentucky under Hal Mumme was a dream come true if a player became the starting QB. He would have the opportunity to throw the ball on the majority of the snaps, and would lead the conference in several passing categories. There would be very few times that he would be criticized by Mumme with most of Mumme's criticism going to the receivers, running backs, and offensive linemen. He must be a special type of person however, or his teammates may come to resent him for his special treatment and protection by Mumme. In Mumme's four years of spring football, he allowed only two quarterback competitions and he changed the results of one of those when he didn't like the outcome. If Mumme ever again becomes a head coach at any level of college coaching, I would strongly recommend a QB recruit to understand this fact. He may not be given a chance to compete for the starting job or he may win the starting job and have it taken away by Mumme if he is not Mumme's choice.

LESSON #15—Many things in life will happen to you over which you have no control. Some will be good and some will be bad. You cannot change those events, but you do have complete and total control over how you respond to what happens to you. Hal Mumme unjustly removed Dusty Bonner from the starting QB position at the University of Kentucky. Bonner had no control over the situation since he had already won the true competition on the field. He did have control of his response to these unjust actions. His decision was to go play where he was wanted and would be treated fairly. Bonner's decision to not dwell on being treated unfairly and to be proactive in his future made him a winner on the football field and in life. Your responses to what happens to you in life will determine the quality of life you lead.

CHAPTER 16

EGO, ARROGANCE, & EMOTIONS

Lesson 16—It is human nature to enjoy watching someone fall from grace and distinction. Remember, no matter how high you sit on your pedestal, you are one swift swing of an ax away from falling on you face. The same people you once looked down upon will now be gazing down on you.

Flaws

A great offensive football coach who has a huge ego might survive in the SEC. A great offensive coach who is arrogant might survive in the SEC. A great offensive coach who wears his emotions on his sleeve might survive in the SEC. However, a great offensive coach with a huge ego, unmatched arrogance, emotional immaturity, and a simple lack of integrity has no chance to survive in the Southeastern Conference.

Hal Mumme was a great offensive football coach when he worked at it. He was not the Offensive Coordinator at the University of Kentucky; he was the Head Football Coach. The ability to be a trusted leader is much more important than the ability to score points. As with all walks of life, the higher you move up in the financial and leadership world, the more your true integrity or lack thereof will begin to show itself. The highest stage of college football is the SEC, and it moves a coach into a glass house for the entire world to watch his every move. Mumme moved into his glass house and it didn't take very long for his weaknesses to take control of his destiny.

Two statements from John C. Maxwell's *The 21 Irrefutable Laws of Leadership* would best describe Hal Mumme's lack of true leadership: (1.) Maxwell stated, "The real test of leadership isn't where you start out. It's where you end up."[2] Mumme started his job at the University of Kentucky as the "chosen one" to bring excitement, energy, and wins to the Commonwealth. Players, fans, and media were excited and hopeful. He ended his career accepting a $1 million buyout, having numerous NCAA violations against his program, a coaching staff and team in disarray, blaming everyone except himself for the problems, and never stepping up in public, like a real leader, and addressing his critics. (2.) A quote from John Morley, "No man can climb out beyond the limitations of his own character."[3] Mumme surrounded himself with several "yes-men" as advisors and confidants. Some of these were men whose character couldn't have helped Mumme. His limitation of true character prevented him from ever being a quality leader.

Emotions on His Sleeves

The plastic bottle flew out of his hand and narrowly missed free-safety Anthony Wajda's head. Mumme screamed at Wajda at the top of his lungs about the defense giving up a 99-yard drive for a touchdown prior to the ending of the first half. Mumme continued his ranting and raving at senior linebacker Jeff Snedegar, who stopped and stared at Mumme and then calmly told Mumme, "Stop fumbling," then walked into the defensive locker room.

Mumme's emotional outbursts were commonplace and the players and assistant coaches had come to expect them at any given time. Their effect had long since gone awry. I have seen several good football coaches use emotion to truly motivate a team, but their methodology was much different than Mumme's. They normally planned an outburst and very seldom if ever made the emotional outburst personal. On the other hand, Mumme made many things personal in nature. Snedegar's calm reply was perfect. Mumme had a difficult time when players like Snedegar and defensive tackle Mark Jacobs would calmly and boldly stare at Mumme during one of his tirades. His yelling and screaming became almost comical.

Game day emotional outbursts were detrimental to our chance at victory. You could expect to see more towel throwing and screaming at officials on a nationally televised game than on a regular Saturday afternoon game with no TV exposure. Mumme seemed to believe that he was trying out for an Academy Award winning role when we played on TV. He was pure theater. SEC officials seemed to wonder if this guy was for real as he argued several calls they made. On more than one occasion Mumme told the team we would have to overcome the officials as well as the hostile SEC crowd. Numerous times I would have to tell Mumme to "forget it" and quit screaming at officials and to call the next play. Mumme was a great game day technician when he stayed cool and calm and methodically worked his magic against an opposing defense. When he began his ranting, raving, and cursing, he seemed to lose focus and our offense suffered as a result.

The office staff as well as the coaching staff would see Mumme's common emotional outbursts. One day as he walked out of the office at Commonwealth Stadium he stopped and re-entered the front door. He then proceeded to curse the receptionist at the front desk. She would later tell the other members of the office staff about Mumme's emotional outburst and about his cursing her, but she never filed a complaint because she loved the Wildcats and her job.

I was eating lunch with my wife and kids at a local Chinese restaurant when my cell phone rang. Mumme was on the other end of the call and he was cursing and screaming so loudly I couldn't hear him. I walked outside the restaurant to hear Mumme scream, "Don't ever have that !@#$ Craig Clayton or any of your other western Kentucky friends on my campus again!"

Craig is the Head Football Coach at Hopkinsville HS and one of his players, Brandon Hayes, was scheduled to come on an official visit. We had only recently entered the recruiting picture with Hayes, and Clayton had worked hard to encourage Hayes to visit Kentucky. Hayes had agreed to visit and Kentucky had chartered a private plane to pick him up. When Clayton arrived to take Hayes to the plane, Hayes had a change of heart and decided not to visit Kentucky. Clayton had called me and was visibly upset and embarrassed about Hayes' decision. I told him I understood and when a 17-year old kid decides to not cooperate there is nothing you can do about it. Clayton was one of the coaches who originally signed the petition to help Mumme get hired at Kentucky, but Mumme was furious. He told me I had caused this embarrassment and he didn't care that we had just entered the recruiting picture of the highly recruited Hayes, because every Kentucky kid should immediately drop any school that had recruited him when Hal Mumme and Kentucky called.

When Mumme quit screaming and cursing me I re-entered the restaurant and my children asked, "Who was that screaming on the phone?"

I told them that it was Coach Mumme and they all smiled, because I had used Mumme as an example many times in telling my children what not to do and how not to act. I only recently told Clayton about Mumme's demand. Hayes signed with Arkansas.

Emotions are an unpredictable thing. True leaders learn how to control their emotions and use them to everyone's advantage. Some people wear their feelings on their sleeves, however, and Mumme was one of those highly volatile people. His failure to control his emotions would eventually play a role in his downfall.

Arrogance and Ego Out of Control—The Prediction

David Morris, previously the Head Football Coach at Mercer County High, had come to visit our spring practice in April 1998. Hundreds of high school coaches from Kentucky and surrounding states had joined Morris to come to the UK spring football practice and clinic to learn about the successful and exciting "Air Raid" offense. Morris and I had coached together at Mayfield High and Mercer County and are very close friends. "How much has Mumme changed?" Morris asked.

I laughed and responded, "Watch him today at practice and you'll get to see. He'll chew some assistant's butt out today in front of all of these high school coaches just to let them know that he's a big-time college head coach."

We were in the middle of our "Inside Period" when I called out the next play. The play required a split end to move in tight and Garry Davis was the designated player for that call. Davis however was running 1-on-1 routes versus the defensive backs, just as he did everyday. We had never used a split end in the Inside Period in our two years of practices. Mumme normally would have been watching 1-on-1, but for some reason on this day he had decided to watch Inside Period. "Where the !@#$ is Garry Davis?" Mumme screamed at me.

"He's doing 1-on-1," I replied.

"It's your !@#$ job to get him here Franklin and if you can't do it, I'll hire someone who can." Mumme shouted.

I went and got Davis and we ran the play with Davis in. Mumme had made a prophet out of me. In front of hundreds of high school coaches he had decided to curse me and threaten my job.

David Morris grabbed me after practice and laughed, "Well Franklin, you were right. He (Mumme) put on a show."

Other high school coaches would comment to me during the spring of 1998 and at summer camp in 1998 what a noticeable difference there was in Mumme and many wondered out loud if his first new raise and contract had gone to his head. He was definitely not the same man who had taken the job in late 1996 or was he? A wealthy friend once told me that money doesn't make you good or bad, it just reveals your true character more. Mumme would prove that statement true and the spring of 1998 was just the beginning of what would become a more arrogant and egotistical coach and person.

Travis Atwell, Billy Joe Miles, Larry Ivy (I'll Show Them I'm Running This Show)

Several coaches from Western Kentucky had called me to tell me about a great athlete from Hancock County High named Travis Atwell. They all said he could do it all: run, catch, throw, tackle, and lead. Mumme had received a call from, at that time, Senior Associate Athletic Director, Larry

Ivy, telling him that UK Board of Trustees member Billy Joe Miles of Owensboro had called to request that we look at Atwell. Mumme was upset Ivy had called to mention the recruiting of a player and Mumme made it clear he had no intention of offering Atwell a scholarship, regardless of how good he might be. "Larry Ivy and Billy Joe Miles need to take care of their own business and let me run this football program," Mumme told me in December 1999.

I eventually saw Atwell play twice, once in November at a muddy game in Mayfield and finally at the state championship in December in Louisville. The first game left me not quite sure how fast he was, but the second game on a dry field left no doubt that he could play receiver in the SEC.

Mark Peach, the Head Coach of Atwell, told me he had sent a video to Bassett and I went to Bassett's office to find the tape. After watching the video, I was amazed. I told Bassett I thought we were making a mistake in not offering Atwell a scholarship.

We had signed only a few players from Western Kentucky in our three previous classes and I felt Atwell was worth my getting Mumme upset, so I decided to try a different approach. I invited Mumme into my office and told him I had just watched a great player on video. When Mumme asked who it was I told him that I wasn't sure of his name, but I would look it up after he watched the tape. Mumme sat and watched the highlight tape of Travis Atwell, not knowing who it was. When the video was almost over he said, "That kid can play, let's get him."

I replied, "Coach, that's Travis Atwell of Hancock County." If looks could kill, I would have been dead.

Mumme stared at me and said, "Franklin, I told you about Ivy and Miles pressuring me to recruit that kid. He can walk on but I will not give him a scholarship!"

"Coach, the kid is a great student, great player, and of great moral character. He fits exactly what you say you want as a receiver, 6'2" 190 pounds and runs a 4.5 forty. Lets forget Ivy and Miles and just sign him." I said.

"I offered the kid a chance to walk on. Tell him to take it or leave it. I'm running this football program." Mumme stated as he stood up and walked out of my office.

Atwell would not be offered a scholarship by Mumme and would eventually sign at Toledo University with a team that would defeat Penn State and go 10-1. To conclude his high school career he was named Mr. Football, and in the Kentucky-Tennessee All Star game was named the MVP while leading the Kentucky football all-stars to one of their few victories over Tennessee. Mumme won his little "power contest" with Ivy and Miles, but eventually lost the war. After Mumme "resigned" from UK, Atwell decided to transfer to Kentucky where I'm sure he'll enjoy a good career.

They Don't Have Hal Mumme $Money$

In December of 1999, Hal Mumme perceived himself as the hottest coach in America. He once told Sonny Dykes and me that LSU " . . .had Dennis Erickson money, but not Hal Mumme money." Erickson was a former national championship coach at Miami, Head Coach of the NFL Seattle Seahawks, and current coach in one of the top five turnarounds in college football history at Oregon State University. Mumme had just stated to us however, that neither of these programs could afford Hal Mumme. Standing in front of a group of UK boosters at a function in Louisville in the spring of 2000, Mumme told them he had turned down offers from North Carolina, North Carolina State, LSU and Texas Tech. I am sure the A.D.'s from all of those colleges would like to be informed of their offers to Mumme, especially North Carolina because they didn't fire Carl Torbush until the end of the next season. I believe Mumme confused a call of interest with an offer for a job as being one in the same. In 1997 Mumme had told me during dinner that the University of Texas had called and offered him the job when they hired Mack Brown away from North Carolina.

From the end of the first season at Kentucky, Mumme occasionally talked about what new jobs he might be offered or in his mind, had already been offered. His biggest and boldest talk would always be about the NFL. After Mumme's first pay raise took him from approximately $300,000 yearly to the $450,000 range in his second season, Mumme was ready to demand a big raise after the 1998 season that took us to the Outback Bowl. Mumme and I were flying in a private jet to visit a recruit when he asked, "Would you leave UK to coach in the NFL with me?" I replied, "Sure."

Mumme went on to tell me he was not happy with Newton's offer of $650,000 and the buyout part of the contract was also very weak. He stated it was time to shop around. A few weeks later, Newton would return to Mumme with a much better offer, according to Mumme, which would pay him up to $800,000 per year and had a much stronger and more favorable buyout arrangement. The agreement would be signed and Mumme announced to the staff what a great guy C.M. Newton was and he would be at UK forever!

That forever would only last one year, as Mumme began to have Morriss make calls to his NFL contacts to see what the interest in Mumme was. His belief was he could get $2 million per year and control of personnel. Morriss would later tell me his NFL contacts laughed at Mumme's belief of his worth. They told Morriss to tell Mumme he might get $700-800,000 per season with no control of personnel, if someone became interested in selling tickets with Mumme's offense. This dose of reality seemed to put Mumme back in focus to concentrate on pursuing only college jobs and not the NFL.

There aren't many teams that want head coaches coming off 2-9 seasons with dozens of NCAA violations attached to their program, so I would venture December 2000 was probably the first year of Mumme's time at Kentucky that he wasn't considering what team was going to pay him millions to leave the Bluegrass.

A UK alumni and booster faxed this letter (see Insert E, page 150) to me in January of 2001, after calling to inform me Mumme was cutting my throat to various people.

I'm not sure if Hal is still taking the trip to Montana, but I'm sure that if you send him the $30,000 he will take you somewhere. It takes quite an ego for a coach with a 2-9 season and dozens of NCAA violations under his watch to offer this bargain trip. Shoot, I don't blame him, there's probably some Internet gurus like 'rbs' who would give him more than $30,000 if he would bring Bassett and Major along with him.

They Only Come For Me

During Mumme's press conference on Monday following the 2000 Tennessee game, someone asked him if firing any of the coaches would hurt UK's recruiting. Mumme replied recruits came to UK because of Hal Mumme, not the assistant coaches. Someone had forgot to inform All-SEC tight end Derek Smith and All-SEC freshman team running back Chad Scott. They had told Larry Vaught in an article a few days prior that I was one of the main reasons they came to Kentucky and without me they would have gone elsewhere.

I don't state this fact to brag on myself as a recruiter. I only want to give an example of how far removed from reality Mumme's ego had taken him. Head coaches have very little contact with players being recruited and the assistant coaches are the primary contacts during the recruiting process. Most head coaches in college football realize this and surround themselves with coaches who can recruit effectively. Mumme's statement was a slap to assistant coaches throughout college football.

Conclusion

Ego, arrogance, and emotion make up a portion of all people. It takes strong people surrounding a leader to not allow him to go overboard on any

Montana With Hal
Title Sponsor Package – $30,000

- One Home Game in the Box with June Mumme - 2 people

- One all expense paid trip to an Away Game of your choice - 2 people

- Announcements on the Radio "Hal Mumme Quarterback School" presented by "YOUR COMPANY"

- Full Scholarship to 2001 Fantasy Camp - 2 people

- An afternoon of golf with Coach Mumme and a member of the coaching staff at Champions - 6 people

- All expense paid 3 night / 4 day trip to Montana to go fly fishing with Coach Mumme - 2 people

- Special Game Package - pre-game sideline passes, tickets to the game, parking pass, picture taken with Coach Mumme, pass to the post-game press conference - 4 people

- Company logo displayed in the camp facilities, on the camp T-shirt, and in the camp booklets

- Four autographed footballs personalized to people of your choice

Insert E. A letter received by a UK alumni and booster.

one of these qualities. Mumme's flaws in these categories eventually led to his downfall. No real leader can survive with flaws in each of these areas.

LESSON #16—It is human nature to enjoy watching someone fall from grace and distinction. Since the beginning of mankind, humans have taken some pleasure in watching people be knocked off their pedestals. The more success you have, the more people will look into your glass house at your daily lives and eventually you will be found lacking in some areas. If you cannot handle your ego and emotions and you become arrogant in your daily living, not only will people enjoy watching you fall they will help speed up the process as well. Mumme's huge ego, untimely emotional outbursts, and consistent arrogance would eventually cause his dramatic downfall at Kentucky with such speed that some people are still in shock. Always remember, no matter how high you sit on your pedestal, you are only one swift swing of an ax away from falling on your face and looking up at those same people you once looked down upon.

CHAPTER 17

A PURE & SIMPLE LACK OF INTEGRITY

*Lesson 17—The true measure of your character and integrity is
what you would do if you thought no one would ever find out.
Discipline is doing the right thing when no one is watching. It is
our job to keep our leaders in check by exposing their actions, good
and bad, when their power begins to impact the lives of others.*

A Bad Snap (Or Was It?)

The game was winding down to its final seconds and it looked like the
1998 UK Wildcats were going to dramatically win with a last second field
goal. We had beaten LSU in similar fashion at Baton Rouge and now we
were on the verge of upsetting Georgia. The non-perfect snap came, was
bobbled and the kick never took place as Georgia escaped with a 28-26
victory over the Outback Bowl bound Cats. The players accepted the last
play as hard-luck and moved on to the next game. There was very little, if
any, debate as to whether a bad snap or mishandling of the ball had caused
the kick to not be attempted.

The 1998 season highlight video would eventually clear up the question
of whose fault it was, but no one seemed to care except Hal Mumme. You
see, the holder on that botched field goal attempt was Mumme's son Matt
and Mumme allowed it to be made perfectly clear to everyone who saw this
video that it was Jimmy Haley's bad snap, not Matt Mumme's mishandling
that caused the field goal to not be attempted. I'm sure Haley's parents
would have allowed Matt to be blamed if they were the Head Coach with
the final editing decision, not their son.

No, I don't really believe that! I believe most parents who happened to
be a head football coach in NCAA Division I would treat all the players as
if they were their own children. I believe a highlight video would simply
show the play and let the people watching make their own conclusions. The
snap was slightly off-center and I could easily blame Haley or Matt Mumme
for not performing perfectly, but it is an issue that never needed to be
publicly addressed.

Hal Mumme's allowing blame to be placed on Jimmy Haley for the botched last-second field goal attempt in the 1998 Georgia game is a classic example of a simple lack of integrity. Number one, it wasn't completely true. Number two, it didn't matter if it was Haley's fault alone, it should have never even been mentioned. Matt Mumme's accomplishments on the field spoke for themselves. He had earned the players' respect with his quality play on fake punts and mop-up duty as a quarterback. He certainly didn't need his father allowing Haley to have the blame solely placed on him for what was a team loss.

Lightning

My father taught me at a very young age there was an element of nature you never wanted to take a chance with; lightning. While playing golf as a young pre-teen, Dad taught me to respect lightning and to *always* immediately seek cover if any bolts came down, no matter how far away they seemed. When I became a head football coach, my teams would never take a chance with lightning. I once had a superintendent send an order to me to take the field as he took cover in the school building. After refusing his order we eventually cancelled the game and played it the following night. Several trees at a nearby golf course were struck with bolts of lightning that evening and I never regretted my decision.

At a spring practice in April of 1998 I would get the opportunity to witness Mumme's lightning philosophy. We were practicing on the Cooper Drive field when I noticed several bolts were coming straight down at what looked to me to be a threatening distance of only a few hundred yards. "Coach, there's some pretty bad lightning a couple of hundred yards ahead. We might want to go to the indoor facility." I said.

"I'd rather our team get hit by lightning than to have a player tear up his knee on the turf in the indoor." Mumme replied. After watching a few more bolts come down Mumme stated, "When God is ready, he will get you no matter if its lightning or not." A few minutes later Mumme would yell for the team to take cover as it became obvious we were ready to get hit hard by a storm. I was about 30 seconds away from walking off the field before Mumme called us all off. I wasn't quite ready to let Hal Mumme's relationship with God determine my children's future without a father.

I've always had to wonder about "macho coaches" who decided to show their toughness and ignorance when lightning began to strike. There should be a rule for these coaches who decide to gamble with lightning. These coaches should stay on the field alone, as lightning strikes, to prove to their team how tough they are. I'm sure the players and assistant coaches would 'win one for the Gipper' if that one in a million lightning bolt hits the coach and as Mumme implied, 'God decided it was your time.' The rest of us would like to go inside and stay safe.

Mumme's decision to delay our exit from the field was probably based on his belief that it was safe. There was some type of weather equipment used by the field maintenance crew that gave specific weather warnings that Mumme may have been waiting for the results before removing our squad. It was his comments and my respect for lightning that alarmed me.

An Embarrassing Night on the Road

Gosh, what a tough job recruiting is! It was mid afternoon and I was eating an early dinner with Mumme and Defensive Line Coach Tommy Adams in downtown New Orleans. I had never been to downtown New Orleans before and I was quite impressed with the sights of the French Quarter. Mumme and Adams were going to visit defensive lineman recruit Bennie Mills, who would eventually sign with Florida. I had been recruiting Ronald McClendon earlier in the day and was going along for the ride with Mumme and Adams.

Adams had done a good job recruiting Mills and he was strongly considering Kentucky along with Florida. Mumme and Adams discussed Mills briefly at dinner and Adams told Mumme he was concerned with Florida. After Mumme had his second drink (Makers Mark or some other Bourbon he had requested) Mumme moved his arrogance notch up a couple of levels. I had been on several in-home visits with Mumme over the years, but this was the only time I had ever witnessed him drink Bourbon before an important in-home visit. Kentucky Bourbon was one of the reasons Mumme liked Kentucky, and he had a tendency to say whatever came to his mind when he had a couple of drinks. I thought to myself that this could be an interesting night and it sure was!

The night began smoothly and I could tell Adams had done a solid job gaining the trust of Mills and his family. There was a definite connection between the family and Adams. The recruiting class of 2000 for Kentucky desperately needed a quality lineman and this visit was deemed crucial. All Mumme had to do was earn the respect and trust of the family, as Adams had already done, and UK would have a great chance of landing Mills.

Somewhere early in the conversation between Mumme and the Mills family the discussion of Florida came up. Adams and Mumme told Mills we desperately needed him and that he could probably come in and start as a freshman. Mills replied to Mumme that he felt and the Florida staff felt that he had a chance to play as a freshman at Florida. Mumme said, "No, you won't. No freshman defensive line recruits play at Florida." Mills replied that Florida's coaches were good men and they wouldn't lie to him.

Mills also had done his homework and knew which defensive linemen were graduating. Mumme's voice and tone seemed confrontational as he again told Mills and his family he would not play as a freshman at Florida. After a few of these quotes by Mumme, Mills' father stepped in and told Mumme, "Coach, Florida has not said anything negative about you or Kentucky or any of your assistants, and I would appreciate it if you didn't talk in a negative tone about Florida."

Mumme responded, "I'm telling you the truth and they're lying."

It seemed Mr. Mills and Bennie were becoming agitated with Mumme's near belligerent attitude and the night ended very quickly with the three of us leaving knowing any chance we had to sign Mills had gone out the door.

Although Mumme was probably right in his assumption that Mills wouldn't play as a freshman at Florida, his tone seemed to almost demean the Mills family for believing Florida. It was the most awkward night of my recruiting experiences and I was embarrassed to be a representative of the University of Kentucky. The Mills family showed great restraint to keep from throwing us out earlier in the evening.

The Speech At Crooked Stick

Arrogance and liquor also played a role in Mumme's talk to a group of alumni at Fuzzy Zoeller's golf course in southern Indiana, in the summer of 1998. We had played an alumni golf tournament earlier in the day and Mumme had a few drinks before his designated speech to the group of former UK athletes. One of the UK alumni asked Mumme how he felt about losing two in state Kentucky recruits to out of state colleges. Mumme responded, "!@#$ any kid who doesn't bleed blue and white." The UK alumni clapped and screamed in approval. This was the type of coach they wanted. Forget everybody who didn't bleed blue and white.

I wonder how those same people would have felt if that was their 18-year-old son whom a prominent figure had just denounced to a group of 100 or so for not choosing Kentucky as his college. At least this occasion was not in the home of a recruit but among a group of adults who shared the same passion for the Wildcats as Mumme.

If I Want Your Opinion I'll Give It To You

The 2000 summer Fantasy Camp provided Mumme another occasion to display his arrogance after a few drinks. The group of fantasy campers made up of 21 to 70-year-old men was engaged in a question and answer period with Mumme and the UK coaching staff. Fantasy camper and alumni Bob

Comstock was talking to the group about some of his observations from attending many practices over the last couple of years. Evidently Mumme thought Comstock had talked too long so he interrupted Comstock with this request, "Bob, shut the !@#$ up. If I want your opinion I'll give it to you." Some of the campers nervously laughed and others sat stunned in silence. Bob mumbled something as Mumme continued to talk. He looked visibly shaken by Mumme's comments.

Comstock was one of Mumme's strongest supporters and had gathered a group of businessmen to form the "Air Corp" which provided tens of thousands of dollars in private donations to fly Mumme around the country in a private jet instead of on commercial airlines. Later that night Mumme approached Comstock and laughed about the incident telling him the had done it in jest because he knew that Bob could take it. I've never quite understood what was funny about trying to humiliate another human being in a public setting, but Mumme seemed to enjoy it. Comstock evidently tolerated Mumme's ridicule because he remained one of Mumme's strongest supporters throughout Mumme's tenure as UK's Head Football Coach.

I am totally not against anyone 21 or over drinking Bourbon or sharing stories under the influence of alcohol. I have certainly participated in drinking my share of alcoholic beverages at times in my life and have made errors in judgement as a result. However, there is a time and place for everything and if you have a tendency to be obstinate and arrogant, there is a good chance the right amount of alcohol may push your comments over the edge. It definitely seemed to have that effect on Mumme at various times.

A Unique Approach to a Tragedy

The phone rang at our home and as I answered I could tell my mother was noticeably shaken. "Tony, there has been a wreck and Ernie, Curt, and Ricky are all hurt bad." I jumped in the car and raced to the Caldwell County Hospital and entered the emergency room to find several of my friends already there. Ernie Rickard and Curt Jones would both die from injuries in the accident as well as the drivers of both vehicles. Ricky Williamson would spend months in intensive care before eventually recovering and continuing to live a productive life.

Caldwell County High School gymnasium was full as we eulogized Curt and Ernie in December of 1975. I was an 18-year-old senior, and 25 years later I can still feel the hurt and pain of losing two memorable friends. *If We Make It Through December* was the song played as the funeral came near its end. I have never forgotten Curt and Ernie and many times each year they still fill my heart with pleasant memories from our childhoods.

Most of our coaching staff at Kentucky had lived long enough to go through at least one tragic loss in their lives. In November 1998 each member of our staff would have the chance to offer their condolences and experience in handling a tragedy as center Jason Watts would be involved in an accident that seriously injured Watts and fatally wounded defensive lineman Artie Steinmetz, and Eastern Kentucky University student Scott Brock.

Tragedy has a way of bringing out the best and worst in people. A football staff should be similar to a family sharing in the good and bad and relying on each other in time of tragedy. Mumme never gave all of our staff that opportunity during this time of tragedy. We witnessed first hand Mumme's feelings toward us one week later after the 1998 Tennessee game, which followed the tragic wreck. "Get the !@#$ out of my locker room and leave me with *my* team." Mumme instructed all of the assistant coaches and other personnel. He did offer Newton the opportunity to stay. Players later told us about Mumme's speech in which he threatened the players about drinking in the future. Mumme would say later in 2000, after announcing the firing of several assistants, that our coaching staff had "chemistry problems." I wonder why there would be bad chemistry when your head coach throws you out of the locker room as if you are an outsider to address *his* team about a tragedy that affected all of us.

My high school football coach, Al Giordano of Caldwell County HS, could teach Mumme a tremendous amount about being a real head football coach. Coach "G" was like a second father to his players and was like a big brother to his fellow assistant coaches. During the aftermath of our tragic wreck in 1975 with similar circumstances to the 1998 Kentucky tragedy, Coach "G" was the foundation of strength, love, and family unity for everyone. No coaches or players were slighted and he never once referred to the Caldwell County Tiger football team as *his* team. It was a community loss and Coach "G" was the emotional leader because he truly felt a strong love for everyone hurt in this tragedy. Coach "G" didn't see a need to ban his assistant coaches to address *his* team.

If Mumme had only asked all of us on the staff, not just his confidants, I'm sure he could have received some valuable advice that might have helped him in his search for better staff "chemistry." He also would have received a gift from one of his assistant coaches who would have given him the phone number of Al Giordano. This assistant would have told him that Coach "G" has been through many tragedies in his 40-plus years of coaching and would be a valuable mentor to help him through a tough situation.

According to Guy Morriss, who related his story to me, there would eventually be a decision made by Mumme, supposedly through the advice of Newton to not allow Jason Watts to attend the senior banquet. Thank God some seniors of the 1998 Outback Bowl football team had the courage to stand behind their conviction of friendship and morality and boycott this banquet, which was eventually cancelled. Would it be politically incorrect to allow an eventually convicted drunk driver to attend a Division I "Next Great University" banquet? What would the press say? Thank God those 1998 seniors didn't care about the public or media's reaction and just did the right thing: they supported a member of their football family with no judgment of his actions.

Newton would later drive through a "Zero Tolerance" policy for a UK student athlete who was convicted of drunk driving. Many media members would applaud this decision, as would many members of the public. It certainly satisfied specific groups in society. I wonder how many times, in the lives of those involved in making this decision, they have gotten behind the wheel after one, two, or more drinks. Zero tolerance might have knocked out some UK athletic coaches and administrators over their career if not for pure luck. They simply weren't caught or because of who they were, were let go. Thankfully, Larry Ivy had the courage to abolish the, in my opinion, emotional and politically based "zero tolerance" when he became Athletic Director.

I have no doubt Mumme and Newton had more to worry about than Tony Franklin, Tim Keane, or any other assistant coaches during this tragedy. I'm sure that their intentions were pure and ethical in their own minds, and I'm sure they both helped numerous people during this tragic experience. I just happen to disagree with their style and substance. Both men could learn valuable lessons from Al Giordano. Coach "G" will probably die a much poorer man in possessions than Newton or Mumme, but a much richer man in my eyes.

Summer Camp and Camp $Money$

It didn't take me very long to learn about Hal Mumme and summer camp money. Summer camps at Division I universities have two primary purposes: (1.) To showcase the university and athletic facilities to potential recruits whom the coaches will also closely evaluate, and (2.) To provide extra income for assistant coaches. The summer camps at Kentucky under Mumme would become some of the longest camps in all of college football with the staff working as many as 18 days during the summer. They would also become some of the "strangest" paid camps in all of college football with the assistant coaches pay ranging from as little as $2000 to as high as $20,000 or more. The number of campers and the amount of money taken in had little to do with how much assistant coaches were paid. Mumme told me my first summer I could expect to make around $10,000 since he would pay me two camp shares for running the camp. Instead, my actual pay was around $3800 for two weeks of some of the most stressful work of my life, not including the four months of preparation work. It was a good lesson for me, because I knew not to ever believe Mumme again about camp money. The director of the summer camps at Kentucky could be paid a million dollars in cash and I wouldn't want to do it again.

Chris Hatcher and Kwyn Jenkins eventually ran the summer camps in 1998-1999 and Rob Manchester and Kwyn in 2000. Jenkins worked most of the year doing something towards preparing for upcoming camp. Hatcher would make close to $20,000 for running the camps and Jenkins would eventually make as much as $9,000. However, Manchester was cut dramatically his first year as Camp Director from the $20,000 paid to Hatcher to less than $5000.

Something startling happened to the 2000 summer camp money! Mumme had told the assistant coaches he didn't take any money out of the summer camp fund. Several Division I head coaches in football don't take any money from their camps, leaving all the funds to be divided among assistants and other staff who worked the camps. After the news media did some investigating they found that Mumme had paid himself around $20,000 while most of his assistants made between $3000-$5000. Mumme also paid his son-in-law $2500 for two and half days of camp work, which included his primary job of shooting a radar gun to see how fast the quarterbacks were throwing the football. Mumme also allowed his wife, June, to use $2600 from the camp funds for a social outing to take the assistant coaches wives on a daylong trip. Some of the wives were under the impression that Mrs. Mumme was paying for the trip from her own personal money, not camp money that could have been paid to their husbands. Morriss and Major each made over $10,000 for their specialty camps and other camps combined. Bassett was paid more than $8000 for his camp role. I made over $5000 due to my running of a Fantasy Camp as well as other camp work minus over $1000 in personal expenses I chose to use to learn a marketing campaign for the Fantasy Camp. Other assistant coaches made approximately $3000 for their 18 summer camp workdays.

The camp discrepancy in money and the length of time required to work the summer camps was a source of agitation for some of the assistant coaches. Most would have rather been told they were receiving no money and that it was just a part of their job than to have high expectations of income that was never realized by most assistants. According to Mumme, chemistry problems were a factor in Mumme's firing several assistant coaches. When the head coach makes $800,000 per year and most of his assistants make $60,000-$100,000 per year and this head coach takes $20,000 for himself and pays a family member a much higher daily rate than his assistants, do you have to wonder why there might be a chemistry problem?

Conclusion

John C. Maxwell says in his book, *The Right To Lead*, "The truly great leaders are not in leadership for personal gain. They lead to serve other people."[4] Perhaps that is why Lawrence D. Bell remarked, "Show me a man who cannot bother to do little things and I'll show you a man who cannot be trusted to do big things."[5] Mumme had assistant coaches and staff members drive him as if they were his chauffeurs; he had secretaries serve him coffee as if they were servants. He eventually didn't want to fly unless he was in first class or on a private jet. In the meantime, Kentucky Head Basketball Coach Tubby Smith, slept in the dorms of his summer campers and ate meals at their tables. Smith won an NCAA Championship, but he spent many hours daily doing his own work at camps, where as Mumme, with the exception of his quarterback camp, spent as little time as possible. Personal gains and accomplishments are noteworthy, but not nearly as important as what you become on your journey to your destination. Mumme accomplished several noteworthy milestones in his coaching career. The man he became on his journey was much less noteworthy.

LESSON #17—The true measure of your character and integrity is what you would do if you thought no one would ever find out. Houston Nutt, the present Head Football Coach of Arkansas, once spoke to a group while still the Head Football coach at Murray State. Nutt said, "Discipline is doing the right thing when no one is watching." Integrity and character are not what the public sees, it's what they don't see their leaders do in private that steer the course of mankind. It is our job to keep our leaders in check by exposing their actions, good and bad, when their power begins to impact the lives of others.

CHAPTER 18

THE AUTHOR AND THE MUMME SPLIT

Lesson 18—No matter what people do to hurt you or defame you, remember the greatest man to ever live received a much worse fate than we could ever imagine. Don't expect truth and honesty from people and don't be disappointed when they fail to meet your expectations. When you expect little in return, you'll be plenty surprised when truth and loyalty emerge in a relationship. Value those few select people who stand by you in times of hardship for they are more valuable than gold.

OC—$100,000—Oklahoma—Central Michigan Assistant of the Year

When Chris Hatcher decided to take the Head Coaching job at Valdosta State University in December 1999, Hal Mumme gave me the title of Offensive Coordinator with a $30,000 pay raise. I had reached a goal in life of making $100,000 per year and was also the Offensive Coordinator at my dream school, the University of Kentucky. Bob Stoops, Head Coach of Oklahoma, would call me in January of 2000 and talk to me briefly about the possibility of replacing the departed Mike Leach as an assistant on his staff. Mumme would call SEC commissioner Roy Kramer to ask for his assistance in recommending me for the Head Coach job at Central Michigan University. In September 2000 Mumme would nominate me for the AFCA Assistant Coach of the Year and write a note to Barry Terranova of *American Football Quarterly* suggesting he shop me around as a potential Division I head coach. My professional career was going better than ever and Mumme was listening to me and treating me with more respect than ever before.

With all these positive things happening, I must have been in absolute heaven. I wish I could say that was true, but it wasn't. I knew if I didn't get out of the job with Mumme at Kentucky it would only be a matter of time before things blew up. Too many bad things were happening and some bad characters were gaining more and more power. I tried to get a shot at the offensive coordinator job at North Carolina State, but to no avail. In February 2000, on National Signing Day, Guy Morriss and I hoped a fax from a Memphis high school stand out did *not* come through. We both believed if he signed at UK it would probably mean the beginning of the end for our football program. The rumors on the recruiting road were strong about Melrose coach Tim Thompson and Bassett making a deal for the players' services that involved more than playing time promises. The fax came through and all of our worst fears would start to appear. Although that player may not have known about any arrangements made by Thompson and Bassett, it would become evident, almost a year later, Bassett and Thompson had arrangements working that involved more than football playing time.

Bonner/Franklin/Mumme

The earlier chapter concerning quarterback Dusty Bonner relayed the events and how Bonner's demotion took place; however, it didn't detail my mistakes in the Bonner decision. As just mentioned, in the spring of 2000, I had many positive things happening in my coaching life. When Mumme made the decision to unjustly take Bonner's job away from him, I should have immediately resigned. Although I firmly believe in a head coach's right to make any football decision he chooses, the Bonner decision was different. It didn't meet football criteria I believe to be rational. It looked and smelled like a rat from the moment Mumme began to rationalize and explain the decision.

When I went home and discussed the Bonner demotion with my wife, I discussed the possibility of resigning my job, but I ended up taking the selfish way out. I justified my staying as the only lucid thing to do because of the time of the year. There was no way that I could get a good college job in the summer; therefore, I decided to stay and to hope I was wrong and that Mumme was a pure genius. I hoped the decision would work out and we would win enough that I could leave him at the end of the season and find a good offensive coordinator job.

In writing this book, I have made several critical observations about other men I worked with. I have been truthful in all of my observations so I must be truthful about this next statement. Tony Franklin acted selfishly and against his own moral standards when he didn't immediately resign after Mumme's demotion of Bonner. There are no excuses for my behavior at that critical time, and I will never be able to justify my lack of judgment no matter how I try. I was merely wrong!

Florida 2000

As mentioned in an earlier chapter, Mumme had decided to coach defense when we were preparing to play the Florida Gators in September

2000. I had more freedom in game planning than at any time of my coaching career at Kentucky. Fourth down would be a "go for it" down Mumme told me and I scripted several fourth down situations and plays we could run against the Gators. To note, we successfully converted 6 of 7 fourth down attempts. Our offensive game plan worked well as we put up more than 500 yards on offense and 31 points in "The Swamp." We had an incredible offensive output against the Gators but not near enough as Mumme's defensive plan looked like a Major's defense as it gave up 59 points.

The Florida game would be one of my proudest accomplishments as a coach at the University of Kentucky. Although Mumme called the plays on Saturday, it was my work and planning that gave us an opportunity to exploit the Florida defense.

After Mumme and I had our falling out Mumme would tell an amazing story about the Florida game. According to Tim Keane, Larry Ivy's good friend and Kentucky booster Talbot Todd, told Keane that Mumme gave an explanation of how Florida scored so many points against us. Todd told Keane that Mumme said Franklin made the *defensive* game plan against Florida. I'll have to admit it looked like a defensive plan I would have made, because I hadn't coached defense since the early 1990s at Calloway County HS. Mumme's excuse making had reached an all-time high as he had found a way to dodge responsibility in an incredible fashion—blame your offensive coordinator for your defensive shortcomings.

LSU, "You're Nothing But A High School Coach"

Mumme had just finished his lecture of how all of our offensive players stunk up the LSU game and we had all given him our corrections. He began to draw our new game plan for the Georgia game when I interrupted him and asked, "Coach, we've told you our corrections. I'd like to know what you plan to do to correct the quarterback."

Mumme replied, "I thought he played well."

"Could you explain to me why on the opening drive of the game on a third and one when we ran Early Right 619 he didn't throw the ball to an open Derek Smith versus man coverage?" I asked.

"I don't remember that play." Mumme stated.

I repeated my statement and Mumme replied, "Oh yeah, Jared had pressure on him and couldn't get the ball to Derek."

"No sir, there was no pressure, I have the video cued up to that play and I'll be glad to go get it." I replied.

"You don't even know what !@#$ pressure is, he had pressure! Do you have anything else to say?" Mumme angrily asked.

"No sir that will be it," I replied.

When the meeting ended I left for my office and seconds after I entered Mumme followed. He asked, "Do you have a problem?"

"Yes I do. You've blamed everybody on our football team for our problem except the quarterback. You've publicly blasted players by name and you're starting to hurt our team and Jared by not making him responsible for his part." I replied.

"Give me some examples." Mumme requested. I reached in my desk and pulled out a list of big plays for the season and began to go through Lorenzen's errors that Mumme had blamed another player for. My door was now shut and Mumme asked, "What would you do if you were the head coach?"

"I would start Shane Boyd as quarterback." I said.

"With over half the season gone?" Mumme asked.

"No sir, I would have done it three weeks ago if I were head coach. It's the same problem Jared had in the spring and I disagreed with you then, but I supported you publicly because you are the head coach and that is what I'm supposed to do!" I stated.

"You need to quit pouting and coach!" Mumme, with his face now red, said.

"I'm not pouting I simply disagree with you and you asked me my opinion and I'm giving it to you." I replied.

"You're pouting just like you did when you came to me and asked to be offensive coordinator and wanted more money. You're nothing but a high school coach that I took up and gave a job and now all you do is pout," Mumme emphatically stated.

Mumme's memory had become very short and selective. He gave me a chance! What a joke! He wouldn't have been at Kentucky had it not been for the work of me and several other high school coaches. The time was right now for me to do what I should have done when he demoted Bonner.

"You need to find me a job and I mean a good job as an offensive coordinator at a good school. A coaching friend of mine, Terry Curtis, a high school coach in Alabama said when you can't support your head coach it's time to leave and I don't support you anymore. I don't believe in you and I especially don't believe in how you are treating our players," I strongly said.

"Do you know what you are saying?" Mumme asked.

"Yes sir. You helped Hatcher and Leach get jobs and you can help me. I love Kentucky and these players and I'll bust my butt coaching and recruiting until something else happens," I said.

"Mike Leach was with me ten years before he took a job and you need at least another five years under me before you know enough to be a real offensive coordinator," Mumme snapped.

Remember, this is the same Mumme who had recommended me for the head-coaching job at Division I Central Michigan and to Bob Stoops at

Oklahoma to replace Mike Leach. However, Mumme was doing what he always did in a football discussion when he didn't want to hear the truth: he was attacking me personally. "You can't get a good job, you're nothing but a high school coach," Mumme repeated.

"I don't want your help and I don't need your help. I'll take care of myself!" I seethed.

Mumme stood up and said, "When I leave this room it's over. Are you sure?" "I'm sure," I replied and Mumme left my office.

Everything happened pretty much the way I expected. I had decided after Mumme's post-game speech at LSU that it was time to confront him regardless of what it cost me. Mumme had told the team, "I hope you're happy boys. I've been a head college coach for 12 years and you get to be known as the first team to have *me* shutout." It was strictly about his ego and nothing else. I had enough. When I got home early Sunday morning I told my wife someone had to step up and tell him the truth and that it might cost me my job. Laura agreed it was the right thing to do, so she wasn't surprised when I came home Monday night and told her what had happened.

The personal attack on me was the fourth in my relationship with Mumme and his comments about my being "just a high school coach" were comical. I don't think he believed high school coaches were inferior; rather it was just his way to try to hurt me for telling him something he didn't want to hear. Mumme had complimented me in the spring for not being confrontational with him and knowing when not to argue, but the fact that we were losing and our offense was struggling was too much for his ego to endure. He did what he always did during the four years we worked together; he made it a personal situation rather than a professional matter. I felt relieved that it was almost over. I could coach my butt off the rest of the season, continue recruiting, and put the word out on the college coaching circuit that I was looking for another opportunity. Now, I had to hope he could behave as a professional and we could finish the season and our relationship as professionals. I should have known better than to expect that miracle. Professionalism was the farthest thing from the reality of what he would do during the next few months.

Georgia, Back To Work

After embarrassing offensive performances, Mumme returned to work with a vengeance. If he had approached each week the way he did after the LSU game, I believe we would have won four or five more games in 2000. His preparation time for opponents had a tendency to vary from week to week, but he occasionally would become invigorated and study video for hours at a time and when he did he was very talented as an offensive coach.

The 2000 Georgia defense was the perfect match up for Mumme's comeback to coaching. They were a soft zone coverage team and very seldom blitzed. Lorenzen did much better versus a non-blitzing team and Mumme did a superb job preparing him for the Bulldogs.

On Thursday, however, a freak accident would lead to the strange events I related earlier about Mumme's high level meeting including Jodi Gillespie, Scott Highsmith, and Mike Major to decide if Lorenzen or Shane Boyd would play quarterback versus Georgia. Lorenzen eventually got the call and had his greatest individual performance of his young career, blistering the Georgia defense for a career high and Kentucky passing record of 528 yards in a 30-34 loss.

The events surrounding Lorenzen's thumb injury on Thursday were made even stranger because of Mumme's comment to me about Shane Boyd. Mumme told me, "There's no way Shane Boyd will play this year. I wouldn't do that with only four games left. I won't blow Shane's red shirt year no matter what."

When Lorenzen hit his thumb on the helmet of an offensive lineman and trainer Jim Madaleno told Mumme it didn't look good, Mumme would get tested on his statement. Although third team quarterback Mark Perry was quite capable of leading our offense, Mumme decided to ask Boyd what he wanted to do. Boyd's answer was easy. He wanted to play. Mumme walked Boyd down from the scout team where he had been playing Georgia's QB all week and announced to the offense that Boyd would be the QB Saturday versus Georgia. The entire offense was excited about Boyd leading them. As Mumme walked off the field to the sideline, he could hear the excitement from the team. Mumme walked up to Derek Smith and said, "This may be a blessing."

"This may be what our team needs." Smith said.

"If I'd known you felt that way, Derek, I'd have made this decision earlier, but I was afraid how you would react." Mumme replied.

Smith looked at Mumme and emphatically stated, "Coach, I just want to win. I don't care who the QB is."

We redid the entire team offensive practice and when it was over Mumme addressed the team and told them Jared was out and Shane would be the QB. Derek Smith said, "Guys, Shane Boyd is going to lead us to a win."

Boyd then stood and said, "Fellas, there's four more games to play. Jump on my back because I'm going to take you to a bowl." There was a wild yell from the defensive players as Boyd seemed to energize them.

Mumme would eventually change his plan after Lorenzen's miraculous recovery from Madaleno's early diagnosis of a possible season-ending injury. The team seemed slightly deflated when Mumme told them Boyd would probably not play unless Jared struggled. Lorenzen rose to the occasion and put on a gutsy and classic performance as he, like most competitors, played better when he had a threat of losing his job. The team wasn't down on Lorenzen, they just felt Boyd might have been the spark to change the season around and were looking for a spark to rally around.

Mumme came to my office Monday morning following the Georgia game and announced to me, "You need to know that Jared Lorenzen will be my QB as long as I'm here and Shane Boyd will not play until Jared leaves for the NFL. If you don't agree with that then you need to leave, but if you can support it then I will forget last week and you can stay."

"I made myself perfectly clear last week. This has nothing to do with quarterbacks. This is about my not believing in you as a head coach anymore. My decision is strictly professional." I said.

Mumme replied, "We've been friends for too long to end it this way. I just got mad when you dared to question me, especially since I took you out of high school and gave you a job. I'll help you get a job as an offensive coordinator. Have you talked to Sonny (Dykes)? There's going to be some movement in the Big 12 Conference."

"I talk to Sonny every week." I said.

"We need to make sure we can get you a job by spring practice or else you'll have to resign at that time so I can hire a coach for the spring." Mumme said.

We agreed and Mumme left.

For the final three weeks of the season Mumme chose to not include me in the game planning and practice schedule and there was very little communication between us with the exception of game day. I bit my tongue everyday and kept my cool because I hoped that maybe Mumme would actually honor his word and be a professional. How stupid could I be? He soon showed me he wasn't capable of being professional and I would quickly discover what his real plan for me was.

The Smear Campaign Begins

A reporter sent me an e-mail from someone using the code name of "rbs." This Internet frequenter sent a memo to several members of the news media telling them that Franklin may not be returning to UK because of "family concerns." All season long, "rbs" was releasing his inside information and he was now giving opinions, which included my family. There was no doubt in my mind what was happening. Another newspaper reporter also called me to tell me he was sorry about my family situation. I asked what he was talking about and he told me about an e-mail he had received from "rbs."

The spin machine had begun to start its campaign of propaganda. Bassett had a following of Internet groupies who believed most anything he told them and I believe he released inside information to spread his message whenever he wanted it out. Mumme had already begun to talk to administrators and key boosters about me and I believe that he was spreading the news that I could be leaving. Mumme and Bassett worked together to control any possible damage they felt my leaving UK football might cause them. Boosters who normally went out of their way to talk to me after practice now dodged me like I was infected with the plague. "rbs'" e-mail to the press was, I believe, Bassett's way of spreading a rumor that would smear my name. "rbs' " reference to my family was a declaration of war. Mumme and Bassett had stepped out of bounds by including my family, and I would not sit back idly and watch them spread false rumors concerning my family life.

Oscar Combs and Lonnie DeMaree, writers for *The Cats' Pause* and *Wildcat Championship Football* respectively, would tell a reporter later in the week I was going to be fired because I wouldn't cooperate in recruiting. I believe Bassett's smear campaign was continuing with Combs and DeMaree, who were frequent visitors of Bassett's office. Both men seemed to believe his philosophical agenda at times, or else they simply enjoyed hearing a good story.

Mumme just couldn't help himself. Being professional was totally out of his reach and with Bassett nearby he had the perfect "hatchet man" to spread his propaganda. I believe Mumme's goal was two fold: (1.) Blame the season's problems on me. (2.) Portray me as a malcontent who caused internal problems in recruiting.

Mumme's inability to act professionally in our disagreement and parting of ways and my belief that he used Bassett to do his dirty work would lead me to meet with A.D. Larry Ivy to request his help. I will go into the details of that meeting later.

The Mumme Propaganda Machine

Mumme and Bassett both would eventually warn fellow coach Dan Lounsbury to stay away from me if he wanted to continue coaching at Kentucky. Bassett would tell Lounsbury on the practice field, "See these millionaire boosters. They watch whom you talk to and hang out with. You need to be careful about being seen with Franklin if you want to keep your job." Mumme would bring Lounsbury into his office in mid-November and tell him Tony Franklin "is poison," and that I was making up lies about Bassett, that Bassett had done nothing wrong, and if Lounsbury wanted to keep his job he should to do three things: (1.) Do whatever Bassett tells him. (2.) Have no contact with Tony Franklin. (3.) Not talk to anyone else about taking a job irregardless of the opportunity. Mumme also told Lounsbury our offensive problems began because he named me the offensive coordinator.

When the rumors of improper ties involving Kentucky and Memphis Melrose began to arise Mumme needed a diversion to take responsibility away from him. Because of my split with Mumme and my eventual meeting with Ivy he had the perfect scapegoat: Tony Franklin. If he told enough people the story, maybe he could get them to believe it and take some of the heat off himself. He might even persuade boosters, fans, alumni, and the Kentucky staff to direct their anger at someone else. It was a great plan that resembled something out of the Bill Clinton administration and it worked for a while.

Mumme began to tell people Franklin was the main problem, not Bassett. Bassett, according to Mumme, had done nothing wrong except for a couple of minor NCAA violations. Franklin was leaking information to the press, the NCAA, and UK compliance, according to Mumme. He went so far as to tell one staff member that, "Franklin is the number one enemy of the University of Kentucky" and another staff member that Franklin "made up lies to frame Bassett." He told one staff member that "Franklin made up these lies about Bassett because he was so afraid to go home and tell his wife that he had given up this great job I (Mumme) had given him that he wanted to get me (Mumme) to fire him."

The blabbering excuses by Mumme were farfetched even for him. He had completely gone overboard in his attempt to cover his own backside. Talbot Todd, the previously mentioned booster and close friend to Larry Ivy, would tell Mumme's Personal Assistant Kwyn Jenkins, "If Mumme ever talks about you the way he does Franklin, I'll hit him in the mouth." Todd is a friend of Jenkins' father and has known Kwyn since childhood.

Inside Sources

Amazingly, just like in Nazi Germany or other times in history, if you tell a lie often enough people will eventually begin to believe it. Mumme and Bassett did a masterful job for several weeks of getting fans, boosters, alumni, and staff to believe their propaganda and lies. The Internet groupies led by "rbs" preached the conspiracy theory and pointed the finger of blame as if they really knew the facts. The Internet groupies even falsely planted the thought that Franklin was being paid by *The Courier Journal* for turning over information.

Each Internet groupie always cited their information to be reliable and from an "inside source." You cannot blame some of these groupies for wanting to believe the conspiracy theory. It made more sense than the stupidity of the reality of what really happened. No one could really believe the arrogance and ignorance of what eventually would become the true story once the facts began to surface.

Some of these "inside sources" were people who had daily contact with Bassett and Mumme. There was some information, such as Mumme's behind closed door conversations with me in which he called me selfish and told me that I needed to spend several more years like Leach before moving on, that had to come from Mumme. I believe that those people, along with others close to Mumme and Bassett, spread the information for them.

Once the "reliable" sources joined in with their daily updates of what new conspiracy took place the previous day, the freaks jumped in. There would eventually be threats and suggestions to others as to what they should do with this "Benedict Arnold" traitor named Franklin. My brother called to tell me that someone had put my daily jogging path on the Internet with suggestions on what someone should do if they saw me.

Prior to the tumultuous end of my coaching career at Kentucky I didn't know what an Internet message board or chat line was. Dan Lounsbury kept telling me to read the Wildcat Chat lines but I had no idea what I was getting into when I finally decided to read this information. The Internet freaks, goons, and cowards all have a common trait: they hide behind a fake name and can write whatever they wish with no repercussions. Men and women with absolutely nothing in their own lives can obtain a sense of power and importance by sending something via the Internet that grabs the other readers' attention.

Incredibly, when the hard facts of Bassett's wrongdoings became accepted as truth, many of these Internet groupies began to spin new conspiracy theories. There was something missing, however, as my name disappeared from later boards and they turned their hatred and vengeance toward new targets.

Conclusion

I used Hal Mumme and Hal Mumme used me. We were never friends, we were merely associates who occasionally had to socialize with each other.

If not for realities of life and economics I would have left him after one year. That didn't happen however and, because of my selfish pursuits of furthering my college-coaching career, I got exactly what I deserved. In my opinion, Hal Mumme and Claude Bassett did everything in their power to try to destroy my reputation in my home state. The price I paid for my selfishness was two and a half months of hell when I was portrayed as a vengeful destroyer of UK football. Then the facts revealed more of the truth. I even received phone calls and letters from some of Basset's cronies who wanted me to know they were lied to. They hoped there would be no hard feelings. Gosh fellows, why would I have hard feelings? It simply cost me my coaching career.

LESSON #18—In my mid-twenties, my mother and I had a discussion that would change my outlook on life. We sat on the front porch of my parent's home in Princeton, and I explained to her how several people had disappointed me. My mother reminded me of a story of a man much greater than I could ever hope to be whom had been betrayed by his closest friends in his most desperate time of need. She reminded me if his friends could betray this man, then how could I expect any better treatment from mine? That man was Jesus Christ. I was not a deeply religious person, but the story struck a chord with me I have never forgotten. No matter what people do to hurt you or defame you, remember the greatest man to ever live received a much worse fate than we could ever imagine. Don't expect truth and honesty from people and don't be disappointed when they fail to meet your expectations. When you expect little in return, you'll be pleasantly surprised when truth and loyalty do show up in a relationship. Value those few select people who stand by you in times of hardship for they are more valuable than gold.

CHAPTER 19

THE DEATH OF THE EGO

Lesson 19—Be careful if you decide to roll in the dirt, because you will get dirty. If you choose to get dirty, don't cry when you are exposed. If you do the crime, be willing to do the time.

"The Bonner Ghost"

Hal Mumme signed the beginning of his own demise when he initiated the Dusty Bonner debacle. He never correctly estimated the potential damage to the morale of a team when one of its favorites was treated with injustice. Mumme's ability to convince himself of anything he wanted to believe was one of his strongest assets as well as one of his major shortcomings. His belief to make James Whalen a player worked like magic, but his miscalculation of the Bonner fiasco was born out of an idea that, I believe, was self-promotional in nature.

Tim Couch and Dusty Bonner were both products of Chris Hatcher's coaching and I believe Mumme was getting tired of hearing how great of a coach Hatcher was. He wanted Lorenzen to be his very own protégé which only he would get the credit for. It's really sad to think a Division I Head Coach would have to boost his ego in such a perverted way. Trust me, Mumme's ego, in my opinion, was very capable of such a deed.

Karma, the Gods of football, and all the other terms that might describe spiritual intervention played a part in the 2000 Kentucky season of 2-9, as well as revealing the eventual recruiting scandal. Everyone must pay for their misdeeds and sins against good in the end. Sometimes people have to wait until after death for their punishment or payback to take place, but usually the initial phases of punishment begin on Earth. Hal Mumme's punishment for his unjust treatment of Bonner would initiate his own self-destruction. It's a shame the players and fans had to also pay for his misdeeds.

Major Gone—Mumme Not Far Behind

Major made the statement if Newton had still been the Athletic Director Hal Mumme would still be the football coach at Kentucky. That is one of the few times I could ever say I agreed with Major. The naming of Larry Ivy as the athletic director to succeed Newton was not something Mumme was very excited about. He publicly supported Ivy's promotion because Newton told him to do so. Privately, however, he was very concerned and with good reason. If Newton had stayed on as A.D., in my opinion, not only would Mumme still be coaching at Kentucky but also so would Major.

Ivy's style of management would be much more hands on when dealing with coaches, whereas, Newton being a former coach, would allow Mumme to control his coaching staff. Ivy would eventually say Mumme and Major made the decision for Major to resign, but I seriously doubt it. The pressure put on Major through Ivy began before the season and was evident to most everyone familiar with the program. When Mumme began to meddle with the defense during the early part of the season, it was evident the Major/Mumme honeymoon of many years was nearing it's end.

After Major "fell on the sword" for Mumme, as Mumme announced late in the 2000 season, it was also announced Major would move into an administrative position within the football offices. This move would eventually be reversed and Major would be totally out of the Kentucky football program.

The resignation of Major and eventually Bassett's removal was a strong move by Ivy which could have saved Mumme and given him a chance to become a tremendous success as a head coach. Mumme, however, couldn't handle Ivy's guidance and eventually, despite all of Ivy's efforts to help Mumme save himself, Mumme would find enough rope to hang himself and his career.

The Melrose Connection & Tim Thompson

On Monday morning, Equipment Manager Tom Kalinowski asked Bassett, "Where are all the sideline jackets you gave the Melrose kids?"

"I'll get them for you later," Bassett replied.

We had just been drilled by Mississippi State, but the weekend was a Claude Bassett "coup" as he had the recruits from the "infamous" Tim Thompson and Memphis Melrose for an "unofficial" visit. The players and coaches from Melrose evidently left the Kentucky campus with more than just a promise of playing time. Kalinowski joked with me daily about the jackets being "on the way back from Memphis."

When Bassett and Mumme decided to enter into the Memphis Melrose "sweepstakes" for players, they were entering a dangerous game which neither one was competent enough to play. Tim Thompson, the gifted football coach at Melrose, had caught my attention the first year I joined Kentucky. A high school coach had told me Thompson was "shopping" his players as a package deal to colleges with him going as an assistant coach. Later in my career, Thompson had gained a rumored reputation for selling his players' services for several thousand dollars to the highest bidder. Thompson would eventually receive a three-year suspension from coaching at Melrose. He would also be a prominent figure in Bassett's NCAA wrong-doings, including his acceptance of a $1400 money order from Bassett.

Any type of common sense should have warned Bassett and Mumme to stay out of Melrose. Richard Ernsberger, a *Newsweek* magazine editor and writer, had written a book called *Bragging Rights* detailing college football in the South. Ernsberger dedicated an entire chapter to Memphis, which included high school coaches Tim Thompson and Lyn Lang and the rumors of their unscrupulous methods of handling their college recruited players. Warning signs were everywhere, all one had to do was open his eyes to see if a coach was going to *discreetly* cheat and buy the services of players, this would not be the best place to hide. Most coaches and many fans in south-eastern college football knew the rumors pertaining to what was going on at Memphis Melrose and Memphis Trezvant. Most programs with any decency either backed out or proceeded recruiting with great caution. Not Bassett and Mumme, they went full throttle and after signing stellar defensive tackle Dewayne Robertson in 2000, Mumme and Bassett put on the full court press for 2001 with the courtship of Tim Thompson.

The 2000 summer camp was one of the greatest displays of "butt kissing" in the history of college football. Mumme and Bassett treated Thompson, his staff, and players as if they were royalty. One day Bassett escorted the Melrose coaches into Kalinowski's Nike locker room and each coach left with his arms full of Kentucky apparel. Amazingly, they did it in broad daylight in front of visiting high school and college coaches. That was pure Bassett at his best. Several high school and college coaches left whispering about the Kentucky/Melrose connection.

Mumme eventually told members of the UK football staff that Thompson would be joining them as the new Receivers Coach. Bassett was making sure that Thompson stayed happy by sending money to him. It looked as if Kentucky and Thompson were about to consummate a marriage, with Thompson trading his players services to Kentucky in exchange for money and a college coaching job. If not for the ignorant and arrogant openness of the sideline jackets being distributed to the Melrose players at the Kentucky vs. Mississippi State game, I believe Thompson would have been hired as an assistant coach at the University of Kentucky. He would have been coach-ing at Kentucky when the NCAA began their investigation. Mumme was in the process of trying to hire Thompson even after the release of the book *Bragging Rights*.

Thompson was a good football coach and would have been a good college coach. His players respected him and followed him. There was no need for him to sell his players' services. It took away from the many positive things he did for his players. He eventually blamed me, taking the advice of Mumme and Bassett, for not being hired at UK. All he needs to do is look in the mirror to find the person he needs to blame.

Mumme's pre-game speech on Thursday before the 2000 Tennessee game included the point emphasizing we needed to beat the Vols because they cheat in recruiting. Amazingly, he said it with a straight face, as Morriss and I looked at each other and laughed. Mumme and Thompson were made for each other and they would both end their 2001 coaching careers in the same fashion. Both were avoiding the press under extreme duress as the truth had appeared and broken their mystique.

The End of the "Big Man"

Bassett's last days as a Kentucky coach were the work of a master plan coming to its ultimate destiny. His power had become almost one in the same with Mumme's. His opinion was the only one that Mumme seemed to need. His expertise in defense, recruiting, and coaching personnel was becoming the main voice Mumme listened to.

Coincidentally as his power had reached its ultimate height, his weaknesses were killing him. Inside his heart he must have known he had made some fatal mistakes which might come back to haunt him. Bassett had left a paper trail a mile long as well as a group of people whom he had consistently mistreated who were ready and willing to provide critical information he had left behind.

The Memphis deal was Bassett's grandest notoriety. He was getting recognition throughout the South and he surely loved the notoriety that came from his association with Thompson. Bassett once told me he looked forward to an NCAA investigation because he believed he could lie his way out of anything. I strongly believe Bassett wanted to get caught cheating. He wanted to have the chance for martyrdom that Dave Baker would give him in a comical televised interview. I had told my father and others a year in advance that Bassett wanted to be a martyr. Baker's interview gave him that chance as Bassett told Baker that he alone was responsible for the $1400 money order to Tim Thompson. He had "fallen on the sword" and

Baker rewarded Bassett with his praise for being a "Big Man" for telling the truth and taking the blame. His martyrdom was now official.

Mumme had earlier been shocked on the Sunday following the 2000 Tennessee game when Ivy had called Bassett and Mumme to his office to present Bassett with a surprise. A copy of a $500 check made payable to the University of Kentucky that Bassett had signed and cashed was presented to Bassett. According to Ivy, Bassett had no explanation which could justify his action and after Ivy's request, Bassett resigned on the spot, assuring that he could continue getting paid his $120,000 salary through June of 2001 or until he secured other employment before July 2001.

Mumme was furious. He had lost his right arm with Major and now he had lost his left arm, Bassett. Ivy was trying to save Mumme and the university from Mumme's own ignorance. If Mumme had realized Ivy was trying to help him and dropped his ego for a few months, he could still be making $800,000 a year instead of $250,000 per year for the next four years. Instead, Mumme stepped up his attacks on me, and his defense of Bassett.

Bassett and Mumme had spent several moments behind closed doors the last few weeks of the season. Whatever their plans had been were now in deep danger of blowing up. As Mumme stepped up his "blame game," documents and testimony began to show Mumme's defense of Bassett was strictly diversionary. Bassett was guilty of much more than a couple of minor violations as Mumme had told an office staff member while placing the blame on this author.

Bassett became obstinate and obnoxious in his rise to power at Kentucky. I believe he intentionally hurt people on a regular basis. Make no mistake, however, he was Mumme's designated hatchet man. Everything Bassett did, in my opinion, was under the implied or direct consent of Mumme. He may not have known everything in detail, but he knew the direction that Bassett was headed and by saying nothing, if that were the case, he gave his implied consent.

You can read the NCAA or UK compliance report to see the details of the violations committed by Claude Bassett under the watch of Hal Mumme. If Mumme knew of the violations then the NCAA should punish him; if Mumme did *not* know, then the NCAA should punish him. A head coach of a Division I school that could allow the number of violations under his watch by one of his top assistant coaches is unforgivable. If a booster had committed these violations, then maybe there is a legitimate excuse that you didn't know. However, if it is one of your top assistants, there is no excuse.

Hal Mumme, Mike Leach, Claude Bassett, and an Oklahoma Recruit

Leach and Bassett were both followers of the Mormon faith and both went to BYU, but that was where any slight similarities between the two ended. Bassett and Leach clashed early in the Mumme Era at Kentucky, and there was a noticeable dislike for each other that they both expressed to me on numerous occasions. Leach's recruiting or lack of recruiting, as Bassett would say, was a sore spot with Bassett. Mumme was in a dilemma trying to balance the power between the two of them.

The success Leach had at Oklahoma as their Offensive Coordinator in the 1999 season seemed to bother Bassett even more than Leach's presence at Kentucky. Leach and I were never close friends, but I respected the fact that he, having given up a law degree in order to coach college football, had paid a huge price to be a successful college coach. He was the total opposite of Bassett, as Leach seemed to be mostly honest and a strict follower of NCAA rules. It was Leach who first told me of Bassett's background being a fabrication of lies, such as his supposed Harvard earned master degree in constitutional law.

During a staff meeting in 1998, Bassett was giving instructions on recruiting as he passed out a recruiting manual. Leach asked a question and Bassett looked at Leach as if he were totally ignorant for asking the question. Bassett proceeded to talk to Leach in a degrading and sarcastic tone when Leach exploded. He cursed Bassett loudly and challenged him in front of the staff. Mumme sat in silence as Bassett did what he normally did when his bullying and belittling techniques were challenged to his face. He backed down, changed his tone, and talked to Leach respectfully.

Leach's leaving Kentucky in 1999 was perfect timing as he and Bassett were ready to go off on each other. I always felt the best way to get a good job with Mumme's blessing was to get to the point where Major and Bassett both wanted you gone. Once you reached that point, Mumme would help you leave. It definitely worked for Leach.

During Leach's one short year at Oklahoma, he and Bassett would have an opportunity to match wits again. Leach told me over the phone that a top defensive line recruit, who also visited Oklahoma, had been taken on a shopping spree while on his official visit to Kentucky. Leach asked me what I thought about him telling Mumme and I advised him to do so. I also told Leach I didn't feel like Mumme would do anything. The purpose of Leach calling Mumme and informing him was to try to protect Mumme because Leach still was loyal to Hal then as he is today. Another assistant coach at Oklahoma had told Leach that the recruit had told him of the violations while he was later visiting Oklahoma after his UK visit. Leach's phone call to Mumme led to a predictable move by Mumme. According to Hal, he asked Bassett and Bassett said that he didn't do it. Mumme never filed a report to the UK compliance office and the matter would not enter into an official inquiry until approximately one year later when the investigation of other wrongdoings at Kentucky would create an opportunity for the incident to reappear.

The failure of Mumme to report Leach's warning of this possible NCAA violation would eventually play a vital role in Kentucky's buy out of Mumme. The effort by Leach to protect his ex-boss and warn him of Bassett's misconduct and Mumme's decision to not report the incident would give Kentucky some leverage when deciding to negotiate a settlement with Mumme.

Bassett later told me of Leach's call to Mumme, and I acted as if I didn't know. He was furious and vowed to "get Leach." Approximately 11 months later I believe he took his shot at paying back Mike Leach. I was in Bassett's office to tell him about a recruit late in the 2000 season. I told him the recruit had just visited Texas Tech, where Leach was now the Head Coach, and had enjoyed his visit. Bassett blurted, "We don't have to worry about Tech. A (former Coach) just called me and told me Leach is going to be fired after the season."

I told Bassett, "I could care less and I don't want to hear about it," and I walked out of his office.

Claude Bassett had just told a man, who had not spoken to him except for professional reasons in weeks, an absurd story about Mike Leach getting fired. His ability to conjure up stories and blurt them out to the next person in his sight would even include his enemies. Bassett was truly frightening, especially because he had his group of reporters and Internet groupies who believed every word out of his mouth.

I called Leach later that day and told him about Bassett's story. Dave Baker, who I believed to be one of Bassett's message boys, would print a brief note in *The Cats' Pause* magazine that an inside source had told him Mike Leach may be dismissed from TTU at the season's end. I wonder who Baker's inside source was? In my conversation with Leach I told him he could use my name as his source if he wanted to question Bassett or "The Former Coach." Leach and I both knew "The Former Coach" was too classy of a man to have delved into such rumor mongering especially with Bassett. After talking to "The Former Coach," Leach called to tell me "The Former Coach" said he had never had such a conversation with Bassett. Texas Tech University and Mike Leach threatened legal action and shortly thereafter Baker resigned from *The Cats' Pause*. *The Cats' Pause* also printed a retraction. Bassett's attempt to smear Leach, in my opinion, had worked just the opposite, as Leach's administration came to his defense in a strong show of support.

If Mumme had listened to his former assistant coach's warning about Bassett and acted strongly, he could still be the Head Coach at the University of Kentucky. The Memphis fiasco probably would have never happened. You have to ask yourself why Mumme didn't vigorously pursue this evidence that came from Leach, a coach who had worked with him loyally for 10 years. Maybe Mumme didn't pursue the truth with vigorous effort because he already knew what Bassett was doing. When you look at all the evidence, it is hard not to come to that conclusion.

Conclusion

Hal Mumme spent a great deal of time in November and December of 2000 and January 2001 unjustly blaming me for many of the problems in the Kentucky football program. Everything from a 2-9 season to a NCAA investigation became the work of Tony Franklin, according to Hal Mumme. If he had spent those same moments taking total responsibility for *his* football team and *his* football program, as he had reminded all of his assistant coaches after the 1998 Tennessee game that it wasn't our team, it was his team, then he could have survived and possibly even thrived. He cried wolf as long and loud as people would listen to him because, I believe, he knew that there was dirt and he didn't want anyone looking. Ivy tried hard to save Mumme from his own ego and his ignorance, but Mumme could not stop blaming others long enough to realize Ivy was trying to take care of him. There is only one reason I believe Mumme ignored the warnings of Leach and refused the guidance of Ivy; Mumme was dirty and couldn't get out of the dirt long enough to save himself. An NCAA investigator, Jim Elworth, asked me in May 2001 if I thought Mumme was in over his head, having only been a small college head coach before Kentucky and therefore, he relied on Bassett because of his Division I experience. Absolutely not! I don't believe that! I believe Mumme knew everything and occasionally helped orchestrate Bassett's strategies. Mumme is an extremely smart man. He is simply, in my opinion, lazy and unethical. Those two characteristics have caused the demise of many leaders and Mumme was just the next one in line.

LESSON #19—If it looks like dirt, walks like dirt, smells like dirt, and hangs around with dirt, there is a good chance it is dirt. Be careful if you decide to roll in the dirt, because you will get dirty. Hal Mumme was surrounded with dirt. He was warned about dirty deeds and dirty actions. His response was to point the finger at others and to promote the doer of the dirty deeds. In my opinion, Mumme laid in dirt and he got real dirty. If you choose to get dirty, don't cry when you are exposed. If you do the crime, be willing to do the time.

CHAPTER 20

THE BUCK STOPS WHERE?

Lesson 20—"Few things are more dangerous than a leader with an unexamined life." We should never sit back and accept the word of someone simply because they are an authority figure. Strongly examine the lives of people who make decisions and the reasons they make those decisions. When they are wrong, tell them. When they become arrogant, abusive, obstinate, and unethical, rise up and overthrow them.[5]

Martin Luther King, Jr. once said "The ultimate measure of a man is not where he stands in moments of comfort and convenience, but where he stands at times of challenge and controversy." When will Hal Mumme, C.M. Newton, Larry Ivy, or Charles Wethington deliver a rousing speech that says "I'm embarrassed this happened under my watch. I'm responsible because I'm in charge and the buck stops with me! I can assure you it won't ever happen again under my watch."

Has anyone else noticed Kentucky's leaders reluctance to grab the microphone and take total responsibility? Claude Bassett is *not* solely to blame.

Will The Real Leader Please Stand Up?

Claude Bassett returned from his meeting wearing a look of victory with then Athletics Director, C.M. Newton. It was the fall of 1997 and Bassett was furious with Sandy Bell's insistence he do everything by the rules. There would be no "gray area" with Bell watching Bassett like a hawk. I believe she had strong suspicions about Bassett's rule breaking early in his tenure at Kentucky. Bassett told me, "I got Sandy Bell off my !@#$ and now I can do some real recruiting." Bassett went on to tell me Newton was going to see to it that Bell backed off and let him have more freedom. Considering the number of lies told by Bassett over the years I knew him, there is a possibility this Newton/Bassett meeting was just another fabrication by Bassett, but I strongly suspect the meeting took place. Although Bell would probably never admit it because if she did she would most likely be fired, I believe Newton had Bell back off Bassett to give him more leeway.

When Sandy Wiese was told to meet Sandy Bell in late November to provide information and documents to reveal recruiting violations, she drove to Bell's new home in Garrard County for the meeting. Bell had suffered a broken leg and was struggling to travel, but her explanation for Wiese coming to her house was something different. According to Wiese, Bell told her C.M. Newton and the SEC investigative office recommended Wiese meet Bell at her home because the records would then not be open to the press under the open records laws. I'm sure there is a good explanation. I'll wait to hear!

Newton's legacy has been portrayed as a man representing everything right about college athletics, a man of unquestionable integrity who always did the right thing. He enjoyed a tremendous honeymoon with the press that continues today. When Newton speaks, the whole world of college athletics stops and listens. He is a man of considerable power both inside and outside of college athletics. You can read *Newton's Laws* to hear his own story of greatness as told by Newton to sports writer Billy Reed. My own father, a longtime UK fan, believes Newton is as close to perfection as anyone comes. Like most fans, Dad takes Newton's word as if it were the gospel.

When I was in junior high school, I read a book by Robert Penn Warren called *All The Kings Men*. This novel was based on the legendary Louisiana governor Huey Long and his powerful political machine of the 1920s. There would come a time in Governor Willie Starks' (the fictional character supposedly modeled after Huey Long) reign as governor that he needed to find dirt on a respected judge. All of his advisors told him Judge Irwin was beyond reproach, that he had no dirt. Stark told his advisors there was always dirt on everyone. Yet, on some people you have to dig a little deeper to find it. I've always remembered Willie Starks' advice and it has always proven to be true. Everyone has dirt in their lives they hope will not be discovered. There are no exceptions to this rule. Some public figures are more fortunate than others in their ability to hide their dirt from the public.

Newton is no different than you or I. He isn't perfect and his words should not go unquestioned. Betty Boles Ellison delivers several facts in her book *Kentucky's Domain of Power, Greed, and Corruption*, that would cause any person with common sense to question Newton's sparkling legacy. My own reading of Newton's account of how he came to hire Mumme as the Head Football Coach at the University of Kentucky was enough to let me know that telling the whole truth was not a requirement to becoming a legend. I revealed earlier the story of Newton's hiring of Mumme and I can guarantee you my account is accurate.

Why in God's name would I, "nothing but a high school coach," as Mumme eloquently described me, decide to question the legacy of the great Newton? That's a good question. My advisors tell me I'm committing career suicide by writing anything negative about the gallant Newton. Well, guess what, it doesn't matter. It's my belief that Newton and Mumme have already used their power to spread the message in the college football community that Tony Franklin is a "rat." The false message came from within the UK athletic administration that I was the leak to the press. The press had their sources of leaks throughout the Mumme Era and all of them knew I wasn't their leak. When it became evident I was not the leak, Newton and Wethington, as well as others refused to acknowledge they were wrong about me! The damage that Newton can do to me is over. If I never coach college football again, then so be it. My life's value is not going to be judged by whether I coach college football. My goal in writing this book is to tell the truth and Newton is an important part of that story. Janetta Owens once told me, "The truth doesn't change from day to day." Newton had a role to play in the absurd conditions that UK football is now under. He definitely was willing to accept the praise when Mumme's 1998 team went to the Outback Bowl and he certainly needs to step up and accept his responsibility for the debacle that now exists.

I don't think Mumme would wipe his nose if Newton told him not to. Newton could have provided Mumme with invaluable guidance in staff cohesiveness and relationships. With the numerous times Newton watched practice he was too astute to not see the blundering of Major's defensive coaching philosophy and strategies. With one swift move, Newton could have guaranteed Mumme more success by simply moving Major into a cushy administrative position. Fifty percent of Mumme's problems would have disappeared that day. The staff and player morale would have jumped enough notches with Major gone that even Mumme would have had a much more difficult time "screwing it up." Ivy would eventually have the insight to do what Newton refused to do: get Major off the field.

I believe Newton was tied into the inner circle of college athletics with more information at his fingertips than any other Division I Athletics Director. He could have made a few phone calls and had most any information he wanted at a moment's notice.

I had more contact with Newton in the hiring process of Mumme than in my four years combined as a coach at Kentucky. My only sit-down meeting with Newton while coaching at Kentucky came during my first few days of employment. Mumme and Newton called me to Newton's office to address an anonymous letter from a "UK graduate'" with deep concerns that I had gambled in my past. I told Mumme and Newton there had been times in my younger life where I had participated in gambling, but I had not been able to afford that leisure activity for a few years with the exception of betting thoroughbreds occasionally. Newton asked me if I needed "help," and I responded that I felt my past gambling was not a problem. Mumme later told me I wasn't the only staff member to have gambled in their past and not to worry about it. I've wondered many times since that day to how many anonymous letters Newton had a similar response, especially since former Kentucky Basketball Coach Rick Pitino and current Athletics Director Larry Ivy were both involved in the horse racing industry. Whoever wrote that anonymous letter certainly did a good job if they wanted to scare me. I refused to go near Keeneland for a year with the other coaches because I was scared of another anonymous letter being written. I've narrowed the candidates down for the author of that letter to three people. It's probably one of the same cowards who thrive on the Internet with their secret code name.

When Mumme's clean image began to be questioned by reporters in January 2001, Newton came to his rescue telling reporters that Mumme was a man of integrity and family values. I felt extremely heart warmed to know the arrogant, egotistical, low-integrity man I had worked under for four years was just faking it. You see, C.M. Newton had just spoken and all the evidence made no difference now because we were all supposed to take his word. Shoot, I couldn't wait for Newton to publicly announce that Tim Keane, Darrell Patterson, and Tony Franklin were good family men and men of integrity. I'm sure he is just waiting for the right time.

Ivy would tell me in February 2001 that Dr. Charles Wethington and Newton both believed Mumme's story until the end. The facts were unimportant. They both falsely believed I had continuously released information to the press and the NCAA. They were embarrassed that their Golden Boy (Mumme) was publicly exposed to be far less than perfect. Although they both accepted the praise for hiring Mumme, they didn't seem to want to take the responsibility for his shortcomings. Ivy told me that Newton and Wethington both blocked my chance to be rehired as Offensive Coordinator when Morriss requested it. To hire me back would have been an admission that their Golden Boy was actually lying all along, and, it would have taken stand-up leaders to do that. These guys were too concerned about their legacies to step up and do the right thing.

Newton's accomplishments in college athletics are well documented and I'm sure he is worthy of the accolades he has received. His contributions to Kentucky have been many and I had always been a Newton fan from afar. We all make judgements good and bad, about people without really knowing them. Newton is no different. I can judge him much better now as I had the opportunity to watch him in up-close action. What I saw reminded me of a lesson I learned a long time ago; no one is as good or bad as they appear. I'm sure Newton considers me a "little peon" who doesn't matter, however, he surely misjudged my character and tenacity. He should have chosen another scapegoat. It would have been a lot easier.

"What More Do You Want? Do You Want Blood?"

"What more do you want? Do you want blood?"[7] Dr. Charles Wethington asked the UK Board of Trustees in the spring of 2001. I wish I could have been there to see our fearless leader of the "next great university" address this group of people selected to oversee the running of the University of Kentucky. How dare these people ask tough questions! Everybody cheats, we just got caught. That was the attitude expressed by some die-hard Wildcat fans and a board member. Wethington seemed rattled by the fact that not everybody in the state of Kentucky was buying the story which the Kentucky leadership was spinning.

Dr. Charles Wethington seemed to be a relatively nice man who genuinely wanted Mumme to succeed. After all, Wethington, like Newton, had gone out on a limb to hire this unknown Division II coach from Valdosta State, and he had enjoyed Mumme's modest success the first three years. Wethington occasionally would come to practice and ride the "power" golf cart with Bassett. He also made an appearance at the coaches' offices in the middle of our 2-9 season to show his support.

Leadership starts at the top and rolls downhill. When you are the leader of a Division I state university, the most visible people working for you are the two who make more money than you: the head football coach and head basketball coach. If you're not aware of what they are doing then you better wake up quickly. It may not be right, but I promise you, more people are going to notice your good and bad activities in football and basketball than will ever notice your top professor finding a cure for some deadly disease. It is impossible to watch the daily activities of all of your subordinates or employees, but when a fire starts to burn in your high profile athletic programs, it is probably a good idea to get personally involved in a big way.

If you were President of the University of Kentucky and your Head Football Coach was under an intense investigation, would you want to know the truth? Let's assume that the answer is yes. Would you then want to talk to an employee whom your Head Football Coach has told you has consistently lied and fabricated stories to the press and others if you suddenly find out that those supposed fabrications were true?

Dr. Charles Wethington had absolutely no interest in finding out the entire truth. He never made an attempt to talk to me and on February 9, 2001, refused to meet with me after my request for 30 seconds of his time. My request was to have Dr. Wethington tell me to my face what Ivy had told me in an earlier meeting Wethington had said behind my back. According to Ivy, Wethington stated he believed Mumme's story that I was the source of the problems for the UK football program. Mumme would later excitedly tell another coach that, "Wethington had blocked Franklin's return."

After my press conference to a group of Kentucky reporters, in which I publicly announced Wethington's refusal to talk to me and his refusal to rehire me, I received a call from Wethington's office on February 13, 2001. A Wethington assistant said Wethington wanted to inform me he would talk to me after the investigation was complete. I told the Wethington assistant I would never hear from him. I am still waiting for his call.

Charles Wethington did not want to talk to Tony Franklin. I would have told him things he didn't want to hear including the truth. It is much easier for him to ride off into his "legacy sunset" with his own fairytale memories of Mumme and his regime than to actually look in the eyes of someone who would tell him his last big football coaching hire as University President was a man who embarrassed the state of Kentucky. Maybe Wethington didn't want to really know the truth.

Larry Ivy—A New Legacy Begins

Rob Manchester, the stepson of Larry Ivy and Graduate Assistant football coach, entered my office the week of the 2000 Mississippi State game and said, "Somebody's got to do something about Bassett." Rob was a Paducah Tilghman graduate and we felt a certain kinship with both of us having played and lived in the western part of Kentucky. I had told Rob the entire Memphis deal was going to blow up and put our football program back to the "black-eye reputation" of the late 1970s. Very few people loved UK football anymore than Rob, and he and I both were upset that flagrant cheating and abuse by Bassett were eventually going to get us in NCAA trouble. "You can trust Larry. I think if he knew how bad it was he would do something to stop it," Rob said.

"If I talk to Larry, I'm risking everything," I said, "I'm probably going to anyway, this whole program is going to blow up and it's just pure arrogance and stupidity. I've got to talk to Larry for other reasons anyway."

Guy Morriss later came into my office, after Rob had left, and we discussed the same scenario. Guy and I decided we should both talk with Ivy to see if he could discreetly do anything to stop Bassett before it became an investigation. Neither of us trusted Mumme to handle it. We both thought Mumme knew what Bassett was doing but was too arrogant to understand he was going to get caught because of Bassett's flagrant public flaunting of the Memphis Melrose group.

Guy had a personal relationship with Ivy and felt like he could trust Ivy to keep their conversation private. He was right, to my knowledge Ivy never told Mumme that Morriss had been to see him prior to the Mississippi State game. According to Morriss, he told Ivy the Memphis relationship was going to explode on us and that Bassett was becoming too flagrant in his abuses. Morriss also told Ivy Bassett was going to have the Memphis coaches and players in that weekend and Bassett was going to be paying cash for a hotel room at the Hyatt, which was a brazen NCAA violation. Ivy, evidently, chose to not do anything to prevent the incident, instead waiting to see how public the problems were.

An Attempt To Escape

Morriss later went with me to the University of North Carolina in December 2001 to interview for a co-offensive coordinator position. He was certain, just as I, that Kentucky football under Mumme was finished. New North Carolina Head Coach John Bunting and Morriss had played nine years together in the NFL. Although I gave 95% of a 6-hour clinic to Bunting of what we would do with their offense, Morriss was the key to the job because Bunting knew him. We knew at the end of the interview that Bunting liked what he saw. After it was over, he called us into a back room and asked us if we were "clean" with the NCAA. We both assured him that we were and the next day we had Sandy Bell call him to tell him that we were clean. We were both to be blindsided, however, by the national release of Claude Bassett's $1400 money order. North Carolina had nothing to do with us after that.

Guy and I were both disappointed the North Carolina situation didn't work out. We had been excited about the opportunity to run our offense with a real defensive coach and a head coach who didn't worry about stats, but was only concerned with victory. It is astonishing how things work out sometimes. Morriss would not be the Head Coach at the University of Kentucky right now and I might not have written this book if we had gone to coach the UNC Tarheels.

Ivy/Franklin Meeting—#1

Larry Ivy and I met at the Campbell House restaurant on a weeknight following the 2000 Kentucky vs. Mississippi State game. My purpose of calling Ivy for the meeting included three primary goals: (1.) Request his help to have Mumme and Bassett stop their smear campaign against me to alumni, coaches, staff, and others; treat me with respect and honor his commitment to try to help me pursue other coaching jobs after the season as he had promised. (2.) Follow up Morriss' visit and warning to Ivy of the potential blow up concerning Kentucky and the Memphis Melrose connection. (3.) Request his assistance to prompt Mumme to be professional and include me in game and practice planning so that I could increase our chances to be successful in the remaining games.

I have already mentioned the Internet report released by "rbs" saying I had "family concerns." I told Ivy I would give him the opportunity to shut Mumme up first, and that if he failed to do so I would take matters into my own hands. My explanation for wanting to leave Mumme after I found future employment was also given and Ivy said that he understood. We discussed the football situation and I told him Mumme would be a much greater coach now that Ivy had taken measures to get rid of Major. The dismal offensive point production would entice Mumme to go back to work because his offensive genius label, had been damaged, and that hurt his ego. I believe Ivy had absolutely no intention of doing anything but trying to help Mumme succeed. Mumme was still filling up Commonwealth Stadium and Ivy felt with some new assistant coaching blood maybe Mumme could win again.

The conversation about Memphis was enlightening. I told Ivy if Bassett and Mumme wanted to flagrantly cheat to get players it was their business. Ivy responded, "Sometimes you've got to cheat to get a good player." I told Ivy I would not be a part of that, but they could cheat all they wanted.

"The problem you have is not necessarily cheating, it is flagrantly taunting your cheating in public," I said.

The 2000 summer camp UK apparel escapades in front of visiting coaches, the sideline warm-up jackets from the Mississippi State game taken to the Lexington Bluegrass Airport, and the dinner at Malone's with another group of parents and recruits on official visits which included the unofficial visiting group from Memphis, were all examples of flaunting your cheating. I told Ivy he might want to read Richard Ernsberger's book *Bragging Rights* before he made a national announcement that he was hiring Tim Thompson to be his new assistant football coach or his career as Athletic Director might be short lived.

Our conversation's goal was to solve my problems with Mumme in a professional way and to let Ivy quietly solve the Bassett problem. When I left Ivy he was appreciative and I was fairly certain that Ivy would try to solve the problems with a strong verbal reprimand to Mumme. He implied he would simply try to help Mumme put a lid on Bassett and move on. Bassett was a concern to Ivy, but he hoped by letting Mumme handle it, there might be no need to do anything else. There was no doubt in my mind when I left Ivy he wanted to keep Mumme as his head football coach and, if possible, try to start "damage control" with the Memphis situation without having to involve compliance if possible. I felt confident he could accomplish his goals if Mumme willingly cooperated.

The following morning Mumme walked into my office and for the first time in several days spoke to me with civility. He was nervous and giddy, and I could tell Ivy had already said something to him. What happened after that was pure stupidity on Mumme's part. For some reason, of which I am still not sure, Ivy felt he had to report to Bell the possibility of the sideline jackets being taken by the Memphis group. I think Ivy must have felt there was too big of a chance for others to find out because, as I had told him, several people were aware of the jackets being gone. Mumme then went absolutely nuts! He began his full-time smear campaign against me immediately to anyone and everyone who would listen. Instead of keeping his egotistical mouth shut and letting the news run its course, Mumme blabbered to everyone that nothing was wrong and that Franklin had framed Bassett. I had hoped my meeting with Ivy would force him to finish the year in a professional manner and that with Ivy in control he could fix Kentucky's problems with Memphis before they became public. Instead it blew up because of Mumme's ego. He cried wolf so many times that eventually no one wanted to hear him. I strongly believe if Mumme had simply stepped up and came clean with the public, he would still be Kentucky's Head Football Coach. A simple apology with a full acceptance of responsibility and his immediate firing of Bassett would have probably stopped the entire investigation and 90% of Kentucky's problems would have never been exposed. Instead, as in most instances in history, the cover-up and denials would become worse than the actual problem.

Ivy/Franklin Meeting— #2

During our first meeting, Ivy asked me if there was any hard paper evidence on Bassett that he could use to fire him. I responded, "There are a million. All you have to do is look."

A week later Ivy called me at my house and said, "I want that fat !@#$. Do you have anything at all that I can use? He is going to !@#$ up this whole program if I don't get rid of him now."

"Where do you live?" I asked.

Ivy gave me directions to his town house, and five minutes later I arrived and handed Ivy a document I had kept a copy of since the summer camp of 1999. Hatcher had come to me and asked for advice on how to handle the now famous Vernon Cooper letter. Cooper had sent Bassett a $500 check for UK Camp Funds, but Bassett had cashed the check himself and Cooper's letter was demanding to know what happened. Cooper had written the letter to Janetta Owens because of her long time friendship and trust. Janetta gave the letter to Hatcher who was Camp Director and he immediately came to me. I had advised Hatcher on many issues of camp, as Mumme had asked me to do when Hatcher had taken over the camps from me in 1998, and this was a possible major problem for him. I told Hatcher he better handle it swiftly because Bassett would try to make it Hatcher's fault if he got the chance. Hatcher took care of the incident by advising Bassett to send $500 back to Cooper and also to write an apology letter. When Hatcher left for Valdosta State, he asked me to keep a copy of the letter and check in my camp files and I did so. When Ivy decided to fire Bassett the letter and a copy of the cancelled check were all he needed.

I believe Bassett had tried as hard as he could to destroy my life. He even convinced a big-time UK fan and pal from my hometown to turn against me and join his attempt to smear me. If I had enough moral fiber about me I would have delivered him a long time before, but I was abiding by the "good old boys" philosophy that you keep your mouth shut no matter what. I waited until he personally hurt me and my family before I helped to deliver him his walking papers. If he and Mumme had left me and my family out of their smear campaign, I would have selfishly decided not to assist Ivy, but this had become personal through their calculated attacks. I felt no remorse for assisting Ivy because of their vengeful actions. They actually believed I would sit passively and allow them to smear my character with no response. They made a sever error in misjudging my character and resolve.

Ivy was now deeply concerned about how fast and how far the Memphis deal was going. He asked for help. I told him that Bassett's recruiting assistant, Sandy Wiese, had documented everything for two years, at my suggestion, in order to protect herself. I believed Bassett would have placed any blame on her if she had not kept records. Wiese trusted me and I told Ivy if he needed her to help him I would ask her to comply under one condition; Ivy must promise me she would keep her job or a similar paying job at Kentucky and he would also keep Mumme from abusing her. Ivy promised me he would do both. He called me a few days after our second meeting and I reaffirmed with Ivy she would be protected if she told the truth. Wiese honored Ivy's request and she provided documents that enabled a thorough investigation by UK compliance. Her honesty saved the University of Kentucky from much more severe penalties by the NCAA. If not for Wiese's openness and honesty, the NCAA would have investigated Kentucky on their own and the Kentucky football program would be in a worse predicament than it currently is. I assure you, several officials and some boosters don't want a more thorough outside investigation.

Ivy's meeting with Wiese opened up his eyes to just how blatantly flagrant Bassett's violations had been. In my opinion, he knew there was no way he could keep all of the violations from the press because too many people knew. It was time to start damage control, and that meant involving Bell.

Mumme continued playing the blame game, even after he was made aware of the facts. Wiese's recruiting duties and administrative duties were immediately and dramatically cut and Mumme confronted Wiese after her meeting with Ivy and asked her why she had not come to him first. Wiese did not go to Mumme first because she felt it would cost her her job. Mumme had previously questioned Sandy's reporting of other actions by Bassett and had left her under the impression he didn't want to hear any negative reports about Bassett. She trusted Ivy would honor his word because I had promised her he would.

Ivy blatantly lied to me. He used Wiese to get documents and information that would help Kentucky look as if they had done a thorough job of self-investigation. Once they had finished using Wiese, and they were sure she couldn't hurt them with any more information, they would look for a way to get rid of her. I strongly suspect Mumme and Bassett used the remaining student workers and office staff to look for "dirt" to give the university information that would justify the firing of Wiese. I believe through Bassett's instructions, he directed a student office worker to the documents Kentucky used in her dismissal. It's my belief that although Bassett was gone, through Mumme and others, he was still able to direct a revenge attack against Wiese.

Why would Ivy allow Bassett to still have any input in any of the university's decision making? I believe Bassett and Mumme forced Ivy's hand by threatening to reveal more information than Ivy was willing to have exposed. Those details will be revealed later. I am sure Ivy and UK officials would say they dismissed Sandy because of her involvement, by being Bassett's assistant, in his recruiting violations and because they had no choice since she "violated university policy." If Kentucky was going to dismiss everyone who had violated university policy then there would be several more people not employed at the university. No, this was a selective firing. Ivy and Kentucky sacrificed Wiese because, in my opinion, they believed she would not fight back and that she was expendable. She didn't have 20 years of dirt on Ivy or other administrators at Kentucky like others may have.

Ivy/Franklin Meeting—#3

My cell phone rang and it was Ivy on the other end. It was late January and Ivy requested my help one more time. His request was a little different than our other meetings. Ivy said, "I need something on Mumme. Do you have anything?"

"Meet me at my house in 30 minutes and we'll talk," I replied.

By this time I knew that Ivy was totally untrustworthy, but I didn't care. If there was anything that I could do to help send Mumme on his way out of Kentucky, I would be happy to do it. Mumme had spent two solid months doing everything in his power to attack my character with malicious lies in my home state. I was going to go after Mumme myself, but I had planned to wait until after national signing day to hold a press conference and to tell of his many childish actions. I didn't want to hurt Kentucky's recruiting for their next Head Coach because I was certain Mumme would hang himself and force his own firing before the 2001 season kicked off.

To my knowledge, the only information I gave Ivy that was used in Mumme's dismissal was my confirmation of Ivy's question about Leach having called to warn Mumme about the recruiting violations that occurred during the visit of the defensive lineman who later visited Oklahoma. Mumme had also once told me to ask a high school coach to change the transcript of a defensive lineman whom we had signed but was struggling to qualify. I never asked! That request, however, was my word against Mumme's word and that wasn't enough. I wish I had something of more substance because I certainly would have liked to repay Mumme for the two months of hell he had recently put me through.

"What more do you all need? The man has been in charge of this program for four years with his closest confidant publicly breaking dozens of NCAA rules. I can't believe you need anymore than that. Pay him off if you have to. It will save the university money in the long run." I continued, "There is no way you'll ever convince me he didn't know what Bassett was doing and if he didn't know, you should fire him anyway for being incompetent."

Ivy left my house after a less than a 30-minute question and answer session. I didn't feel he thought they had enough to fire Mumme without paying him, but I thought his knowledge of the Oklahoma recruiting incident was enough. Later on, I was informed the Oklahoma incident was one of Ivy's biggest piece of evidence used to buy out Mumme.

Not turning in the evidence of possible violations on the recruitment of the Oklahoma recruit would become Mumme's nightmare. It would cost Mumme a lot of money as Ivy and Kentucky now had a legal reason not to pay Mumme because he had possibly violated his contract by personally knowing of the breaking of NCAA rules. Why then did UK pay Mumme $1 million over the next four years as part of his terms to leave? Did Mumme have something on Ivy and Kentucky or was Kentucky just being nice to a coach whose program was guilty of breaking dozens of NCAA rules?

The Buyout

Mumme's lawyers looked at Ivy and the Kentucky attorney and told them their offer of $200,000 in "severance pay" was not enough. The Texas-based attorney representing Mumme wasn't about to accept this original lowball offer.

Ivy and the Kentucky attorney implied they didn't have to pay Mumme anything, since they had Mike Leach's testimony implicating Mumme in a possible NCAA violation concerning his failure to notify the UK compliance office about an Oklahoma high school recruit's improper recruiting trip to Kentucky. According to Ivy, Mumme had clearly violated his contract and Kentucky didn't have to pay him a penny.

There have many criticisms concerning Mumme over the last year, but no one could criticize him when the subject was money. He may have been lacking in some areas, but when it came to collecting money for himself, Mumme was very shrewd. He certainly knew how to take care of himself. And he might take anyone down to collect his money.

*The Mumme legal team and Hal told Ivy and the Kentucky lawyer Leach had just spent several moments on the phone with them and he was **not** telling them the same story Ivy and his attorneys were spinning. The Mumme team also informed Ivy if he was so interested in pursuing the **entire** truth of NCAA violations they needed to extend their investigation back to the years prior to Mumme's arrival as Kentucky's head coach. The investigation must include "Booster #1" and "Booster #2," two of Ivy's close friends and confidants, and their role in securing Kentucky recruits in the past.*

What a game of poker Mumme and Ivy were now playing! Who would blink first? Was there dirt on "Booster #1" and "Booster #2" or was Mumme simply taking a wild shot in hopes of getting more money? Ivy and the Kentucky attorney made a contact with other sources and then changed their original offer. The $200,000 had ballooned to $1 million to be paid over four years. The Mumme team decide to accept this offer of "severance pay."

On more than one occasion Mumme had bragged to me about how much money Kentucky would have to pay him if they fired him. "Booster #1" and "Booster #2" inadvertently became Mumme's best friends in his time of need. Mumme wasn't paid his full contract buyout of more than two million dollars which he would have been entitled to had he not broken his contract, but he shrewdly negotiated a pretty good payout for a man who had clearly violated his contract.

Who told this story of hard-core poker and how in the world did Tony Franklin get a blow-by-blow account? You have to understand the ego of Mumme to understand how I, of all people, could get this story. This is Mumme's Story told by Hal Mumme. He relayed his buyout to someone close to me who called and gave me the details as told to them by Mumme.

Although the story is paraphrased with the conversation dialogue not being exact, it is the gist of how Mumme described the negotiation. His ego wouldn't allow him to keep his mouth shut.

"Booster #1" and "Booster #2", The Good Old Boys Are In Charge

Ivy tried to save Mumme from himself, but it had been an impossible task. However, when it came time to fire Mumme, Ivy's own dirt or friends with dirt, had cost Kentucky $1 million. When Ivy decided to go after Mumme, he had forgotten a cardinal rule in life: don't throw stones if you live in a glass house. Ivy's long time friends "Booster #1" and "Booster #2" were in Ivy's glass house with him.

"Booster #1" had been a visible part of the UK athletic program for years. In my four years at Kentucky I got to listen to him brag on more than one occasion about his financial help in securing Kentucky players in the past. I always thought he was full of hot air. If a man had to brag about cheating to buy players then he was desperately trying to accommodate for other shortcomings in his own life. His self-proclaimed love for Wildcat football was second to his desire for attention. An old friend of mine pledged over $1 million to Kentucky and I've never heard him once need to brag to a group of people about his love for Kentucky and I guarantee you he never bought a player.

Mumme and "Booster #1" were occasional social partners. Did "Booster #1" open his mouth one too many times and brag to Mumme about his past contributions to Kentucky players? My guess would be a definite yes!

"Booster #1" seemed to know every detail of the Kentucky football fiasco. "Booster #1" was occasionally hanging out with Mumme late in his tenure as UK's Head Coach and since Mumme was telling stories, I'm sure "Booster #1" had to jump in with his own. I believe on negotiation day, some of "Booster #1's" stories came back to haunt Ivy.

I received a phone call immediately following the Kentucky/Larry Ivy press conference that announced Mumme's "resignation." A reporter who had called me numerous times over the last 90 days was giving it one more shot. My standard answer to all reporters was that I would have something to say, but not until after national signing day.

The reporter said, "Tony, 'Booster #1' just told a group of people that you had a two-hour meeting with Larry Ivy yesterday and gave him the information to fire Mumme."

I replied, "Well, I was in Mayfield yesterday, I'd have to say that's not true. I wish I could take credit for it (Mumme's firing), but I'm afraid I cannot."

The great UK football lover, "Booster #1" evidently couldn't keep his mouth shut again. I assume Ivy had told "Booster #1" about Ivy's 30-minute meeting several days before at my house, but the story was better now that it was a two-hour meeting the day before, not several days before. "Booster #1," thanks for giving me the credit for getting Mumme fired, but I just can't honestly accept it. I promise you I would if I could.

I wasn't around "Booster #2" as often as "Booster #1" and I didn't hear him brag about past recruiting purchases at Kentucky. He did, however, tell me in the summer of 2000, that he was currently involved in the attempt to secure a UK recruit and asked my opinion as to how good the player was. I told him that the player was definitely needed and he assured me he was going to get it done. That player did not sign with Kentucky, so I'm not certain if "Booster #2" was just trying to show off or if that player got a better offer, or simply refused to be bought.

"Booster #1" and "Booster #2" are two of Ivy's close friends and top confidants. All of the UK fans, alumni, and boosters should be happy to know with them advising Ivy, the UK athletic future is bright. Unfortunately, high moral and ethical standards may not be top priority.

I originally planned to print the name of "Booster #1," especially since he has had no trouble using my name as a scapegoat. My decision to not use his name is based on protecting former and current players at Kentucky. It has nothing to do with protecting him.

Ivy/Franklin Meeting—#4 The Final

My final meeting with Larry Ivy came on February the 8th or 9th at his office. I called Ivy and told him I wanted to look him in the eye and have him tell me to my face why they (Wethington and Ivy) had refused Guy Morriss' request to bring me back as his offensive coordinator. Ivy told me that Wethington and C.M. Newton had both falsely believed Mumme's stories that I had released information to the press and made this embarrassment for the university. Morriss had previously told me Wethington had given him an ultimatum to take the head job without me or else not take the head job period. Ivy told me he tried to tell Wethington and Newton not to blame me, but they wouldn't listen.

This meeting took all of two minutes and I heard all I needed to hear. Ivy had become extremely predictable during the past couple of months. He used people to accomplish his immediate goals, and then played a political game to cover his own butt. I have no doubt Ivy wasn't fighting very hard to clear my name.

Ivy will have to stay on his toes to survive at Kentucky. He played both sides of the fence during the investigation and I'm sure that he's made more enemies than this author. I'll be watching the daily newspaper to follow his career closely.

Franklin's Final View

Ivy, Newton, and Wethington all played a role in the fiasco that took place at Kentucky. Ivy was the most proactive of the three, making some early tough decisions to try to prevent Mumme from hanging himself. When his efforts failed, however, he sacrificed his integrity and honor by allowing the dismissal of Sandy Wiese and by paying off Mumme.

Newton was portrayed as an innocent bystander who had briefly begun to enjoy his retirement when suddenly things fell apart for Mumme. Many would like to think Ivy was in charge when all the trouble started, but that simply is not true. Newton was Athletic Director during some of the violations, as well as continuing today as a well-paid ($50,000 per year) consultant to the Athletic Department, and stood by Mumme even when it was evident that Mumme was lying. Publicly, it appeared to me, that he had hung his old buddy Ivy out to take all the heat.

Conclusion

I spoke to Ivy and Ivy only. I never released any information to the press, UK Compliance, or the NCAA until after they talked to every UK personnel they needed. My only time to release information to the press came after Mumme's dismissal and national signing day. All of the reporters I had supposedly released information to sat in my home waiting to hear my story for the first time in early February. Several of those reporters had called me on an almost daily basis to lure me into talking. Some used creative techniques to try to pry information out of me. I refrained each time. I was eventually vindicated by most of the rumormongers and the reporters who followed this story daily. However, Wethington and Newton decided to continue to believe the stories, or did they? Did Ivy ever tell them about Morriss and my early conversations with him and his failed attempt to control the leakage about Bassett? Did he tell them that our meeting's goal was to save UK football, not destroy it? NO, I doubt it. I think Ivy eventually used me as his scapegoat. I believe Ivy let Mumme, Newton, and Wethington think I was releasing information to the press, compliance and the NCAA because it allowed him the freedom to pursue Bassett and eventually Mumme without seeming to break the "good old boys code." Ivy wanted to portray himself as sympathetic to Mumme in the beginning and he wanted to show them he was forced to fire Mumme in the end. All three men had a common trait: cowardice. Not one of them had the courage to step up, to ever tell the truth, and to say, "I'm in charge. The buck stops here. I'm embarrassed that this happened under my watch. I promise all those responsible will be terminated and this will not happen again under my watch." No, they all had other agendas. Newton and Wethington were protecting their precious legacies and Ivy was just starting one.

The easiest thing to do was to find some "schmuck" to lay off as a "rat" and push the blame and the anger of their cronies onto someone else. Their only problem was that they picked the wrong "schmuck." They should have done better research. My father and mother taught me at a young age to not be afraid to stand alone and fight for what's right, no matter what the cost. You see, Mr. Ivy, Mr. Newton, Mr. Wethington, and Mr. Mumme, I truly don't care about what you and your cronies think. A man leaves this world with nothing but his integrity, and I can promise you that your combined efforts can't touch mine. You guys made a calculated mistake. You picked the wrong scapegoat. The truth should not hurt, but for you men concerned about image and legacy, the truth will hurt.

LESSON #20—John C. Maxwell states in his book, *The Right to Lead,* "Few things are more dangerous than a leader with an unexamined life." [6] When a leader decides he is almighty and the public is his servant rather than his being a public servant, then we have a potential disaster. History teaches us that leaders who go unchecked by the public can easily become tyrants. I taught history for 15 years and I know history teaches lessons if we are willing and observant enough to recognize the facts. We should never sit back and accept the word of someone simply because they are an authority figure. Strongly examine the lives of people who make decisions and the reasons they make those decisions. When they are wrong, tell them. When they become arrogant, abusive, obstinate, and unethical, rise up and overthrow them. Never forget, the men and women who founded our country refused to allow their leader's policies to go unexamined.

CHAPTER 21

THE FUTURE

Lesson 21—Opportunity knocks at unexpected times. You must be prepared to take its challenge when it arrives. Don't complain about the timing of the opportunity, just take it and run. It may never come again.

Wildcat Football Forever

The University of Kentucky will eventually find the right coach to take this program to the next level and maintain it. The coach is out there somewhere right now. He will be a man who doesn't make excuses, believes in winning with integrity, and is strong in character. He won't listen to all the old timers excuses of why you have to cheat to win, and he will be heavily influenced by the history of newly successful programs like Toledo, Northwestern, Oregon State, and Kansas State. He will find a way to overcome the minor obstacles of winning at Kentucky.

Football can be successful at Kentucky on a consistent basis. It simply takes the right leader. I believe that Guy Morriss can be that leader; however, Dr. Wethington seriously handicapped Guy from day one when he refused to let Guy hire his first choices as assistant coaches. If Morriss gets a fair shot with new president Lee Todd, then he could very well be the leader the Kentucky fans have waited for. If Morriss does not get that shot, then I hope Todd personally takes over the search for a new head coach, because if Ivy is in charge, then Kentucky fans can expect more of the same.

Kentucky football can win big and win consistently. It simply takes the right man and the right vision.

Guy Morriss

New University of Kentucky President Lee Todd is from Earlington, Kentucky, a small town in western Kentucky close to my hometown of Princeton. I spent many days in Earlington as a child with my Uncle Roy Lamberth and his children. I know that Lee Todd has true down home roots and a real work ethic background. I have never met him, but I get a strange feeling he will be a no-nonsense, strong ethical leader. I believe he will judge Morriss simply for his performance and leadership ability as well as his character.

If Guy will stay clear of the Ivy "cronies" and some old-time political boosters and simply coach to the best of his ability, I believe he will thrive. Guy must realize that he has the job he has so clearly wanted and make every decision based on simple football common sense. He must *not* listen to some of the very same men who supported him for the job and helped him to obtain it. Play football now, not politics, and he can be the man Kentucky has wanted for years. I have a strong suspicion Ivy's power and decision-making ability will dwindle considerably now that Todd has taken over.

Morriss must acknowledge that Mumme did do some great things while coaching at Kentucky and not totally eliminate all of Mumme's practice philosophy or offensive style. The recruiting classes of the previous four years need to be utilized to the best of their abilities. If Morriss will make the 2001 offense use their weapons effectively, then he can recruit to his new style of play in the future, but he must win now.

Don't blame the past coach for all the problems. Don't make excuses about a lack of talent. Don't complain about having to speak for free at alumni and coaching functions. Don't berate coaches or players in public or in the press. Don't listen to people who don't matter. Find a way to win now. Find a reason why rather than a reason why not. Treat every player as if he were your own son. All of these preceding comments are pieces of advice that I would give Morriss, but he hasn't asked me so I just have to hope he reads my book.

Morriss can be a winning head coach if he uses the proper moral characteristics. Don't change Guy, not even if it costs you your job or you will be a true hypocrite. I'm hoping you can win and thrive at Kentucky, but I hope more that you win as a person and don't stoop to the lack of integrity that your predecessor and some of your supervisors now possess. You were a good mentor and a good friend at one time and I wish you the best.

My Future

My goals in life have always consisted of making a dramatic difference in the lives of young people. Very soon I will embark on a new adventure of seminar presenting, success and goal workshops, public speaking, and writing. My desire is to teach the valuable lessons that I've learned in my 44 years on this planet and provide a pathway for young people to reach their dreams with as few obstacles as possible.

Hal Mumme

Mumme will reappear as a head coach somewhere. C.M. Newton has enough power to find Mumme a job. Hopefully he will have learned some valuable lessons and can reach his potential as a coach. If he ever learns to control his ego and his emotions he could be one of the top college coaches in the country. He's incredibly talented as an offensive mind and if he is able to put together a good staff, he will make some A.D. look smart for hiring him. It will be interesting to see how long he can keep his mouth shut about the Kentucky fiasco. My guess is he will eventually start "singing." It will be interesting to hear his story. I can't wait!

Claude Bassett

If Kentucky fans and coaches think they've heard the last from Claude Bassett, they're crazy. He'll continue to use some of his media puppets to stir some controversy—even if his name isn't attached to it. Incredibly, he still has some media and Internet groupies who believe his stories and help spread his propaganda. He'll make another big splash, its just a matter of when. If he decides to write a book about his experiences I would love to publish it! We would have to make it a novel, but I believe it would be a best-seller!

LESSON #21—Opportunity knocks at unexpected times. You must be prepared to take its challenge when it arrives. Don't complain about the timing of the opportunity, just take it and run. It may never come again. Guy Morriss has a once in a lifetime opportunity. The conditions aren't perfect, but that is why he has the opportunity. Make it happen!

EPILOGUE

In the summer of 2000 one of my favorite parents in all of my recruiting experiences came to Lexington to bring his son on a visit. Jim Clausen is a former high school coach and current insurance executive in Los Angeles California. His oldest son, Casey is currently the starting quarterback at Tennessee and his middle son Rick was a senior quarterback to be that we had offered a scholarship, and his youngest son Jimmy may be the best of all the Clausen athletes. Rick was offered by several major colleges before signing with LSU in February of 2001.

Jim and his beautiful wife Cathy had brought Rick for an unofficial visit in the spring and were coming back because they liked Mumme's offense and they loved the SEC. We were the leader for his services, and it looked like it was between LSU and us. I had begun to like the Clausen family, and I had enjoyed listening to Jim and Cathy talking about their philosophy of raising their children. I knew Rick was incredibly sharp as a young man and wouldn't want to hear any outlandish recruiting stories or sales pitches.

When I finally got a chance to be alone with Jim I broke the news to him, "Jim, I can not in good faith tell you that this is the right place for your son. I've grown to respect and like you and your family, and I must tell you since your son is a quarterback, his likelihood of being treated fairly is not good. I'm very uncomfortable with what happened to Dusty Bonner this spring and I must be honest with you. There are several things happening here in this football program that make me uncomfortable, and I'm afraid we are on the verge of a scandal. If you are comfortable sending your son here knowing those facts, then I would love to have him, but I wouldn't be able to live with myself if I lied and told you that he would have a fair shot at playing QB or that our program was in good shape."

"Tony, I deeply appreciate your honesty and friendship. We will discuss everything after we get back to California," Jim replied. Rick Clausen committed to LSU shortly thereafter and Jim Clausen eventually called me in January to thank me for not getting his son involved in the mess at Kentucky. I speak to Jim Clausen from time to time and consider him a friend. I look forward to watching his sons Jimmy, Rick and Casey playing football the next few years.

Many UK fans, some college coaches, and athletic directors will think my honesty with the Clausens was a disloyal act to Kentucky and Mumme. I strongly believe in loyalty, but I do not believe in blind loyalty or loyalty to a position. Loyalty may begin because of trust, but it must be continued because of one's actions and character. A leader cannot and should not expect loyalty when he loses his integrity and direction.

My loyalty is now, and always will be first and foremost, to do what I believe to be the right thing when I have a choice. When my threshold of tolerance is tested, then I must look inside to my gut and decide if I can cross my line of values. I have crossed lines of what other people's concept of right and wrong are, but I can't cross my own, for I must be able to sleep at night and look at myself in the mirror when I awaken.

I am not a "goodie two-shoes" or a straight and narrow thinker. Breaking NCAA rules to the point of buying the services of players or paying parents or coaches is something I personally chose not to do, but I don't condemn or dislike everyone who has done it before or who will do it again. It simply crosses over my threshold of tolerance. I personally believe it makes no sense to buy players in today's political climate. You don't gain anything in the long run, because if you win, you will always be tainted by the fact that you did it by cheating.

True & False

My accusers and critics tried to portray me in several ways in which the reader of this book may still be slightly confused. Let me set the record straight on my role in the Mumme era recruiting and coaching scandal of 2000-2001. The following rumors and accusations were floating around during November-December of 2000 and January-February 2001. I will answer each one honestly and distinctly.

- I turned in the recruiting violations to UK compliance—FALSE. I refused to talk to Sandy Bell or any UK compliance person until they were near the end of their investigation and until they had guaranteed me that they had already talked to all other coaches and others in the investigation. My first discussion with Sandy Bell would be near the end of January.

- I wrote letters and sent memos to the NCAA reporting violations—FALSE. I met with the NCAA investigator Jim Elworth at my home in May 2001. This was the first and only contact of any nature with the NCAA in my college coaching experience.

- I released information to news media members that contained facts of recruiting violations, including several Memphis Melrose violations—FALSE. Although questioned hundreds of times, including snow covered reporters knocking on my front door, I refused to give media members information concerning recruiting violations. Although I know some of my former fellow coaches did contact media members and point them in the right direction to find dirt regarding the investigation, I did not do so. My fellow coaches watched in silence as I received blame for what they purposely leaked. My information to the press was given in a press conference after the dismissal of Mumme in February.

- I talked with Larry Ivy about the possible recruiting problems from the Memphis Melrose/UK involvement—TRUE. I met and talked with Larry Ivy and Larry Ivy only. I have given those exact details earlier in this book and have included most of the details from the meetings.

- I conspired with Guy Morriss to have Hal Mumme fired—FALSE. Guy and I probably should have conspired to have Mumme fired, but we didn't have to. Mumme was doing a good enough job of getting himself fired. He certainly didn't need our help. If I could have predicted the scenario that happened, I certainly wouldn't have had my blowout with Mumme. I would have waited until his departure and instead of writing this book I would be game planning for the next game as UK's Offensive Coordinator.

- I conspired to have Claude Bassett fired—FALSE. I definitely helped Ivy in any way possible to make it easier to fire Bassett. My assistance was not a conspiracy; it was simply a matter of handing over the truth on a man who was attacking me and my family. Several employees would have gladly done the same, if asked. My only regret is that I didn't do something about him two years prior. However, in my opinion, it would have been a waste of time as some of the top officials already knew about Bassett anyway and were allowing him to go about his daily cheating with their implied consent. If I had done anything earlier, I believe it would have fallen on deaf ears, just as other reported Bassett violations had with Mumme.

Potential Future Employers

If you want a good football coach who relates well to young people, works endlessly to help you succeed, is a proven successful recruiter, and knows how to run a creative, explosive, and fun offense, then give me a call. However, there are some major liabilities of which you need to be aware:

- Truthful—I will actually tell you the truth if you ask me my opinion, so if you're looking for a "yes-man" to agree with your every move, then I am not your guy.

- Not Blindly Loyal—If you do something unethical to hurt innocent people and are the type of person who is untrustworthy and emotionally immature, I will not follow you, and I will not ask others to risk their children's well being on your behalf.

- Will Not Flagrantly Cheat—If you're looking for a coach to make payments to high school coaches, players, or parents, then I'm not your guy. If you treat people fairly and with respect then I can possibly look the other way for a brief time, but I won't feel good about winning without integrity and will soon leave you.

- Can Be Vindictive—If you are a classic bully and hurt people intentionally and one day decide to attempt to destroy my character, I will attack you with every legal means possible. This may include, but not be limited to, a true book that exposes you for what you really are, and a lawsuit.

I'm sure that this limits my possible college coaching jobs. The coaching circle is still full of "good old boys" network and they don't like it when someone doesn't conform to their Mafia type style of management. However, I believe that somewhere out there is an athletic director and head coach with high ideals and independence who could care less about the "good old boys" network and would like to hire someone exactly like me. I'm looking forward to meeting you both. Until then, I'll do more important things in life.

My final thought is one of regret. In my selfish method to leave Hal Mumme, but to use him and his much-needed reference to land another offensive coordinator job in college football, I didn't get an opportunity to say good-bye in proper fashion. I left without looking him in the eye because of my fear that I couldn't control my anger and would physically do something to him that would cost me more than my coaching future. It is not my style to miss the face-to-face final good-bye, but I guess it wasn't meant to be. All of the things that I would like to have said had to wait too long, but they are finally said in this book.

Conclusion

I have desperately tried not to be overly negative in this book. My intention was to tell a true story of events that have significant meaning for my life and the lives of others. There is no doubt that some purely innocent family members will be hurt by the portrayal of their loved ones in this book. We are each loved by some of our family members in spite of all our misdeeds and warts. Sometimes we are so totally blinded by loyalty to our loved ones that we refuse to see their misdeeds. I wish that I could have written a totally positive book about nothing but good deeds, but I couldn't. It would not have been true. I'm sorry some young people have to hear bad stories about their parents. I only hope that their parents take a long look in the mirror and think twice before hurting innocent people again in the future.

Never in my wildest dreams did I imagine in September 1996, when I started a process to get Hal Mumme the job at Kentucky, that five years later I would be writing a book of this nature. That is what makes life so grand! We never know what is lurking behind the next door. I can't wait for tomorrow to see what is going to challenge me next. Life is truly about the journey, not the destination, and I'm excited daily about the newest journeys that await me.

LESSONS SUMMARIZED . . .

LESSON 1
No matter how outlandish or impossible your dream seems you can accomplish it with a solid plan and by taking immediate and consistent action! However, be careful what you dream because it may come true.

LESSON 2
Phenomenal success takes place only when you are willing to step outside of your comfort zone and expand your circle of influence. Nothing spectacular ever takes place without a willingness to risk everything.

LESSON 3
Leadership does not care who possesses it. There is not an age requirement or experience requirement to be a good leader.

LESSON 4
True friendship is based on caring and honesty. It will survive rough days and tumultuous times.

LESSON 5
All you can do is all you can do, but all you can do is enough.

LESSON 6
The public owes itself the responsibility to not blindly believe any facet of the press without legitimate questioning of the particular reporter's agenda. Read and watch the media daily with a skeptical eye, but be thankful they exist for they truly help prevent corruption and tyranny.

LESSON 7
Success can happen for any business, team, or government as long as you have determined and flexible people dedicated to a cause and selfless in their actions.

LESSON 8
There is an incredible strength in numbers. Every monumental movement has started with one person who is passionate about their beliefs. If

you are truly committed and have a worthwhile idea, thousands will follow you.

LESSON 9

Talent in some people is obvious, while you must dig deeply to uncover value in others. The digging, however, can provide phenomenal returns when you reach and unveil its worthiness.

LESSON 10

Don't ever love a job or a position more than you believe in doing the right thing. Right is right and wrong is wrong. Don't be blinded by your ambitions in your quest for self-promotion.

LESSON 11

Good and evil are constantly at war with each other. Take notice of this conflict and fight to prevent evil from winning the war. Strong ethical leadership can bring out the good in a person and eradicate the evil.

LESSON 12

Beware of the man with the silver tongue for he can make you believe events you saw with your own eyes disappear as if they never happened.

LESSON 13

Be careful with whom you choose to associate because we all become similar to those whom we work with, live with, and are friends with. Pick you friends with meticulous care. They could be your final downfall.

LESSON 14

Yes-Men will get you fired. Hire people who will tell you the truth, not what you want to hear. Hire people who want to be better than you and when they surpass you, hire someone else better than them. Success comes to a team or business when no one cares who gets the credit. A true friend tells you the painful truth every time not just when it's convenient for him.

LESSON 15

Many things in life will happen to you over which you have no control. You can't change those events, but you do have complete and total control over how you respond to what happens to you. Your responses to what happens to you in life will determine the quality of life that you lead. Control your responses.

LESSON 16

It is human nature to enjoy watching someone fall from grace and distinction. Remember, no matter how high you sit on your pedestal, you are one swift wing of an axe away from falling on your face. The same people you once looked down upon will now be gazing down on you.

LESSON 17

The true measure of your character and integrity is what you would do if you thought no one would ever find out. Discipline is doing the right thing when no one is watching. It is our job to keep our leaders in check by exposing their actions, good and bad, when their power begins to impact the lives of others.

LESSON 18

No matter what people do to hurt you or defame you, remember the greatest man to ever live received a much worse fate than we could ever imagine. Don't expect truth and honesty from people and don't be disappointed when they fail to meet your expectations. When you expect little in return, you'll be pleasantly surprised when truth and loyalty emerge in a relationship. Value those few select people who stand by you in times of hardship for they are more valuable than gold.

LESSON 19

Be careful if you decide to roll in the dirt, because you will get dirty. If you choose to get dirty, don't cry when you are exposed. If you do the crime, be willing to do the time.

LESSON 20

"Few things are more dangerous than a leader with an unexamined life." We should never sit back and accept the word of someone simply because they are an authority figure. Strongly examine the lives of people who make decisions and the reasons they make those decisions. When they are wrong, tell them. When they become arrogant, abusive, obstinate, and unethical, rise up and overthrow them.

LESSON 21

Opportunity knocks at unexpected times. You must be prepared to take its challenge when it arrives. Don't complain about the timing of the opportunity, just take it and run. It may never come again.

P.S. I JUST WANTED TO SAY . . .

There were a few things I wanted to say, but I couldn't fit it into the context of this book. This chapter is just a bunch of STUFF thrown together in no certain order.

Best College Coaches No One Has Heard Of:

- Eddie Gran, the Running Backs Coach at Auburn, is one of, if not the best, Running Backs Coach in the country. Gran added Special Teams Coach to his resume in the 2000 season to go along with his Top Ten Recruiter in the South award, given after the 1998 season. I look for Gran to be a top Offensive Coordinator soon, or possibly a head coach in the next few years.

- Mike Cassano, the Running Backs Coach at the University of Massachusetts, has played a large role in UMass' rise to national prominence. His future is very bright.

- Jeff Durden, the former Offensive Coordinator and Quarterback Coach at Morehead State University, is currently the Running Backs Coach at V.M.I. All the coaches who have seen him work with their quarterbacks at camps heavily respect Durden. His Morehead offense was number one in the nation and someone should name him Offensive Coordinator at a top program soon.

- Sonny Dykes, of Texas Tech University, has as much in-depth overall football knowledge as any young coach in college football. Someone better make him Coordinator fast because he won't be around Lubbock waiting very long.

- Rob Spence was just named Offensive Coordinator at Toledo after serving in the same capacity at Hofstra and Louisiana Tech. He's one of the most talented offensive minds in the country and will make somebody a great Top 10 School coordinator when he gets a shot at the big time.

- Joker Phillips, former University of Kentucky Wide Receivers Coach, was recently named to the same position at Notre Dame after gaining respect of coaches everywhere for the job he did at Minnesota. Phillips is one of the top recruiters in the country and should soon be named Head Coach or Coordinator at a good school soon.

- Gunter Brewer of North Carolina has long been one of the top receivers coaches in the country, and should become a Head Coach or Coordinator within they next two years. His success with Randy Moss at Marshall was phenomenal.

- Larry Johnson, the Defensive Line Coach and Special Teams Coordinator for Penn State, has all the tools needed to make a great Head Coach or Defensive Coordinator. Look for Johnson to get his chance soon.

- Dan Wariner was recently named Quarterbacks Coach at the University of Miami, after enjoying a spectacular offensive year as Offensive Coordinator at Murray State University. Being a great clinician and on the field coach makes Wariner a likely candidate for future head-coaching jobs.

- David Elson of Western Kentucky University has proven he may be as good as any young Secondary Coach as there is in college football. A Division I school will grab him soon!

- Mike Scott of West Alabama and Shawn Bostick of Valdosta State University are two of the top young Offensive Line Coaches in the country. Both should rise rapidly in their careers.

- Darrell Patterson, the new Linebackers Coach at Arkansas State University, has Head Coach written all over him. He simply makes every player he coaches better and he handles stress and adversity well.

Top Coordinators Destined for Head Jobs:

- Jim Chaney, the Offensive Coordinator at Purdue, maybe the sharpest offensive mind in America. His combination of recruiting expertise and offensive genius make him one of the top five coordinators in the country. Chaney's work at Purdue has been nothing less than brilliant. Athletic Directors should be beating a path to his door! It will be a shame if Chaney isn't a Head Coach in 2002.

- Noel Mazzone, the Offensive Coordinator at Auburn has Star written all over his future. He has had the unique ability to adjust to his talent and balance the run with the pass. The leadership skills he has learned from Tommy Tuberville, combined with his offensive expertise, make Mazzone a natural winner for A.D.s looking for quick success. Mazzone will take a top job in 2002.

- Bud Foster, the Defensive Coordinator at Virginia Tech, is one of the major reasons for Virginia Tech's rise to national prominence. His defensive expertise, combined with the people building skills which Frank Beamer has used at Tech, make Foster a natural for success as a Division I Head Coach.

Small College Head Coaches Destined for Greatness:

- Mark Whipple, the Head Coach of Division I-AA Massachusetts, has performed miracles at UMass including the NCAA Division I-AA championship in 1998. Already being courted by the NFL, Whipple should make the jump to a Division I Head-Coaching job soon, before the NFL takes away a top man of integrity from college athletics.

- Mickey Matthews of James Madison University jump-started that program in 1999, and appears headed towards an eventual jump to a Division I Head-Coaching job. Matthews was well respected as a Defensive Coordinator and Secondary Coach at Marshall and Georgia before heading to JMU.

- Joe Pannunzio of Murray State University looks ready to follow in the footsteps of former Racer coaches Mike Gottfried, Frank Beamer, and Houston Nutt, all of whom left the Racers for success as Division I coaches. Pannunzio has energized Murray State and invigorated the fans with an exciting brand of football. The Racers will be lucky to keep him for another two years.

- Chris Hatcher, the Head Coach of Valdosta State University, as already noted, is a steal for the first Division I A.D. with enough guts to hire a Head Coach under the age of 30. He will give fans excitement, but more important than filling up the seats, he will win fast and win big!

With NCAA Restrictions, Why Should a Football Recruit Still Go to Kentucky?

Lexington, Kentucky is one of the greatest small cities in America with plenty of cultural and social activity provided in a safe environment.

The UK athletic fans are second to none. Ninety-five percent of the fans support you with class and dignity, win or lose. If you play hard and show class and character, they will pack the stadium 68,000 strong each week.

The overall football facility is second to none. The combination of stadium, weight room, academic center, indoor facility, and practice fields is outstanding!

Future careers and job opportunities are abundant for players who exemplify class and character. Many millionaires have been made over the years from the contacts and opportunities that former UK football players have made during their playing days in Lexington.

The C.A.T.S. academic assistance program is the best in the country. The only people they can't help are those who refuse to accept their assistance.

The greatest overall bar and grill in America sits in Lexington. *Charlie Browns* is the finest eating and drinking establishment in town for locals and visitors. Win or lose, pre-game or post-game, you can guarantee one thing: owners Dave Fuller and Larry Ellington will have the best food and coldest beer in town ready to serve. I've eaten hundreds of meals in four years at CB's and have never had a bad bite! *Charlie Browns* is reason enough by itself for a recruit and his family to spend four years at Kentucky.

Dr. John Perrine is one of the Wildcats team physicians and he is one of the best family care physicians in the country. Perrine practices medicine the old fashioned way, with extreme caring and individual attention. All Kentucky football players and coaches are lucky to be under his care.

There is no doubt in my mind the Wildcats will one day win the SEC in football. Any young man who chooses Kentucky has a great opportunity to be a part of something special. The Sugar Bowl hasn't got enough seats to hold the number of UK fanatics who will show up to support the Wildcats in a Sugar Bowl appearance.

Stand Up People

- Chris Reid is one of the owners of a group of small banks in Western Kentucky based out of Owensboro named Independence Banks. The Reid family has carved a niche in the banking business by doing business the old fashion way—with a handshake and strong character traits.

Chris provided me with my vehicle the last two years of my work at Kentucky as part of the partner-dealership program that the UK Athletic Department uses. Business leaders provide vehicles for the assistant coaches in exchange for season tickets in football and basketball. After my premature departure from the university Chris received a call to tell him if he wanted to remain in the car dealer program and continue to receive his season tickets, then he should assist in retrieving the vehicle from me. I had balked at turning my vehicle in because my contract said I was to receive full benefits through June. Chris told the Kentucky official I had honored my part of the contract and I could keep the vehicle until my contract expired in June. Although Chris and his family were avid UK fans and the tickets were great business assets for their top clients, Chris did what he perceived to be the right thing: he honored his word to me. It's easy to see why Independence Bank is a true American success story. Chris Reid and his family do business the way they treat people—with integrity, character, and respect.

• Scott Schlosser represents a rare breed of teacher/coach. He believes in a simple method of relationships: treat everyone with respect until they prove they don't deserve it, and then fight for what is right without any regrets. As the Head Basketball Coach at Mayfield High School for many years, Schlosser is well known for his tough, disciplined, hard playing teams. His biggest asset to me, in addition to true friendship, was in training me how to battle the "powers" when an attempt to bully or defame you took place. Schlosser's leadership and advice guided me through rough times and helped me "stay the course" during the turmoil when I considered not fighting the wrong. He is truly a stand up guy.

• Steve Aull, the owner of Sports Warehouse in Owensboro is a true American success story. He has proven time and time again you can overcome the odds with simple determination and not being afraid to dream. Aull's independent sporting goods store has survived and thrived during the times when national chain stores have all but eliminated the independent dealer. Steve taught me a lesson in 1980 I've never forgotten: no one cares what your problems are; it is you and you alone that must make your dreams come true. For 21 years, I've called upon Steve to be a source of friendship and sound advice. His leadership and life story inspire me to not be afraid to take chances.

• David Gallagher of Fulton County, Timmy Schlosser of Franklin Simpson, Ron Greene of Calloway County, David Barnes of Daviess

County, Bruce Raley of Owensboro High, Rush Propst of Hoover High, AL, and David and Joe Morris of Mayfield High called me numerous times during my turbulent days following my early departure at Kentucky. Each call was full of friendship, love, guidance, and nurturing. They simply wanted me to know they believed in me and supported me no matter what! Their camaraderie made me glad I was, and always will be, part of the brethren in the high school coaching profession.

- Current School Superintendent Bruce Johnson of Mercer County and former Mayfield City Schools Superintendent Don Sparks, should give nationwide seminars to every person involved in education. During my 20-plus years of working in the education field I have worked for a few really bad leaders. Sparks and Johnson were different; they had a simple method of leadership I will never forget. They always asked themselves one question before making a decision: will this decision serve the best interest of the students? If the answer was yes, they did it if the answer was no, they didn't. Both men provided hope that effective, non-political leadership stills exist in our education system.

- While recruiting running back Artose Pinner of Hopkinsville High, I encountered two of the most unselfish, determined, and caring people that I have had the privilege of meeting in my life. Winn and Linda Radford knew Artose as a friend of their son Winn IV. They never once looked at him as a football player; they only saw him as a young man with character traits they felt were worth fighting for. The Radfords made it very clear they didn't care if Artose ever played a down of football for Kentucky. They only wanted him to have the opportunity for an education. Their persistence in making sure he finished his education at Hopkinsville strong enough to be eligible to attend Kentucky, along with Pinner's hard work in the classroom, have put him on schedule to graduate on time from Kentucky with good grades. Winn and Linda Radford represent what is good in our society—unconditional caring!

Home Cooked Meals

Recruiting can be a tiresome and monotonous routine, especially if you eat fast food as frequently as most college coaches. Occasionally you are presented with a fabulous home cooked meal that entices you to go home and brag to your wife. Robbie Holmes, the mother of Martez Johnson provided me with undoubtedly the finest home cooking in all of Detroit, Michigan. On three occasions Robbie's mixture of southern vegetables and meats made me feel as if I was back home as a kid sitting at a Sunday feast. Karen Davis, the mother of Jeremy Davis, made the best lasagna I have ever eaten. It was so good my wife eventually called to get the recipe. We have had several lasagna meals with Karen Davis in our minds since then. Thank you Robbie and Karen for making the recruiting road a lot more comfortable.

Scary Plane Rides

I logged well over 300,000 miles in my recruiting trips for Kentucky and for two years I felt that flying was the only way to travel. However, on a two-hour flight from Shreveport, Louisiana to Memphis, Tennessee, I promised numerous times if we landed alive I would never fly again. Mike Leach and I had been recruiting current LSU receiver, Reggie Robinson, and we were heading back to Lexington. A storm had begun to blow in off the Gulf of Mexico, but the airline decided they could avoid most of the rough air. They were wrong! The small jet never could get above the storm and we were tossed for nearly the entire trip. The flight attendant handed out throw-up bags as she crawled in the aisle, while passengers prayed, cried, or did both. Leach was telling me a story during the trip and as always, showed no emotion. Leach, did interrupt his story briefly to say, "I hope this thing lands," before going right back to his story. I was petrified and thought for sure that we wouldn't make it.

When we finally landed in Memphis, the passenger in front of me turned and said, "I knew we weren't going to crash because I have survived one plane crash in my life and no one is ever in two crashes in their life." I wish he had told me this during the flight, not after it.

Leach and I jumped on another small jet from Memphis into Lexington, but flying for me would never be the same. The next few weeks I had bad experiences on two more flights and would eventually decide if I could drive to visit a recruit that would be my preferred form of transportation.

I will miss coaching college football, but I will not miss the daily take-offs and landings from the many airports I visited the last four years.

Answering the Critics

- Why are you bashing the University of Kentucky?

Evidently you haven't read this book. Ninety percent of the people portrayed in this book are portrayed in a positive light. Even the people I have the most difficult problems with are portrayed positively in some manner. However, when you tell the truth, it is not always pretty and it can't be all good. Numerous people who worked for the University of Kentucky did things that caused pain and injury to others. My lifetime admiration and support for Kentucky was not going to stop me from shining some light on their misdeeds.

- It appears that you are vindictive. Why are you so angry?

My former profession as a college football coach is one of the most publicly criticized professions in the world. I understand the nature of the profession and fully accept the football criticism. The attacks that came to me, however, were not football related. They were strictly personal and malicious, at times even including my family. The nature of society promotes and allows the weak to be attacked and maligned. If you allow people to malign you and abuse you, then you deserve what you get. Our country is based upon fighting for individual rights and freedoms. If I am attacked, I have a choice to accept the consequences or to launch a full-scale assault. My past experience has taught me it is always better to be proactive than to sit and hope for the best. Anger is probably not the best word to describe my emotions—challenged would probably be a better term.

- You seem to be obsessed with Hal Mumme. Why?

In November, December, and January my frustration was probably directed more at Mumme than any other person involved. From February until now, however, I have learned new facts which direct my frustration more towards Ivy, Wethington, and Newton. I believe Mumme could have easily been forced to shut his mouth and act as a professional, but because of poor leadership from his superiors, he was allowed to continue his ranting and raving until it was eventually out of control.

- Why do you "cry" now when you were the one to initiate your departure?

  The fiasco that occurred at Kentucky could have easily been avoided with sound leadership and strong professionalism. Ninety-nine percent of the colleges in the country would not have had the final scenario that occurred between Mumme and myself. The reason I "cry" is because I was a part of that 1% and the unprofessional handling of our break-up has possibly cost me my career. If the major leaders involved in this situation had simply done the professional thing, we wouldn't be having this dialogue.

- Why did you write negative items about seemingly minor characters in this story?

  I struggled at times because of my own questioning of whether or not to include some of the minor characters. The reason I eventually included some of those people was because I think we should all be held accountable for our actions, especially if we publicly portray an image that tends to say we are righteous and do-gooders.

- I don't believe Bassett was the only cheater on the staff and since you had success as a recruiter you were probably cheating too!

  Everybody has a threshhold for tolerance. My threshhold of stepping over the line and cheating was defined by certain rules I had for myself. I'm not here to proclaim that I am a "goody-two shoes" or a perfect moral human. Anyone who knows me well knows that is not true. I simply chose not to pay players or coaches. It was a decision I made before beginning my career at Kentucky. Did I break rules? Yes! Everybody in college football breaks rules at one time or another. There are too many to know them all and we all have broken rules. My bottom line in recruiting was to ask myself this question: Does it make common sense to do it or not? Occasionally you could use common sense and still break rules. Compliance even breaks rules sometimes. My conscience wouldn't allow me to get into the exchange of money or gifts for players. I don't begrudge those who do it, I'm just not comfortable with it.

- If Bassett and Mumme had never attacked you, would you have talked to Ivy anyway?

  No! Maybe I was wrong, because the Kentucky fiasco would have been much worse if I had not had my conversation with Ivy. The NCAA would have entered later, on their own, and Claude Bassett, Hal Mumme, and Tim Thompson would have all been working together at Kentucky. The dreaded "Death Penalty" word could even have been thrown around. However, I would have left and been watching from another college had they just been professionals. The reason I even felt comfortable enough to see Ivy was because he was an "Old School" Athletic Director and I knew he would try to fix things if he could. For those of you who want to portray me as someone who saw evil and tried to fix it, I'm sorry to disappoint you, but I've got to be truthful. I could have easily left if only they had acted as professionals.

- Everybody in college football cheats—we just got caught!

You're right and you're wrong. Does everybody have someone on their staff who breaks rules? Yes. Actually everybody on their staff has broken rules. It is impossible not to. The biggest difference in cheater and non-cheaters is the use of money or other goods to entice a player to come to your school. Every college I came in contact with on the road has at one time or another broken a rule. Only a few, however, are actually buying players. Boosters are usually the culprits, but occasionally a coach will also be involved in money or goods exchanges.

- Why don't you go away (move), shut-up, and leave the Wildcats alone?

First of all, this is my home state and I take great pride in being from Kentucky. I'll leave it only when there is a reason, not when a few bullies think they can run me out of state. The reason I won't shut-up is I have no reason to shut-up. My perspective is unique considering my background and inside knowledge of what is going on. Everybody in power should have checks and balances and when they begin to squirm when questioned, you know there is something worth talking about. Finally, I've never done anything to hurt the Wildcats. I was a fan long before the arrival of Hal Mumme and I'll be a fan for years to come.

- You wrote a book to make money and betrayed the trust of your confidants.

I definitely want to make money on my book, however, there is no guarantee. I've self-published, meaning I am personally investing the money to write and publish the book. My future livelihood depends on a certain amount of success in selling this book, so I of course want to make money. As far as betrayal of my confidants, all of those who deserve to know the content of the book have read a pre-published edition and have been given an opportunity to request omissions. The doers of bad deeds who purposely set out to hurt me deserve no act of loyalty and confidence. Each one has the ability to write their own recalling of the events and tell their story. I'd be more than willing to publish their accounts.

- You're a liar! None of these events concerning our leaders ever occurred. You're just a vindictive fired coach who had to make up stories!

I wondered when you would call or write. When my legal issues arrive in court, I'll put my hand on a Bible and tell the same story under oath. If you tell the truth, you don't have to worry about what you've previously said, because the next time you recall the story it won't change.

All other criticisms can be discussed at www.badcoaches.com

END NOTES

1. Mark Story and John Lassetter, *Lexington Herald Leader*, February 2, 2001.

2. John C. Maxwell, *The 21 Irrefutable Laws of Leadership*, Nashville Thomas Nelson, Inc. 1998.

3. John C. Maxwell, *The 21 Irrefutable Laws of Leadership*, Nashville Thomas Nelson, Inc. 1998.

4. John C. Maxwell, *The Rights To Lead*, Nashville: J. Countryman, A Division of Thomas Nelson, Inc.

5. John C. Maxwell, *The Rights To Lead*, Nashville: J. Countryman, A Division of Thomas Nelson, Inc.

6. John C. Maxwell, *The Rights To Lead*, Nashville: J. Countryman, A Division of Thomas Nelson, Inc.

7. *The Courier Journal*, May 6, 2001, Editorial.

8. John C. Maxwell, *The Rights To Lead*, Nashville: J. Countryman, A Division of Thomas Nelson, Inc.

ABOUT THE AUTHOR

Tony Franklin is a born and raised Kentuckian, growing up in Princeton, and graduating from Caldwell County High School in 1976. He received his Bachelors Degree from Murray State University in December 1979 in an exceptional three and one half years. He received his Masters Degree from Murray State in 1988.

Beginning his teaching and coaching career in 1979 and expanding through parts of four decades, he developed a unique style of coaching and teaching. Utilizing his ability to communicate with people through a style of "down home" honesty, Franklin carved his niche in the education environment with a successful high school teaching and coaching career. In 1997 he entered into the college coaching profession and was named the Offensive Coordinator for the University of Kentucky Football Program in the 2000 season.

Honors, including being nominated for the Ashland Oil Teacher of the Year, Top 10 Recruiter in the South, and recognized as a Top Recruiter by *Newsweek's* Richard Ernsberger in his book *Bragging Rights*, were bestowed upon Franklin during his career.

Since experiencing entrepreneurial success in the mid 1980s, the yearning to be his own boss has brought him back to the free spirit environment he so dearly loves. Each day finds Franklin moving in a positive direction to provide service and benefits to others. Today Franklin owns BadCoaches, Inc. which provides various services, including success and goal seminars directed towards high school students; a writing and publishing business; a professional speaking platform directed at businesses, schools, and entrepreneurs; a recruiting consulting business directed towards high school athletes and their parents to provide visibility and advice; and a consulting and seminar business for high school and college coaches interested in obtaining incredible success. For more information about Franklin's businesses, go to www.badcoaches.com

Order extra copies of

Fourth Down
and
Life to Go

Number Requested		Per Book $19.95		6% Kentucky Sales Tax		Shipping $3.00 per book		Total Cost
_____	×	_____	+	_____	+	_____	=	_____

To order by mail, send check or money order
to the address below, Attention Book Orders

Order online at www.badcoaches.com or www.amazon.com

For more free information about the business offered
by BadCoaches, Inc. and Tony Franklin, write to us:

BadCoaches, Inc.
2220 Nicholasville Road
Suite 110, PMB 160
Lexington, KY 40503

or visit our website at www.badcoaches.com